An Actology of the Given

ACTOLOGICAL EXPLORATIONS

A series of books published by Wipf and Stock about actology, which understands reality as action in patterns, and so is an alternative to ontology, which understands reality as beings that change.

ALSO IN THIS SERIES

Actology: Action, Change and Diversity in the Western Philosophical Tradition

Two streams run through western philosophy: one characterized by Being, beings, the unchanging, the static, and the unitary, and the other by Action, actions, the changing, the dynamic, and the diverse. *Actology: Action, change and diversity in the western philosophical tradition*, explores the 'Action' stream as it has wound its way through Heraclitus, Parmenides, Plato, Aristotle, Hegel, Maurice Blondel, Henri Bergson, Teilhard de Chardin, process philosophy and theology, Geoffrey Studdert Kennedy, Ludwig Wittgenstein, and John Boys Smith. The journey enables us to see ourselves, the universe and God in terms of action in patterns rather than as beings that change, and so offers us a complete alternative narrative more in tune with the diverse and rapidly changing world in which we live than the ontology that has shaped philosophy, theology and much else for the past two thousand years.

Mark's Gospel: An Actological Reading

The second book in the series reads Mark's Gospel in the light of an actological understanding of reality. So it understands God, Jesus, and ourselves, as action, change, and diversity. The result is a unique and somewhat unexpected reading of the text, and a distinctive theology to match.

Actological Readings in Continental Philosophy

The third book in the series continues the journey begun in the first. The philosophers studied are Immanuel Kant, Friedrich Nietzsche, Edmund Husserl, Martin Heidegger, Emmanuel Levinas, Gilles Deleuze, Hans-Georg Gadamer, Maurice Merleau-Ponty, Gaston Bachelard, Michel Foucault, and Michel Serres. A whole new way of understanding reality casts new light on their philosophies and raises and answers some significant new questions.

An Actology of the Given

MALCOLM TORRY

RESOURCE *Publications* · Eugene, Oregon

AN ACTOLOGY OF THE GIVEN

Resource Publications
An Imprint of Wipf and Stock Publishers
199 W. 8th Ave., Suite 3
Eugene, OR 97401

www.wipfandstock.com

PAPERBACK ISBN: 978-1-6667-8152-6
HARDCOVER ISBN: 978-1-6667-8153-3
EBOOK ISBN: 978-1-6667-8154-0

07/06/23

He who lives for ever created the whole universe;
the Lord alone is just.
To none has he given power to proclaim his works;
and who can search out his mighty deeds?
Who can measure his majestic power?
And who can fully recount his mercies?
It is not possible to diminish or increase them,
nor is it possible to fathom the wonders of the Lord.
When human beings have finished, they are just beginning,
and when they stop, they are still perplexed.[1]

1. Ecclesiasticus 18:1–7, NRSV.

Contents

Acknowledgements

The philosophical, theological, and social policy roots of this book lie in the author's personal experience, reading, and writing, over the past fifty years, and have benefited from the wisdom of people far too many to number or name. To begin to list them would be invidious. However, I must acknowledge in print the assistance given to me by Professor David Webb and the late Dr. Bill Ross, teachers of the taught modules on the Staffordshire University master's degree course on Continental Philosophy, to whom I owe whatever understanding of continental philosophy I have managed to put together; and in relation to Jean-Luc Marion's philosophy, I must thank Dr. Patrick O'Connor, who supervised my dissertation on Marion's concept of 'the given'. Any errors or misunderstandings are of course entirely my responsibility, and not theirs.

It is a significant sadness that Bill Ross died suddenly and too young in August 2022, and so will not see this expression of gratitude.

Introduction

This book works in two directions. In one direction, it sets out from an actology—an understanding of reality as action in changing patterns, rather than from an ontology: an understanding of reality as beings that change—and it asks how in that context we might understand givens, gifts, and giving. In the other direction it asks what an understanding of givens, gifts and giving might contribute to the development of an actology.

The book builds on the development of an actology in the first volume in the "Actological Explorations" series, *Actology: Action, change and diversity in the western philosophical tradition,* and on a reading of a biblical text informed by the actology in *Mark's Gospel: An actological reading;* and it might be regarded as a sequel to the third volume in the series, *Actological Readings in Continental Philosophy,* which employed an actological understanding of reality to interpret texts written by a variety of continental philosophers and by that means to develop the actology itself. All three of the previous volumes worked with the basic character of actology: reality as action in changing patterns. This fourth volume in the series concentrates on a particular pattern of action: that of giving, and asks how an actology might facilitate our understanding of that, and how a pattern of action that we might call "giving" might help us to develop an actology.

As this book is an exploration of the act of giving, we shall be asking about "the gift," "the given," and so on, but always with an eye on the verb "to give." A gift might be an object, but it is the act of giving that makes the object a gift; "the given" might mean some proposition that we take to be foundational, or some phenomenon, but the fact that it is "given" suggests that there is a past or present act of giving underlying the proposition or phenomenon.

The authors that we shall study are largely chosen for us: it is those authors for whom giving and the gift are somehow central to their concerns. So we shall first of all study the anthropological researches of Marcel Mauss;

secondly, the phenomenological philosophies of Edmund Husserl, Martin Heidegger, Emmanuel Levinas, Jacques Derrida, and particularly Jean-Luc Marion; thirdly, grace—an unconditional giving—in the Juaeo-Christian tradition; fourthly, examples of different givings in social policy; and finally some particular "givens," and some conclusions as to how the act of giving might help us to develop an actology, and how an actological understanding of reality might help us to understand giving, givenness, givens, and the gift.

1

Giving in human society

INTRODUCTION

Gifts are given by human beings to human beings, and so the obvious science with which to study gift-giving has to be anthropology, the study of human behavior; and within that discipline the subdivision of economic anthropology is likely to be the most appropriate: that is, the study of economic human behavior. Given that society changes all the time, we would expect economic anthropology to change all the time, which it does.[1] Significant for our purposes is the "formalist-substantivist" debate, with formalism insisting that the same tools can be used to study any economy, and the substantivist saying that every culture is different so each economy should be studied from within its own assumptions:[2] and so Polanyi suggested that there are three types of economy—"reciprocity, redistribution, and exchange"[3]—and each kind has to be studied separately without assuming that the methods applicable to one will necessarily be applicable to others. As Wilks and Cliggett point out, there are also different kinds of gift-giving, and to study them is important because they form economies with different characteristics, and because

1. Wilk and Cliggett, *Economies and Cultures*, 1.
2. Wilk and Cliggett, *Economies and Cultures*, 3–14.
3. Wilk and Cliggett, *Economies and Cultures*, 8.

1

examining gift giving is a good way to see all the various aspects of human nature in action at one time because gifts can be simultaneously understood as rational exchange, as a way to build political and social relations, and as expressions of moral ideas and cultural meanings. . . . Gifts ultimately show that the dividing lines between rational choice, social goals, and morality are entirely our own creation.[4]

The text that we shall study in this chapter is Marcel Mauss's *Essai sur le Don* (translated into English as *The Gift*), which Sigaud describes as a study of

prestations [services and objects] apparently freely given, yet coercive and interested. Prestations were almost always cloaked in the guise of a present generously offered, even when the gesture that accompanied the transaction was no more than a formalized social fiction which was in fact backed by obligations and economic interest. Mauss claimed that of the various principles that gave exchange its specific character, he was going to study only one by asking two questions: what rule of law and self-interest, in societies of a backward or archaic type, compels the gift that has been received to be obligatorily returned? And what force resides in the thing given that causes its recipient to pay it back?[5]

We shall approach our study of *The Gift* with an understanding that reality is action in changing patterns rather than beings that change: an appropriate choice because a gift is something given, so it is the action of giving that determines that something is a gift. We shall also ask how what we learn about the giving of gifts might develop the actology that we have employed to study gift-giving.

GIFT-GIVING IN ANCIENT SOCIETIES

Archaeology and other sources reveal that before wider political entities such as states developed, ancient societies were on the whole collaborative, not particularly violent, and exhibited sharing economies.[6] More recently, and in continuity with this finding, early missionaries and pioneers in the United States recorded the "potlatches" performed by indigenous tribes. These were sometimes destructive of goods, but were also sometimes

4. Wilk and Cliggett, *Economies and Cultures*, 155.
5. Sigaud, "The Vicissitudes of *The Gift*," 336–37.
6. Widerquist and McCall, *Prehistoric Myths in Modern Political Philosophy*.

exchanges of gifts, generally of items needed by the recipient tribe, with an expectation of reciprocal gifts of needed items in the future. Useful redistribution occurred, as well as opportunities to create status and social bonds.[7]

In his 1924 book *Essai sur le Don* ("Essay on the Gift") Marcel Mauss records different kinds of potlatch: extravagant gift-giving that requires reciprocation, festivals during which tribes exchange gifts, and the conspicuous destruction of goods that requires a neighboring tribe to reciprocate or lose honor. Mauss had studied "the so to speak voluntary character" of these and other gift-giving activities that were

> apparently free and disinterested but nevertheless constrained and self-interested. Almost always such services have taken the form of the gift, the present generously given even when, in the gesture accompanying the transaction, there is only a polite fiction, formalism, and social deceit, and when really there is obligation and economic self-interest.[8]

Mauss employed the terms "*prestations*" and "*contre-prestations*" to express any tribal giving and reciprocation of gifts and services. As an editorial note in the English translation explains, "*prestations*" has no direct English equivalent. The English "services" can be translated as "*prestations de service*," suggesting that "*prestations*" is a pattern of action that is a giving that carries with it some expectation of reciprocation, and that "*contre-prestations*" is the pattern of action that constitutes the reciprocation. Mauss terms the combination a "*système des prestations totales*": a complex pattern of action encompassing a giving and its reciprocation, with the "*totales*" also representing the fact that such a giving and reciprocation is always part of an ongoing and widespread pattern of giving that results in evolving social relationships between individuals or between whole communities.[9] Mauss reserves the word "potlatch"[10] for "*prestations totales de type agonistique*" ("total services of an agonistic type"): that is, where there is a combative element to the complex gift and reciprocation pattern of action.[11]

What Mauss had discovered was

> a quite considerable number of intermediate forms between those exchanges comprising very acute rivalry and the destruction of wealth, such as those of the American Northwest and

---

7. Wilk and Cliggett, *Economies and Cultures*, 156–57.

8. Mauss, *The Gift*, 4.

9. Editorial note in Mauss, *The Gift*, vii; Mauss, *Essai sur le Don*, 6; *The Gift*, 7.

10. The same word appears in the English translation as in the original French.

11. Mauss, *Essai sur le Don*, 7; *The Gift*, 8.

Melanesia, and others, where emulation is more moderate but where those entering into contracts seek to outdo one another in their gifts.[12]

As Mary Douglas explains in her foreword to the *The Gift*, the English translation of *Essai sur le Don*, what Mauss has also shown is that among the tribes that he studied there were no free gifts. Gifts were always with a view to reciprocation, and to the social relationships that the exchange would generate; and she makes the general point that

> by ignoring the universal custom of compulsory gifts we make our own record incomprehensible to ourselves: right across the globe and as far back as we can go in the history of human civilization, the major transfer of goods has been by cycles of obligatory returns of gifts.[13]

Similarly, some North American communities employed gifts to compensate families wronged by murder or some other crime, rather than directly punish the perpetrator.[14] Sigaud suggests that such gifts only appear unconditional if they are isolated from the social systems in which they occur;[15] and Siegel concludes from reading *Essai sur le Don* that at the heart of the systems of gifts that Mauss researched there was a "social force," and that what had led Mauss to his discoveries was

> a Maori word designating a force said to be lodged in the gift that moved it forward in the great systems of exchange of Melanesia. The *hau* compelled the person who received the gift to accept it and it also made that person pass it on to the next person. Eventually the gift returned in another form and from another party, only to be passed on again. . . . One obeys a set of rules, rules that govern exchange, and if not, one is put out of the game. The rules of ritual exchange have their own force, the force of the *hau*. If one does not follow them, one dies. . . . The gift itself embodies the force of sociality.[16]

Frank suggests that Mauss had misunderstood the tribal activities that he had researched by aligning them rather too easily with Roman law and the symmetrical transactions of modern markets. There was in fact a great deal that was not symmetrical, and a significant purpose of the potlatch and

12. Mauss, *The Gift*, 8–9.

13. Douglas, "Foreword," x.

14. Graeber and Wengrow, *The Dawn of Everything*, 42.

15. Sigaud, "The Vicissitudes of *The Gift*," 342.

16. Siegel, "False Beggars," 67, 72, 73.

similar patterns of action was to establish social hierarchy. There was a "verticality" and inequality to what was happening, and not simply "horizontal" exchanges and social bonds.[17]

SENECA

The Roman Seneca, who lived during the first century of the common era, offers a somewhat complex picture: but ultimately he recommends precisely the kinds of symmetrical gift-giving that Mauss had understood to have been prevalent among the tribal societies that he studied.

Although there are places where Seneca suggests that gifts should not be given to someone whom we know will be ungrateful,[18] he expects gifts to be given gladly, without delay,[19] carefully considered in relation to both the donor's ability to give and the ability of the recipient to receive,[20] and preferably anonymously.[21]

> When you ask what return one gets from a gift or good deed, I will reply: "A good conscience."... Why does one give? In order *not to fail to give*, not to lose the chance of doing good.[22]

No gift should ever be regretted, however ungrateful the recipient might be,[23] and any ingratitude on our part is "a serious failing":[24] and in some places, Seneca expresses a clear belief that a genuine gift is possible:

> A certain amount is dispensed; if anything comes back, that's a profit, but if not, it's no loss.... It's a base kind of usury to treat a gift as an account payable.[25]

He also suggests that it is not the object given that matters, but rather the attitude with which it is given:

17. Frank, "The 'Force in the Thing.'"
18. Seneca, *How to Give*, 221, 223.
19. Seneca, *How to Give*, 39–43.
20. Seneca, *How to Give*, 65–69.
21. Seneca, *How to Give*, 47–53.
22. Seneca, *How to Give*, 149, 151.
23. Seneca, *How to Give*, 209.
24. Seneca, *How to Give*, 217.
25. Seneca, *How to Give*, 15.

> Between the product of giving and the gift itself lies a huge gulf.
> The gift is not the gold, or the silver, or any of those things we
> think most important; it's the very intent of the one who gives.[26]

However, while it is the gift and the giving attitude that count, Seneca still
expects there to be an element of self-interest in the giving:

> We should think about what we can give that will bring most
> pleasure in future, what the owners will often bump into so that
> we'll be in their thoughts every time they're in its presence.[27]

When Seneca turns to the question as to how gifts should be received, he
recommends that we should only receive gifts "from those to whom we
would have given,"[28] that we should respond to a gift by "expressing our
joy in a way that the givers can't miss, so they'll get an immediate reward,"[29]
and that we should never respond with ingratitude, hesitation, jealousy, or
greed.[30] What is required is gratitude for the gift, and also gratitude that
our response has given pleasure to the donor.[31] The receiving of the gift is
therefore already a giving back to the donor.

Fundamental to Seneca's understanding of giving is the generosity of
the gods, or of the single god, in relation to the world, our lives, and everything else:[32]

> God gives us very many and very great gifts, without expecta-
> tion of repayment, since god does not need a gift from us, nor
> can we give anything to god. . . . Let's be grateful toward the
> gods, toward humankind, toward those who have done some-
> thing for us or for those we hold dear.[33]

The way in which the gods give is an example to us, as they give "to those
who don't know them, and continue giving to those who are ungrateful . . . Let's give, even if much that we give ends up useless."[34]

There are significant echoes of tribal giving and receiving here, and in
particular an expectation of diverse reciprocities. The giving might initially

26. Seneca, *How to Give*, 21.

27. Seneca, *How to Give*, 33.

28. Seneca, *How to Give*, 79.

29. Seneca, *How to Give*, 81.

30. Seneca, *How to Give*, 83–93.

31. Seneca, *How to Give*, 103.

32. Seneca, *How to Give*, 121–35.

33. Seneca, *How to Give*, 137, 183, 185.

34. Seneca, *How to Give*, 225, 229.

occur without any expectation of return (apart from the donor's own sense of virtue at having given), but it will always take place in the context of a social expectation that reciprocation will be made: not necessarily of return gifts, but of appropriate gratitude. Throughout Seneca's treatment of the subject there is an underlying expectation of social equality between donor and donee, whether an equality already existing, or one facilitated by the gift-giving and subsequent response. In both the tribes that Mauss studied, and among Seneca's ideal Roman citizens, diverse and changing patterns of action are in evidence, and ones not easily summarized: but throughout we find the same pattern of action: giving, receiving, and reciprocating. A consistent pattern of action has emerged, and one somewhat more complex and multidirectional than the unidirectional pattern of action that might be implied by the notion of giving.

A GIFT ECONOMY?

A "gift economy" might initially appear to be "the opposite of the impersonal commodity-producing capitalist system described and condemned by Marx,"[35] but both of them conform to a "give, receive, reciprocate"[36] pattern of action: a three-fold pattern ubiquitous in Roman, Indian, Germanic, and Chinese law[37] and customs, and that survives in social assumptions and arrangements today. "The unreciprocated gift still makes the person who has accepted it inferior";[38] and anthropologists have shown just "how fluid the categories of gift and commodity are as objects move in and out of different social relationships."[39]

Equally fluid is the concept of "reciprocity," of which Sahlins identifies three forms. Firstly, "balanced reciprocity" refers to direct exchange where the reciprocation is the customary equivalent of the thing received and is without delay; secondly, "negative reciprocity" is the attempt to get something for nothing with impunity; and thirdly, close kin tend to share and to enter into generalized exchanges.[40] Wilk and Cliggett give the examples of the potlatch and market exchanges for balanced reciprocity, gambling for negative reciprocity, and caring for children for generalized exchanges, but with a recognition that market exchanges might also be interpreted

35. Wilk and Cliggett, *Economies and Cultures*, 160.

36. Mauss, *The Gift*, 50.

37. Mauss, *The Gift*, 60–82.

38. Mauss, *The Gift*, 83.

39. Wilk and Cliggett, *Economies and Cultures*, 161.

40. Sahlins, *Stone Age Economics*, 194–96.

as negative reciprocity.[41] A spectrum emerges, from "the assistance freely given" in "generalized exchanges" among close kin, to "self-interested seizure, appropriation by chicanery or force,"[42] with "balanced" reciprocity mid-spectrum. Equivalence "becomes compulsory in proportion to kinship distance."[43] And sometimes the goods exchanged can be somewhat irrelevant to the purpose: for instance, gifts given to mark births, marriages, and so on, are a recognition of the significance of the events, of recognition of the individuals involved in the events, and of the emotional turmoil that might accompany such events as marriages. The outcome, as with many other gift exchanges, is strengthened social bonds.[44] Like any scientist, an anthropologist will employ or develop theory that might explain data that they have collected, and they might then seek evidence that will support or disprove the theory. Sometimes different theories will offer different perspectives on the same data, and then we might find ourselves drawing connections between different theories. And so, for instance, Cliggett has shown that both economic and emotional meanings might be "intertwined in complex ways and present as much of a puzzle to those actually engaged in the exchange as they do to an informed anthropologist who is interviewing both parties."[45] A particular case of such an intertwining is the way in which workers who have migrated from rural areas to cities send gifts to relatives in their original communities both to provide for those relatives' physical needs and to maintain social bonds on which the workers might need to rely if they return home.

While what is exchanged is relevant in all of the examples of gift-giving that we have discussed, it is the context in which gifts are given—in terms of the cultures, societies, communities, and individuals involved, the events during which gifts are given, and the social relationships involved—that provides the majority of the meaning of the gift. There are anthropological approaches that look more at what is given than at the kinds of exchange that are going on—for instance, Appadurai asks how the objects being exchanged gain value, and suggests that "exchange is the source of value"[46] and that

---

41. Wilk and Cliggett, *Economies and Cultures*, 162–64.

42. Sahlins, *Stone Age Economics*, 191.

43. Sahlins, *Stone Age Economics*, 196.

44. Wilk and Cliggett, *Economies and Cultures*, 168.

45. Wilk and Cliggett, *Economies and Cultures*, 170.

46. Appadurai, "Introduction," 56.

politics (in the broad sense of relations, assumptions, and con-
tests pertaining to power) is what links value and exchange in
the social life of commodities.[47]

Societies, whether ancient or modern, and whether complex or relatively
simple in structure, exchange "spheres of exchange,"[48] and different spheres
of exchange can ascribe different values to the same object. For instance,
in one sphere of exchange a painting by Picasso might be without price,
but in another it can be bought and sold and by that means ascribed a
value. Perhaps more importantly, in one sphere of exchange people are
"singular" and so are not commodities, but in another they might be
bought and sold as slaves: and perhaps there are aspects of slavery whenever such human commoditization as labor is bought and sold.[49] Objects
are "constructed," and they have "biographies" as they pass through different spheres of exchange. Sometimes we "singularize," and sometimes
we "categorize":[50] that is, we "process" things. They are action in changing
patterns within changing patterns of action; and the ascription of value is
an active and culturally embedded process, and so is as much a pattern of
action as are giving and reciprocation.

Any object can be either a gift or a commodity.[51] This is surely correct,
because, as we have recognized, gift-giving and market exchange are constituted by similar or perhaps identical patterns of action: givings, receivings,
and reciprocations. Both of them are institutions in the sense that they are
both "socially operative systems of rules . . . that structure social interac-
tions"; both represent "the self-transcendence of social relationships . . . according to which individuals orient their behavior";[52] and both can serve
to reduce conflict. The European Union began as a common market in coal
and steel in order to discourage further conflict between European nations;
and Rider suggests that the gift-giving researched by Mauss and others
probably had similar origins.

> In the absence of voluntary exchange institutions, such as
> reciprocity, through which these groups could interact in more
> cooperative ways, their initial external interactions may have
> been characterized by plunder, pillage and war. It is from these
> conflictive relations that more cooperative institutions may have

47. Appadurai, "Introduction," 57.
48. Kopytoff, "The Cultural Biography of Things," 77.
49. Kopytoff, "The Cultural Biography of Things," 82, 84.
50. Kopytoff, "The Cultural Biography of Things," 90.
51. Wilk and Cliggett, *Economies and Cultures*, 165.
52. Cedrini et al., "Mauss's *The Gift*," 694, 688.

been chosen or have evolved. . . . The gift, and reciprocity in general, could have allowed for the evolution of more coopera-tive relations through credible threats of returning to conflict if the gift was not returned. . . . that the original motivation for the return of the gift may have been to elicit cooperation. Only after this cooperation had been attained could the gift then evolve into the social norm that Mauss had observed. . . . reciprocity may have an origin of conflict.[53]

This is not to suggest that the social psychological drivers of the process have evaporated. As Alain Caillé finds,

What Mauss's analyses establish, and on which they continue to rest, is that in human social existence this opposition of the two primary instincts only comes into play when mediated by the opposition between a drive for war, rivalry and individuation on the one hand, and a drive for peace, harmony, alliance and love on the other.[54]

As Wilk and Cliggett point out, the concept of the gift remains

powerful because it demonstrates that all values are produced through human relations and cultural conventions. Value is therefore not an inherent or intrinsic property of things themselves.[55]

The same might be said of values in a market, of course. And as Wilk and Cliggett also point out, "property" is a complex idea, and what we call "pri-vate property" is encumbered with public regulations about what can be done with it. In some cultures, an original owner continues to be somehow invested in a property even if possession has been passed to other people, so it might be best to regard such "property" as "a bundle of rights": for instance, the right to use something for a period of time.[56] A similar situ-ation arises in relation to works of art: however many hands a work of art has passed through, and however many people have owned it, when it is lent for an exhibition it returns to perhaps the most significant kind of

53. Rider, "A Game-theoretic Interpretation."
54. Caillé, "'Marcel Mauss et le paradigme du don,'" 171. Translation by the author. The original French reads as follows: "Ce que les analyses de Mauss établissent, et sur quoi elles reposent tout en même temps, c'est que dans l'existence sociale des hommes, cette opposition des deux instincts primaires ne joue que relayée par l'opposition entre une pulsion de guerre, de rivalité et d'individuation d'une part, une pulsion de paix, d'harmonie, d'alliance et d'aimance de l'autre."
55. Wilk and Cliggett, *Economies and Cultures*, 148.
56. Wilk and Cliggett, *Economies and Cultures*, 167.

"ownership": that of the artist who created it; and whenever a hand-made birthday gift is sent and received, the meaning of the object and of what we do with it will be imbued with something of its creator.[57] However, such perspectives have not really escaped from the significance of the social bonds that generate and are formed or maintained by the gift-giving. As Wilk and Cliggett point out in relation to Mauss's research, "gift exchange is always about social relations . . . An understanding of gift exchange may best be found through an integrated vision that includes all kinds of information, subjective and objective."[58]

> Anthropologists' fascination with gift exchange is an attempt to argue with utilitarianism and to say that in other societies goods are socially (Sahlins) or morally (Mauss) positive, but in capitalist societies commodities dehumanize people and reduce all social relations to markets and money. Gifts and gift economies are attractive because many people hope systems exist that are not purely self-interested and capital-based.[59]

There is some sense in this. In the gift-giving societies discussed in Mauss's *The Gift*, transactions are more about social bonds, social position, honor, and so on, whereas these social aspects are generally less obvious in market transactions, even if they are sometimes present, and less salient today in a culture more characterized by the individual and his or her unique and essentially incommensurable individuality and its attendant needs.[60] Sigaud emphasizes this difference, suggesting that interpreters of Mauss's text had sometimes aligned the meaning extracted from it more closely with modern markets and reciprocity than was strictly warranted, especially as Mauss himself had not mentioned the concept of reciprocity.[61]

> What started out as a text which aimed at drawing attention to problems and putting forth research proposals, came to be seen as a theory, and one which dealt with reciprocity, a concept that Mauss had not even entertained at the time. From a text about law and the economy, it was transformed into a study of economy.[62]

And there is also a difference in the orientations of the different economies, with market economies being more oriented towards production

---

57. Wilk and Cliggett, *Economies and Cultures*, 148.
58. Wilk and Cliggett, *Economies and Cultures*, 171.
59. Wilk and Cliggett, *Economies and Cultures*, 171–72.
60. Coleman, "On Mauss, Masks, and Gifts," 298.
61. Sigaud, "The Vicissitudes of *The Gift*," 354.
62. Sigaud, "The Vicissitudes of *The Gift*," 354.

and consumption, and gift-giving economies more towards social bonds and hierarchies:[63] but there are "no clear-cut, purely moral, purely social, *or* purely utilitarian" systems, and human beings are frequently "illogical" and often "altruistic rather than selfish," and they rarely function as truly autonomous rationally-choosing individuals, which is why "institutions, not individuals, are the main unit of society."[64] Every market economy is just as deeply embedded in "social forces and institutions" as any gift-giving economy might be;[65] and every contemporary gift-giving will be embedded in a market economy, social forces, and institutions, and both the gift-giving and the market economy will have moral, social, and utilitarian meanings,[66] with the moral meaning always somewhat mitigated by the "irony of promoting good through funds harvested from dehumanizing economic systems."[67] All of us contribute to the funds disbursed by the Gates Foundation by buying Microsoft products: and Wilk and Cliggett point out that although we might approve of the Gates Foundations' funding of important medical research, our expenditure on products might also be funding a variety of think tanks that spread climate change disinformation or oppose gun control legislation.[68] Gifts might be morally dubious as well as morally virtuous, and the motives will always be mixed: for instance, a company's charitable giving might be for the purpose of burnishing its image, to gain recognition and prestige, or to atone for the exploitative business methods that might have given rise to the wealth being disbursed.[69] As Wilk and Cliggett point out, gifts are powerful because they contain characteristics of

> self-interest, elements of social integration, and possibilities for establishing or reaffirming moral order . . . they can simultaneously benefit an individual, create a social system, and communicate cultural values of what is important in the world.[70]

Grégoire Mallard takes interpretation of Mauss's *The Gift* in what we might regard as a polar opposite direction. Rather than comparing a modern market-based society with the tribal societies that Mauss researched, he understands Mauss's conclusions as applying to relationships between nations

---

63. Sabourin, "Marcel Mauss," 208.
64. Wilk and Cliggett, *Economies and Cultures*, 172.
65. Panoff, "Marcel Mauss's 'The Gift' Revisited," 65.
66. Wilk and Cliggett, *Economies and Cultures*, 173.
67. Wilk and Cliggett, *Economies and Cultures*, 173.
68. Wilk and Cliggett, *Economies and Cultures*, 173.
69. Wilk and Cliggett, *Economies and Cultures*, 174.
70. Wilk and Cliggett, *Economies and Cultures*, 174.

and between empires both through history and in the modern world.[71] It is in this context that gifts are still given and received, and within which reciprocity is expected.

Later in this book we shall find Mauss's discussion of "the gift," and the considerable anthropological debate about gift-giving that followed, informing a significant dialogue between Derrida and Marion, and to some extent informing the entire philosophical debate about whether "the gift" might be able to function as pure gift rather than as an element in an economy of some kind.

AN ACTOLOGY OF GIVING AND A GIVING ACTOLOGY

Sahlins' brief summary of Mauss's achievement in *The Gift* is "that every exchange, as it embodies some coefficient of sociability, cannot be understood in its material terms apart from its social terms."[72] But what is the "social" here? Social bonds, encountered frequently during our discussion, are patterns of activity connecting the individuals that constitute a community or society: individuals that are as much defined by their relationships as they are by anything else. It is our connections with other people, our surroundings, our pasts, the world that we live in, that either largely or wholly determine what we do and who we become, with the "who we become" best understood as slowly changing patterns of action that tangle with the more rapidly changing patterns of action that constitute our daily lives in society. We are what we do, so we are our social relationships, and in particular we are our gift-giving. Any particular object that is given will always to some extent inform the character of the gift-giving: and so, for instance, to give a hand-made cake will be a different gift-giving from the giving of a shop-bought one, because the hand-made cake carries with it the giving of our time (a giving that we shall encounter when we read Derrida's *Giving Time*), with time here constituted by a sequence of actions in patterns that constitute the making of a cake. But however significant the characteristics and history of the object given might be, it is the action in patterns of the gift-giving that will constitute the gift-giving. So, for instance, if the person to whom something is given does not give money to the gift-giver (at the same time, prior to the gift being given, or after the gift has been given), then we can understand the given object as a gift. Later on an object might be given in the opposite direction, and we shall be able to understand the sequence of actions in patterns as reciprocation. So "reciprocation" means a

71. Mallard, *Gift Exchange*.
72. Sahlins, *Stone Age Economics*, 183.

complex pattern of changing patterns of action, and the objects given might or might not constitute a significant element of that reality. It is the complex pattern of changing patterns of action that constitutes the reciprocity.

This is what we mean by an "actological" approach to an understanding of the gift. Rather than understanding reality in terms of Being, beings, rest, the unchanging, the unitary, and the static, we understand it as Action, actions, movement, change, diversity, and the dynamic, and it is within this latter understanding of reality—within an actology, rather than an ontology—that we can most easily understand the gift, giving, giving back, reciprocity, and the complex social relationships related to these patterns of action, and within which we can understand the pure gift as a pattern of action that transfers something from one person to another without any further pattern of action being generated in relation to the giver or to the person receiving the gift, or in relation to anyone or anything else. However, every pattern of action will change multiple other patterns of action, and potentially every other pattern of action: so to understand gift-giving within an Action understanding of reality—within an actology—is to render the pure gift an impossibility. There will always be repercussions for the giver, the recipient, the reciprocity, the act of giving, and anyone or anything else related in any way to the initial giving. There will always be some kind of reciprocity. The pure gift is what we might call a limit that we can never reach; the point at the end of a spectrum of infinite length. It would be a self-enclosed and isolated pattern of action, and thus an impossibility.

Equally, the actions of giving, receiving, and reciprocating, might contribute to an understanding of actology: indeed, any actology. The fact that a fundamental social fact is a particular changing pattern of action invites us to understand the whole of reality as constituted by changing patterns of action: not only the giving, receiving, and reciprocating, but the gift as well, along with all the players in the complex social activity. There are no unchanging beings here: everything is action in changing patterns.

2

Edmund Husserl's "the given"

INTRODUCTION

Phenomena are given to us: that is, "what appears" appears to us rather than being manufactured by us. And given that Jean-Luc Marion, to whom we shall give two chapters later in this book, concentrates our attention on the givenness of phenomena, and that he regarded himself as a phenomenologist, we must give this second chapter to the founder of Phenomenology, Edmund Husserl. The chapter will discuss Husserl's phenomenology, and particularly the givenness at its heart, in order to understand how an actology might contribute to an understanding of phenomenology and how phenomenology might contribute to the development of an actology.

HUSSERL'S PHENOMENOLOGY

In 1907, in five lectures on his new philosophical method, Husserl studies the possibility of a phenomenological critique, that is, "the possibility of the knowledge of the possibility of knowledge, not the possibility of knowledge in general."[1] The method of the lectures is to follow the development of

---

1. Hardy, "Translator's Introduction," 3.

Husserl's own philosophical journey from a Cartesian understanding of the problem of knowledge to a phenomenological resolution of the problem.[2]

Husserl begins with a "natural attitude" within which our attention is turned, "in acts of intuition and thought," to "*things* given to us."[3] We then generalize, and find "logical relations," agreements, and contradictions. It is when we suspend the natural attitude and turn instead to a "philosophical attitude" that we ask such questions as "How can knowledge go beyond itself and reach its objects reliably? . . . How do I, the knowing subject, know—and how can I know for sure—that not only experiences, these acts of knowing, exist, but also what they know exists?"[4] What is required in order to answer such questions is not such positive sciences as psychology, but rather a "phenomenology"—"a method and an attitude of thought"—and first of all a "*phenomenology of knowledge and known objectivity*."[5]

GIVEN PHENOMENA

In his second lecture, in order to counter the radical skepticism that he found in contemporary and previous philosophy,[6] Husserl begins with Descartes' radical doubt, and understands, with Descartes, that only knowledge of our own thought can be certain knowledge. He replaces Descartes' "attempt to doubt universally" with an *epoché*, a "cessation,"[7] that brackets out our assumptions about the natural world, and thus "*the whole natural world*,"[8] and that functions as "a first step to laying bare the essence of the act, for example what precisely it *means* to perceive something, remember something, imagine something, and so on."[9] Then follows a "phenomenological reduction"—a "transcendental reduction"—a reduction that encompasses a variety of different "reductions,"[10] and that restricts consciousness to im-

2. Hardy, "Translator's Introduction," 3.

3. Husserl, *The Idea of Phenomenology*, 15.

4. Husserl, *The Idea of Phenomenology*, 17.

5. Husserl, *The Idea of Phenomenology*, 19. Italics in the original.

6. Kidd, "Skeptical Origins," 169.

7. Moran, *Introduction to Phenomenology*, 148.

8. Husserl, *Ideas pertaining to a pure phenomenology*, 61 (§32). Italics in the original.

9. Moran, *Introduction to Phenomenology*, 150.

10. Moran, *Introduction to Phenomenology*, 147.

manence, and thus to phenomena, "appearances": that is, to the "sphere of absolute givenness"[11] internal to our consciousness.[12]

> We accept nothing here but what we find actually given (and, at first, quite immediately) in the field of the *ego cogito*, and . . . accordingly we assert nothing we ourselves do not "see."[13]

> *Every intellectual experience, indeed every experience whatsoever, can be made into an object of pure seeing and apprehension* while it is occurring. *And in this act of seeing it is an absolute givenness.*[14]

And so, for instance, in order to support belief in a world, which Husserl calls "world-belief"—that is, "the assumption that the world is the correlate of infinite intersubjective verification"—we must first submit world-belief to an *epoché*, and then study phenomena. We then find that "world-experience grounds world-belief":[15] for instance, "Having had a concordant experience of tables and of the table in my office, I legitimately expect to see it from the opposite side if I walk around it."[16] As Peterson summarizes Husserl's phenomenological strategy:

> The Husserlian transcendental reduction suspends the external world precisely in order to give the ego over to an alterity that it can no longer know in an immediate way. I can access the other only "indirectly, inside of me." Counterintuitively, the "annihilation" of the world facilitates a nonoriginary relation to the world, which is to say a relation to an otherness that escapes my grasp. Hence, I transcend the world, but the world also transcends me. . . . .[17]

And as Berghofer suggests, this "phenomenology of originary givenness or self-givenness" is the "distinctive, justification-conferring phenomenology" that we might need in order to counter radical skepticism.[18] However, Husserl's "givenness" is not univocal. "The given" is always "what is

11. Husserl, *The Idea of Phenomenology*, 26.

12. O'Connor, "Lecture 1—Husserl's Phenomenology," 1, 3–4.

13. Husserl, *Cartesian Meditations*, 24.

14. Husserl, *The Idea of Phenomenology*, 24. Italics in the original.

15. Stefano, "The Epistemological Contribution of the Transcendental Reduction," 56.

16. Stefano, "The Epistemological Contribution of the Transcendental Reduction," 56.

17. Peterson, *Monkey Trouble*, 27, 71.

18. Berghofer, "Husserl's Conception of Experiential Justification," 154.

experienced, as it is experienced";[19] "the given" is "the given" as "an abstract moment" inseparable from consciousness, such as objective ordered time or a memory;[20] and a further meaning is "original givenness": what is given in perception before any thought-processes take place, as again memories might be[21] as "these and now those past" are "again" given to consciousness . . . as the "pasts themselves"[22] in an "intuitive givenness in an explicit remembering."[23] "Remembering brings the past self to givenness more or less clearly"[24] as "givennesses of a past" are "still retained in consciousness."[25]

What Husserl is seeking is adequate self-evidence rather than immediacy. As Soffer makes clear,

> even seemingly very simple perceptions involve quite complex implicit judgments, which in turn generally require learning, concepts, and language. . . . the category of the given serves to thematize the subjective elements of experience (the immanent) and to show how what is taken by us to be knowledge presupposes and emerges out of these subjective elements.[26]

What is not given is raw sense data: instead, what is perceived is a "'conceptually' apprehended spatiotemporal object,"[27] and any concept of "sensation" "arises in reflective abstraction provided in the course of articulating a theory of perception."[28] The "givenness" might be inadequate, because due to the "spatial structure of things"[29]

> we can never think the given object without empty horizons in any phase of perception and, what amounts to the same thing, without apperceptive adumbration. With adumbration there is simultaneously a pointing beyond what is exhibiting itself in a genuine sense. Genuine exhibition is itself, again, not a pure and simple possession on the model of immanence with its *esse* =

19. Soffer, "Revisiting the Myth," 306.

20. Soffer, "Revisiting the Myth," 306.

21. Soffer, "Revisiting the Myth," 308.

22. Husserl, *Cartesian Meditations*, 19.

23. Husserl, *Analyses Concerning Passive and Active Synthesis*, 69.

24. Husserl, *Analyses Concerning Passive and Active Synthesis*, 138.

25. Husserl, *Analyses Concerning Passive and Active Synthesis*, 371.

26. Soffer, "Revisiting the Myth," 310.

27. Williams, "Is Husserl Guilty," 6371.

28. Williams, "Is Husserl Guilty," 6388.

29. Husserl, *Analyses Concerning Passive and Active Synthesis*, 56.

percipi; instead, it is a partially fulfilled intention that contains unfulfilled indications that point beyond.[30]

INTENTION

Essential to our relationship with given phenomena is the "intention" that we exercise. Because the natural attitude has been abandoned, and a world existing for itself has been bracketed, the intention that we exercise cannot be informed by a world already possessed. Peterson expresses an obvious problem:

> The Husserlian transcendental reduction suspends the world as the condition of our intentional relation to it. Intentionality is utterly impossible without this quasi-worldly transcendence.[31]

That is: what is the content of the intention that seeks out and receives phenomena if there is no existing understanding of the world to inform the intention? A circular process seems to be in mind. Through the inadequacy of our reception the givenness of phenomena might be "inadequate," but there will always be an "accomplishment of consciousness,"[32] and Huang finds that we seek an "optimal givenness"[33] by intentionally steering our perception according to our own interests and social norms.[34] The object then gives itself to our intentional perception.[35]

> The self-givenness of a spatial thing is the self-givenness of a perspectival appearing object that is given as the same in the fulfilling synthesis of appearances intertwining and devolving upon one another. But it is the same object that itself appears now this time in one way, now another time in another way, appearing in other perspectives, always pointing from a perspective to ever new perspectives in which the same object that is exhibited is continually determined more closely, and yet is never determined definitively.[36]

Husserl develops the concept of the "theme" which

30. Husserl, *Analyses Concerning Passive and Active Synthesis*, 56.
31. Peterson, *Monkey Trouble*, 27, 71.
32. Husserl, *Analyses Concerning Passive and Active Synthesis*, 57.
33. Husserl, *Analyses Concerning Passive and Active Synthesis*, 60.
34. Huang, "Normativity and Teleology," 19.
35. Huang, "Normativity and Teleology," 20.
36. Husserl, *Analyses Concerning Passive and Active Synthesis*, 108.

designates the object as the substrate and center of a unitary
interest, more precisely, the entire object toward which the ego
is constantly directed in the mode of attentiveness, while its cognitive interest is satiated by its richer and richer givenness, but
which also strives onward toward newer and newer givenness.[37]

As for the relationship between the whole of something perceived and the
parts that we might discern within it:

Sometimes the givenness of the wholes, their affective promi-
nence and therefore the possibility of grasping them, precedes
the parts, sometimes the givenness of parts the whole. . . . In
immanent time-consciousness we have the stream of givennesses in lived-experience, givennesses that are strung together
temporally with their anticipations which have the character of
an anticipatory believing that is directed-ahead.[38]

However complex and fertile the intentional phenomena and the ways in
which we combine them and abstract from them might be, no transcendence is ever given: hence Husserl's "epistemological principle" that "in
every epistemological investigation, into whatever type of knowledge, the
epistemological or phenomenological *reduction* must be performed, that is,
all transcendence that comes into play here must be excluded," including
any (psychological) transcendence that has attached itself to the *cogitatio*: to
what is thought.[39] And so the "principle of all principles" is

*that every originary presentive intuition is a legitimizing source of
cognition, that everything originarily* (so to speak in its "personal" actuality) *offered to us in "intuition" is to be accepted simply
as what it is presented as being, but also only within the limits in
which it is presented there.*[40]

As Moran puts it:

Husserl's central insight was that consciousness was the condition of all experience, indeed it constituted the world, but in
such a way that the role of consciousness itself is obscured and
not easy to isolate and describe. Husserl therefore constantly
sought to explain how to overcome *prejudices* which stood in

37. Husserl, *Analyses Concerning Passive and Active Synthesis*, 290.

38. Husserl, *Analyses Concerning Passive and Active Synthesis*, 204, 393.

39. Husserl, *The Idea of Phenomenology*, 64.

40. Husserl, *Ideas Pertaining to a Pure Phenomenology*, 44 (§24). Italics in the
original.

the way of the recognition of the domain of pure consciousness, leading to a new beginning in philosophy.[41]

As so although perception is "a phenomenon in keeping with the sense of the positive science we call psychology,"[42] what matters is that

> to every psychological experience there corresponds, by way of the phenomenological reduction, a pure phenomenon that exhibits its immanent essence (taken individually) as an absolute givenness.[43]

It is the phenomenon, and not some subsequent rational process, that is the given and is what is—or, we might say, what appears, or what acts:

> no matter what the status of this phenomenon's claim to actuality and no matter whether, at some future time, I decide critically that the world exists or that it is an illusion, still this phenomenon itself, as mine, is not nothing but is precisely what makes such critical decisions at all possible and accordingly makes possible whatever has for me sense and validity as "true" being—definitively decided or definitively decideable being.[44]

What is given is given not to consciousness as it might be studied by psychology, but to consciousness as the subject—to a "transcendental" consciousness: that is, a consciousness that is the necessary precondition for experience of phenomena.[45] So here we find the same distinction between the transcendent (something existing in itself and separately from our experience of it) and the transcendental (a necessary precondition) that we find in Kant's philosophy: but there is a difference. Husserl is clear that everything "transcendent" must be abandoned (—does this suggest that principles, including the "principle of all principles," should be abandoned?[46]): but that is not the end of his use of the word "transcendent," as, unlike Kant, he suggests a new use for it:

> there is *another sense of transcendence*, whose counterpart is an entirely different kind of immanence, namely, *absolute* and *clear givenness, self-givenness in the absolute sense.* This givenness, which excludes any meaningful doubt, consists of an immediate act of seeing and apprehending the meant objectivity itself as it

41. Moran, *Introduction to Phenomenology*, 61–62.

42. Husserl, *The Idea of Phenomenology*, 33.

43. Husserl, *The Idea of Phenomenology*, 34. Italics in the original.

44. Husserl, *Cartesian Meditations*, 19.

45. Crowell, "Heidegger and Husserl," 54.

46. Marion, *Being Given*, 14.

is. . . . All knowledge that is not evident, that refers to or posits what is objective, but *does not see it for itself,* is transcendent in this second sense. In such knowledge we go beyond what is *given in the genuine sense,* beyond *what can be directly seen* and *apprehended.*[47]

As Rosen points out, the prohibition of transcendence in its normal sense, and Husserl's insistence on a phenomenological reduction to the ego that facilitates a reengagement with a phenomenological world, prevent "the experience of others as singular and other" and also prevent "our phenomenal life" from having "a shape that accounts for the coexistence of empathy to others who are like oneself and hospitality to others as genuine others."[48] We shall soon find Jean-Luc Marion making the same complaint about Descartes' ego-centered philosophy. However, what we have found in Husserl's phenomenology is a pattern of action not dissimilar to the giving, receiving and reciprocating pattern that we explored in the previous chapter. Phenomena are given, we receive them intentionally, and the knowledge that we gain, that is "transcendent in the second sense," then informs the intentionality with which we engage with new phenomena. A circular process is instigated and maintained in much the same way as the gift-giving economy is instigated and maintained.

IDEATING ABSTRACTION

Intentional perception is not our only access to given phenomena. We go "beyond" perceptual phenomena "when we say: this or that phenomenon of representation lies at the basis of this phenomenon of judging; this phenomenon of perceiving contains these or those moments—color contents and the like."[49] So it is not only particular perceived phenomena that contribute to knowledge: "*universals, universal objects, and universal states of affairs*" contribute "*to absolute givenness*"[50] as well, and therefore to certain knowledge, because they are immanent to our consciousness.[51] We sometimes find Husserl ascribing a "quasi-givenness" to such "transcendent objects" as a world separate from phenomena, reserving "absolute givenness"

47. Husserl, *The Idea of Phenomenology,* 27–28.
48. Rosen, "The Givenness of Other People," 333.
49. Husserl, *The Idea of Phenomenology,* 39.
50. Husserl, *The Idea of Phenomenology,* 39.
51. Moran, *Introduction to Phenomenology,* 130.

for phenomena themselves:[52] but we also find him ascribing an "absolute givenness" to "universality,"[53] and by implication to such other universals as time and change. Such *a priori* truths are generated by reflection on acts of consciousness followed by "ideating abstraction":[54] although the existence of time might have been a more reliable example than "the species red,"[55] because the colors of which we are conscious are in fact contingent on their colored contexts, which compromises color as species: something that Husserl might not have realized. Time, change and space are revealed by the phenomenological reduction, and by consciousness's directing of itself beyond itself, to be functions of the "I" being present across different instances of perception and across different spaces.[56]

> At every step the analysis is an analysis of essence and an investigation of universal states of affairs that are constituted within immediate intuition. . . . *Phenomenology carries out its clarifications in acts of seeing, determining, and distinguishing sense. It compares, it distinguishes, it connects, it places in relation, it divides into parts, it separates off moments.*[57]

Like the "abstracted" givens of space and time discussed here, logic and mathematics, which are studied in Husserl's *Logical Investigations*, are as much phenomena as is our experience of the world around us. We experience logic and mathematics: they appear to us.

> We are concerned with a *phenomenological origin* . . . we are concerned with *insight into the essence* of the concepts involved, looking methodologically to the fixation of unambiguous, sharply distinct verbal meanings.[58]

As Rotenstreich puts it:

> Programmatically, Husserl views the logical concept as having its origin in *Anschauung* [intuition]. Thus, he describes the primary synthesis as "ideative universality". . . his ideative universality is grounded in ideas not as universal objects of knowledge, but as they are to be discerned in the subject or the ego, which for Husserl is the basic or primary stratum of knowledge. It is

52. Husserl, *The Idea of Phenomenology*, 35.
53. Husserl, *The Idea of Phenomenology*, 42.
54. Hardy, "Translator's Introduction," 50; Husserl, *The Idea of Phenomenology*, 65.
55. Husserl, *The Idea of Phenomenology*, 42.
56. O'Connor, "Lecture 1—Husserl's Phenomenology," 7–8.
57. Husserl, *The Idea of Phenomenology*, 43. Italics in the original.
58. Husserl, *Logical Investigations*, §67, 153–54.

last from the point of view of our coming to it, but primary from the point of view of that which is the presupposition of all knowledge.[59]

The "phenomenological origin" of logic and mathematics means that they belong with "objects of knowledge" as things in the world, although like such ideas as "change" they are Ideas that are "abstractly apprehended universals."[60] A real world object phenomenally available to us is different in phenomenological structure from time. Real-world objects, such as tables and chairs, can only be given inadequately because evidence is always inadequate,[61] whereas a mathematical formula can be given adequately as indubitable,[62] and might at the same time be understood as a real-world phenomenon via objects and other phenomena, as number might be.[63] Time and change might be different again because they are abstracted from multiple other phenomena. But all of them are phenomena, and all of them are given in intuition,[64] which Rotenstreich describes as

> a categorial form related to what [Husserl] calls "self-givenness." As such, it leads not to knowledge as construction, but to the identity between the content and that which is present or given. It is purely intuitive, referring to the essence and not to the sensuous datum, and it is inherent in ideation.[65]

"Absolute givenness is an ultimate." Whether given in perception, in "representation" by memory,[66] or by universalizing the given appearing objects, such universals as "temporal content in general, duration in general, change in general" can be posited:[67] and so

> thought-forms . . . if appropriately built up, come to consciousness on the basis of given objects synthetically connected in

---

59. Rotenstreich, *Synthesis and Intentional Objectivity*, 2.

60. Husserl, *Logical Investigations*, I, §2, 167.

61. Berghofer, "Husserl's Conception of Experiential Justification," 167.

62. Berghofer, "Husserl's Conception of Experiential Justification," 168.

63. Husserl, *Philosophy of Arithmetic*, 493.

64. Findlay's translation of "*Anschauung*," although he also suggests "envisaging," "picturing," "seeing," which seem to make more sense (Findlay, "Translator's Introduction," lxxxvi).

65. Rotenstreich, *Synthesis and Intentional Objectivity*, 1.

66. Husserl, *The Idea of Phenomenology*, 51.

67. Husserl, *The Idea of Phenomenology*, 44, 49.

elementary acts so as to present states of affairs of this or that ontological form.[68]

Equally "general" might be logic and mathematics. For instance, number is an

> ideal form-series, which is absolutely one in the sense of arithmetic, in whatever mental act it may be individuated for us in an intuitively constituted collective, a species which is accordingly untouched by the contingency, temporality and transience of our mental acts. Acts of counting arise and pass away and cannot be meaningfully mentioned in the same breath as numbers.[69]

Each "something general," whether time, number, or any other abstracted or intuited generality, is immanent in the sense of being given in consciousness, and it is also transcendent, because beyond any particular that might be immanent: so although the phenomenological reduction does not exclude the transcendent in terms of the "really [reelle] transcendent (say, in the psychological-empirical sense)," it does exclude the transcendent "as such, as an existence to be assumed, that is, everything that is not absolute givenness . . . the absolute givenness of pure seeing."[70] This is what a phenomenon is in the phenomenological sense: something "absolutely given."[71]

In this context we can make judgements about objects that appear—for instance, about a particular house, the color, extension, and house of which are phenomena[72]—as "the object of experience constitutes itself in a continuum, and . . . the manner of this constitution is prescribed to it, in that its essence requires just such a gradated constitution."[73] The phenomena have "horizons" which are "given" with them.[74] We cannot see beyond a horizon, but there is something there: and so the house-phenomena indicate towards the horizons of the phenomena and so towards the house. As Moran puts it,

> The "horizon" is constituted by those aspects of a thing that are not given in perception but rather are possibilities which can be given in further acts of perception or reflection.[75]

68. Husserl, *The Idea of Phenomenology*, 52.

69. Husserl, *Logical Investigations*, 8, §46, 110.

70. Husserl, *The Idea of Phenomenology*, 65–66.

71. Boedeker, "Phenomenology," 157.

72. Husserl, *The Idea of Phenomenology*, 53.

73. Husserl, *The Idea of Phenomenology*, 69.

74. Husserl, *Cartesian Meditations*, 45.

75. Moran, *Introduction to Phenomenology*, 162.

Here we arrive at the point in the circular process where phenomena inspire an intention that directs us across horizons and towards the something in particular that we intend, and in general towards the world of objects.[76]

GIVENNESSES

Husserl's argument has led to diverse kinds of givenness: a "given world";[77] givenness of the *cogitatio* (what is thought); "the *cogitatio re-lived in a fresh memory*"; "the *unity of appearances* persisting in the phenomenal stream"; "the *change* in such a unity"; "the *thing* in 'outer' perception"; "the different forms of imagination and recollection"; "manifold *perceptions* and other kinds of *representations* that are synthetically unified in corresponding connections"; the "experienced Other, given to me in straightforward consciousness";[78] "*universality*"; mathematics; logic;[79] and the "structure of the Ego (for example, the immanent temporal form belonging to the stream of subjective processes) . . . I exist for myself and am continually given to myself, by experiential evidence, as '*I myself*.'"[80] Above all, "we stand on the footing of the world already given as existing."[81] It is by studying all of these different kinds of givenness, in the many different kinds of knowing, that the "essence of givenness" can be discovered, and different kinds of objectivity can be understood, such as "real spatial-temporal actuality," "the objectivity of the objective sciences,"[82] and above all the self-givenness of the meaning-giving subject that functions in a way not dissimilar to that of Kant's synthesizing mind but that understands intentionally grasped phenomena as knowledge of the given world.[83]

   Hardy usefully formulates the structure of Husserl's philosophy in terms of transcendence and immanence by correlating immanence (what is within our consciousness) with adequate givenness, and transcendence (what is outside our consciousness) with inadequate givenness.[84] The

76. O'Connor, "Lecture 1—Husserl's Phenomenology," 5, 7.

77. Husserl, *Cartesian Meditations*, 82.

78. Husserl, *Cartesian Meditations*, 90.

79. Husserl, *The Idea of Phenomenology*, 54. Italics in the original.

80. Husserl, *Cartesian Meditations*, 28, 68. Italics in the original. See Rotenstreich, *Synthesis and Intentional Objectivity*, 36, 53: "Givenness on the level of consciousness . . . is self-givenness."

81. Husserl, *Cartesian Meditations*, 34.

82. Husserl, *The Idea of Phenomenology*, 54–55.

83. Luft, "From Being to Givenness and Back," 368.

84. Hardy, "Translator's Introduction," 7.

essences, universals, and so on, given by "ideating abstraction," are therefore transcendent in the sense of being outside our consciousness, but they can be immanent in the sense of being adequately given. The same must also be true of the thinking self as an object of consciousness: it might be outside consciousness, but it might also be adequately given and, because indubitable, might be absolutely given.

Once the question of access to external objects has been tackled, the next problem to be solved is that of correspondence between the act of knowing and the known object, so this too must be brought into the sphere of immanence. In the consciousness, in immanence, object-experiences are completely given, and so although the objects are transcendent, they are immanent phenomenologically: and reflection can then relate the appearances and our intentions to each other, as both are immanent in the phenomenological sense. Hardy sums up the "phenomenological critique of knowledge" as

> to identify, analyze, and describe the various ramified systems of presentation and representation correlated to the various kinds of possible objectivities, and in so doing, identify the forms of evidence which serve to justify belief in the existence and determinations of the objectivities so given.[85]

The question is no longer Descartes' question about how thought can correlate with an existing world, but "how the givenness of objects is intentionally constituted within a consciousness that embraces both the givenness of the empirical mind and the empirical world of which that mind is a part."[86]

Hardy identifies a problem with Husserl's phenomenology. "Intentionality" in the context of the phenomenological project has to leave to one side the question of the existence or non-existence of an external transcendent reality, and so can only refer to the relationship between consciousness and phenomena. The question that Descartes tackled remains unresolved, as any correspondence remains in the immanent sphere.[87] Either any external object must be assumed to exist as phenomena give it when they are organized by the mind into an idea of the object, or we have to say that we should assume that the world is as it is given in phenomena unless somehow proved otherwise. Moran identifies a related problem: Husserl has as much of a problem accounting for personal relationships as Descartes does, as the only route available to Husserl is via analogy, or by a "secondary or indeed

---

85. Hardy, "Translator's Introduction," 9.
86. Hardy, "Translator's Introduction," 9.
87. Hardy, "Translator's Introduction," 11.

tertiary givenness":[88] "Husserl sees the ground for understanding of the mental life of the other . . . as lying in one's own self-understanding,"[89] which implies that the other person is both transcendent and immanent, which in turn reveals the self to be both transcendent object and immanent to the consciousness: and we are back with the problem that Hardy has identified. Marion identifies a further problem that is close to our main concern: that Husserl restricts givenness to objects, rather than understanding givenness as "the ultimate norm of phenomenality."[90] We might develop that idea into a further question: Is givenness given? Given in the secondary sense of an idea based on a generalizing of phenomena? But if so, must those phenomena not already have been given with a givenness that has already appeared?

PHENOMENOLOGICAL DEVELOPMENTS

Whether or not we take these problems to be determinative of the value of Husserl's method, his phenomenology has inspired a significant philosophical movement that has both maintained and used the method, altered it beyond recognition (as we might think Heidegger did by adding a second phenomenological reduction), or taken it further than Husserl did. This last option is the one chosen by Marion, whose philosophy stands firmly within phenomenology at the same time as taking it further by insisting on yet another phenomenological reduction and by centering philosophy on givenness rather than on the phenomena given. As we have seen, there is plenty of givenness in Husserl's philosophy, but there it is a characteristic of the phenomena that are given. The "object that confronts us in life . . . is given, with the originality of the 'it itself,' in the synthesis of a passive experience."[91] The experience might be passive, but it is still human experience to which phenomena appear, and it is the phenomena that are given. In Marion's philosophy it is "the given" that takes center stage.

An important point of contact between Descartes' and Husserl's philosophy is the centrality of the thinking and experiencing ego. It is the ego that is the thinking thing on which the certainty of knowledge of all other reality depends, and the ego to which phenomena appear. As Rotenstreich finds, "The Ego can only grasp and not be a content of grasping. This is the meaning of self-givenness or self-origination."[92] We shall find a similar

88. Moran, *Introduction to Phenomenology*, 177.

89. Moran, *Introduction to Phenomenology*, 179.

90. Marion, *Being Given*, 32.

91. Husserl, *Cartesian Meditations*, 78.

92. Rotenstreich, *Synthesis and Intentional Objectivity*, 54.

centrality of the experiencing ego when we study Marion's philosophy. But more importantly for our theme, we find Marion transforming the status of givenness in phenomenology. Marion sets out from Husserl's understanding of the givenness of phenomena, both in general and in detail: for instance, he follows Husserl in recognizing that givenness is prior to and unifying of some traditional oppositions.

> There is not first the givenness of appearing and then that of what appears, or first that of the object and then that of its mode of givenness. . . . the metaphysical opposition par excellence, the opposition between essence and existence, is abolished in the face of givenness.[93]

Marion has recognized the pivotal role that givenness plays in Husserl's philosophy, which is why he wonders why Husserl never provided a definition of givenness, and speculates that this might be because givenness rather than the phenomena might in fact have been foundational for Husserl.[94] Or perhaps, as we have seen, it was because givenness had such diverse meanings that no consistent definition would ever have been possible.

Coherent with the centrality of givenness to Husserl's philosophy is Marion's recognition that all three of Descartes, Kant, and Husserl, each in their own way, discuss the "saturated phenomenon" that is the quintessential "given phenomenon." In Descartes' case it is "the infinite" that is a saturated phenomenon; in Kant's it is the sublime; and in Husserl Marion finds that "the internal consciousness of time corresponds to . . . the distinctive characteristics of the saturated phenomenon."[95] It is when we get to Marion's own philosophy that we shall find the destination of this phenomenological journey: no longer the givenness of phenomena, but phenomena as the given; and following Heidegger's diversion of phenomenology into ontology, Being as the given as well.

A PHENOMENOLOGICAL ACTOLOGY, AND AN ACTOLOGY OF PHENOMENOLOGY.

But before we leave Husserl, we need to recognize that at the heart of his philosophy, hidden in plain sight, is action in patterns that is the necessary counterpart of the given phenomena. The consciousness that receives the given phenomena is far from passive: it is an active transcendental

93. Marion, *Being Given*, 22.
94. Marion, *Being Given*, 26–27.
95. Marion, *Being Given*, 219–22.

consciousness. The content and meaning of phenomena can only be a relationship between the action in changing patterns that constitutes the subject's transcendental consciousness, and the action in changing patterns that constitute the given phenomena. "Acts of consciousness"[96] are just as constitutive of the phenomena that phenomenology is all about as is the givenness of the phenomena themselves: indeed, without the intentional acts of consciousness there are no phenomena. As Crowell puts it:

> Since such acts condition the givenness of any possible beings, all ontological inquiry presupposes the science of transcendental consciousness.[97]

We might amend as follows:

> Since such acts condition the givenness of any possible changing patterns of action, all actological inquiry presupposes the science of transcendental consciousness.

In relation to both the active consciousness and the giving of phenomena we have only found action in changing patterns. Nothing stands still. Phenomenology is all about the active receiving mind and the giving of phenomena, both of which can be understood in terms of an actology that understands reality as action in changing patterns. Equally, phenomenology contributes to our understanding of actology because it offers us multiple examples of action in changing patterns: the individual person as a complex bundle of action in changing patterns, society likewise, and also likewise the appearing of phenomena as always action in complex changing patterns. In the phenomenological world of Husserl there are no beings and there is no Being. There is Action, and action in changing patterns.

---

96. Husserl, *Cartesian Meditations*, 36.
97. Husserl, *Cartesian Meditations*, 54.

3

Martin Heidegger's "disclosure"

INTRODUCTION

Martin Heidegger's *Dasein*, "being there," understands Being as my Being, because that is the Being to which we have access; and understands my Being as a Being-in-the-world, because I cannot extract myself from the world in which I live and so have no Being other than Being-in-the-world. For Heidegger, it is this Being-in-the-world that is the primary given.

> But is it not contrary to the rules of all sound method to approach a problematic without sticking to what is given as evident in the area of our theme? And what is more indubitable than the givenness of the "I"? And does not this givenness tell us that if we aim to work this out primordially, we must disregard everything else that is "given"—not only a "world" that *is* [*einer seienden* "*Welt*"], but even the Being of other "I"s? The kind of "giving" we have here is the mere, formal, reflective awareness of the "I"; and perhaps what it gives is indeed evident. This insight even affords access to a phenomenological problematic in its own right, which has in principle the signification of providing a framework as a "formal phenomenology of consciousness.". . . Our investigation takes its orientation from

> Being-in-the-world—that basic state of Dasein by which every
> mode of its Being gets co-determined.[1]

It might initially appear, in this passage and more generally, that Heidegger is following in Husserl's footsteps, until we understand that the fundamental phenomenon is not the "I" but "my being in the world," my embeddedness in a broader reality from which my "I" cannot be abstracted. It is no surprise that Husserl understood Heidegger's *Being and Time* as a return to the "natural attitude," because he thought that it was a naturalistic understanding of human being in the world. Heidegger saw it differently: his philosophy was a phenomenological study of *Dasein*, "being there," "being in the world," and so an attempt to understand human being as it gives itself to us.[2]

However different Heidegger's phenomenology might be from Husserl's, we shall find an important similarity: that everything is action in changing patterns. The "Being" that Heidegger studies is a "being in the world," which can only be understood as the changing patterns of action that constitute our being in the world: so just as we found that Husserl's phenomenology demanded to be studied on the basis of an actology, so we shall find that an actological understanding of reality can take us into the heart of Heidegger's philosophy. And just as Husserl's phenomenology contributed to our understanding of actology by offering multiple examples of action in changing patterns, so we shall find Heidegger's exploration of the ontological and the ontic providing us with multiple additional examples of action in changing patterns: examples that dissolve the boundary between the ontological and the ontic that Heidegger regarded as so important.

DASEIN'S GIVENNESS

Although Heidegger abandoned much of Husserl's terminology, we can interpret *Dasein* as immanent to our consciousness, and we can understand the detail of *Sein und Zeit* (*Being and Time*) as phenomenological because of the paired "ontological" and "ontic" aspects of my being in the world, with the "ontological" angst, authentic choices, and so on, that belong to my *Dasein* understood as immanent to consciousness, and the related "ontic" fear, inauthentic choices driven by "the They," and so on, as transcendent aspects of an external world.[3]

---

1. Heidegger, *Being and Time*, 151, 153.
2. Moran, *Introduction to Phenomenology*, 191, 194, 227–28.
3. Heidegger, *Being and Time*, 182, 42–43.

"Phenomenological reduction" does not appear in *Being and Time*, but "givenness" does occasionally, as we have discovered in the quotation at the beginning of this chapter, where, as we would expect, Heidegger privileges the givenness of *Dasein* over other givennesses. Husserl's "absolute givenness"[4] of phenomena has generally been concentrated into Heidegger's "unadulterated givenness" of *Dasein*:[5] "What is more indubitable than the givenness of the 'I'? And does not this givenness tell us that if we aim to work this out primordially, we must disregard everything else that is 'given.'"[6] The same goes for time. A fundamental temporality appears as the time that we experience. "Time temporalizes itself":

> The conception of time as a now-sequence is not aware of the derivation of this time from original time and overlooks all the essential features belonging to the now-sequence as such. As commonly understood, time is intrinsically a free-floating sequence of nows. It is simply there; its givenness must be acknowledged.[7]

However, even though *Dasein* is clearly "given" "ontically" because it is "that which is closest," and time is given as a "now-sequence," they are not *ontologically* closest, simply because they are "in the world."[8] As de Beistegui puts it,

> precisely insofar as being is given from the start, precisely insofar as it is ontically closest, it is ontologically farthest. This is a closeness of which, for the most part, we are oblivious, since we are it, a givenness and a gift we do not acknowledge as such, and which we can take up only in a gesture of appropriation, or reappropriation.[9]

"A bare subject without a world never 'is' proximally, nor is it ever given";[10] and neither is anything else ever "given" ontologically:[11] not even myself,[12] because

4. Husserl, *The Idea of Phenomenology*, 65–66.

5. Cerbone, "Realism and Truth," 254.

6. Heidegger, *Being and Time*, 151.

7. Heidegger, *The Basic Problems of Phenomenology*, 268.

8. Heidegger, *Being and Time*, 36.

9. de Beistigui, *Thinking with Heidegger*, 136.

10. Heidegger, *Being and Time*, 152.

11. Heidegger, *Being and Time*, 129.

12. Carmen, "Authenticity," 293.

in terms of the "they," and as the "they," I am "given" proximally to "myself" [mir "selbst"]. Proximally Dasein is "they," and for the most part it remains so.[13]

Much the same is true of any other givennesses. Sadler's translation of a lecture that Heidegger gave in 1919 is "For something environmental to be *given* is already a theoretical infringement."[14] However, *gegebenes* is here an adjective—"*denn* gegebenes *Umweltliches ist bereits theoetisch angetastetes*"[15]—so it might be better to translate as "for given worldly things are already theoretically inappropriate."

> "Givenness" is already quite properly a theoretical form, and precisely for this reason it cannot be taken as the essence or the immediate environing world as environmental.[16]

As all nouns are capitalized in German we cannot tell whether Heidegger intended "form" here to mean a platonic Form: but whether or not that is his intention, he is clear that the "environing world" is not itself "given," and also that neither "reality," "*Realität*," nor "thingliness," "*Dinghaftigkeit*,"[17] are "environmental characteristics."[18] The world does not exist for me as an independent "given": it is given only along with the absolutely given *Dasein*: my Being-in-the-world. "The history of be-ing" is a history of "whether be-ing gifts or refuses itself."[19] There is no sense here that something has been given and remains as it was when it was given. As Charles Guignon emphasizes, "the giving of the gift" and "the relation of presencing to absence"[20] imply a constant giving of *Dasein* and thus the crucial role of the human being "in the event of bringing to realization an understanding of being."[21]

DISCLOSURE

"Givenness" is not a common concept in relation to Heidegger's "ontological ontology," and is explicitly distanced from the world into which *Dasein* is

---

13. Heidegger, *Being and Time*, 167.
14. Heidegger, *Towards the Definition of Philosophy*, 74.
15. Heidegger, *Zur Bestimmung der Philosophie*, 88.
16. Heidegger, *Towards the Definition of Philosophy*, 75.
17. Heidegger, *Zur Bestimmung der Philosophie*, 89
18. Heidegger, *Towards the Definition of Philosophy*, 75.
19. Heidegger, *Contributions to Philosophy*, 64.
20. Guignon, "The History of Being," 401.
21. Guignon, "The History of Being," 401.

thrown: but the similar "disclosure" is an essential and frequent concept, it fulfils a similar function to Husserl's "givenness," and it expresses a world that is itself disclosed, although the "site" of the disclosure remains *Dasein*.

> "Disclose" and "disclosedness" will be used as technical terms in the passages that follow, and signify "to lay open" and "the character of having been laid open." Thus "to disclose" never means anything like "to obtain indirectly by inference."[22]

> To the Dasein there belongs essentially a disclosed world and with that the disclosedness of the Dasein itself.[23]

An "eventful unfolding" takes place.[24]

As David Webb puts it,

> the movements by which ontological thought arises from the ontic and returns to it are inseparable from one another, and . . . it would be more accurate to say that ontological thought never really leaves the ontic dimension at all. . . . Heidegger conceives of the event of disclosure as a form of movement and . . . understands all movement to be grounded in a formal dimension characterized by continuity. . . . continuity is linked both to the sense of Being as a whole with which fundamental ontology engages, and to the finitude of Dasein as a site of disclosure. To describe the movement between the ontic and the ontological as continuous is therefore to say that these levels belong together, but also to expose a certain condition underlying the relation between the ontic and the ontological, and therefore the very idea of the ontological difference.[25]

Everything is "disclosed," whether ontological or ontic: Being in the world, things "present-at-hand," things "ready-to-hand," the world, understanding, significations, space, Dasein, the Dasein-with of Others, the Other, authentic Being, Dasein in its thrownness, the "there". . . :[26] and by locating understanding of the world in *Dasein's* understanding, Heidegger has

> deprived pure intuition . . . of its priority, which corresponds noetically to the priority of the present-at-hand in traditional

22. Heidegger, *Being and Time*, 105.
23. Heidegger, *The Basic Problems of Phenomenology*, 18.
24. de Beidstegui, *Thinking with Heidegger*, 88.
25. Webb, *Heidegger, Ethics and the Practice of Ontology*, 3.
26. Heidegger, *Being and Time*, 85, 105, 106, 118, 121, 145, 151, 156, 167, 175, 176.

ontology. "Intuition" and "thinking" are both derivatives of understanding, and already rather remote ones.[27]

The "subject-object model" must therefore be abandoned,[28] any propositional truth must be understood to be subordinate to a more primordial givenness of the world,[29] and "*Dasein is its disclosedness*,"[30] with the ontological being disclosed in the ontic. Wrathall therefore finds that "we can say . . . that the disclosure of being consists in our being disposed in a particular way for the world."[31]

Webb draws the conclusion that

> "fundamental" ontological thought is no longer necessarily insulated from the vicissitudes of experience, the changing forms of cultural life and so forth. Second, since ontological thought remains planted in our concrete experience, it is bound to the existential concern over who we are and how we live; that is, ontology is inseparable from ethics.[32]

And negation, an essential aspect of the ontic everyday world, assumes a prior disclosure: "How could negation produce the 'not' from itself when it can negate only if something negatable is already granted to it?"[33] Here "already granted to it" translates Heidegger's *vorgegeben*: "pregiven."[34]

Later on, Heidegger distinguishes between the uncoveredness of beings and the disclosure of their being:

> A being can be uncovered, whether by way of perception or some other mode of access, only if the being of this being is already disclosed—only if I already understand it. . . . The unveiling of the being that we ourselves are, the Dasein, and that has existence as its mode of being, we shall call not uncovering but *disclosure, opening up. . . . with the disclosure of its world* the Dasein is at the same time *unveiled to its own self for itself. . . . a world is disclosed and other Daseins are disclosed with it. . . . The Dasein is its disclosedness.*[35]

27. Heidegger, *Being and Time*, 187; Lafont, "Hermeneutics," 274.

28. Lafont, "Hermeneutics," 267.

29. Wrathall, "Unconcealment," 345.

30. Heidegger, *Being and Time*, 171. Italics in the original.

31. Wrathall, "Unconcealment," 354.

32. Webb, *Heidegger, Ethics and the Practice of Ontology*, 5.

33. Heidegger, *Pathmarks*, 92.

34. Heidegger, *Wegmarken*, 116; Käufer, "Logic," 148.

35. Heidegger, *The Basic Problems of Phenomenology*, 72, 215, 216, 279, 336.

Instead of writing about disclosure and uncoveredness, might Heidegger equally well have written that Being in the world, the being of things, things "present-at-hand," the world, understanding, significations, space, Dasein, the Dasein-with of Others, the Other, authentic Being, Dasein in its thrown-ness, the "there". . . were given? That our Being is given in continuity with the ontic, and in continuity with an ethics of givenness? It is not "a question of things given in advance in their presence," but rather a question of "the eventfulness of things . . . the non-present horizon from out of which they present themselves as things."[36] The problem of Being

> is not a problem constituted by a pregiven faculty of intellection, but by our very being: it is a possibility or a modality of exis-tence, a *Sein-können*, that is, a way—and indeed the supreme way—for us of being (our) being. Thus, we could say, in what amounts to a reversal of the Cartesian *cogito*, that it is insofar as man ek-sists that man thinks. For to ek-sist means: to stand in the Open as such and as a whole, to abide by beings and dwell amid their presence. And thinking is one such way of standing in the Open, one way of being open. Thought is not an absolute point of departure, then, the origin of the question, but already a response, a response to the call of being, or to the fact that man is situated beyond all beings, as this or that being, and thrown in the openness of being.[37]

ES GIBT: THERE IS

There is a gesture in the direction of understanding the givenness of things in Heidegger's employment of "*es gibt*," "it gives": the German expres-sion for "there is," not in the sense that "there is a particular house," but in the sense of "the there, the context or world within which entities can present themselves,"[38] or perhaps more generally our experience of "the something,"[39] or that "there is a universe": that is, a universe exists.

> Being lies in the fact that something is, and in its Being as it is; in Reality; in presence-at-hand; in subsistence; in validity; in Dasein; in the "there is."

---

36. de Beistegui, *Thinking with Heidegger*, 87–88.
37. de Beistegui, *Thinking with Heidegger*, 43.
38. Polt, "*Ereignis*," 376.
39. Polt, "*Ereignis*," 379.

> Sein liegt im Dass- und Sosein, in Realität, Vorhandenheit, Bes-
> tand, Geltung, Dasein, im "es gibt."[40]

As Richard Polt recognizes, the dilemma posed by the "there is" is
inescapable:

> Such questions can never be answered simply by inspecting
> given beings, because when we encounter them we are already
> drawing on a meaning of givenness.[41]

As de Beistegui points out, this is at least as true of ourselves as it is of
anything else because our own being is "a givenness and a gift we do not
acknowledge as such, and which we can take up only in a gesture of appropriation, or reappropriation . . ."[42]

And as Derrida puts it:

> The enigma is concentrated in the . . . *es* . . . which is not a thing,
> and in this giving that gives but without giving anything and
> without anyone giving anything—nothing but Being and time
> (which are nothing):[43]

—"nothing" because Being is not a being, and so does not exist, and time is
not temporal, and neither is it a "thing," so it cannot exist either.[44] Derrida
understands the "enigma" of the "it" in "it gives" ("*es gibt*"), whereas Heidegger interprets it as the occurrence, happening, or event—the *Ereignis*—
which therefore "gives," because "it gives."[45] Derrida's view is that because
Heidegger has gone back "before the determinations of Being as substantial
being, subject or object," he is still able to speak of a gift, as it is not immediately annulled by being an object that is given.[46]

The difference between "given" and "disclosed" is that "given" implies
that something is not there and then it is, and that some agent has done the
giving so that it is now there, whereas disclosure implies that something
has been there all along and that someone or something has revealed it.
In phenomenological terms there would appear to be little difference, if
any. For a phenomenon to be given is for an appearance to be given, which
means much the same as an appearance being disclosed: so perhaps the only

40. Heidegger, *Being and Time*, 26. The German original is quoted in a footnote.
41. Polt, "*Ereignis*," 381.
42. de Beistegui, *Thinking with Heidegger*, 136.
43. Derrida, *Given Time*, 20; "Given Time," 177.
44. Derrida, *Given Time*, 20; "Given Time," 177.
45. Marion, *Being Given*, 37; Polt, "*Ereignis*."
46. Derrida, "Given Time," 180.

remaining difference is that givenness implies a giver, whereas disclosure, the causing to appear, can be of the previously given. So who or what is doing the giving? de Beistigui suggests that

> we live in the epoch or the era in which things manifest themselves as there for us, to be re-presented and re-produced. Their givenness is considered a given; there is no longer a space for questioning them in their origin or givenness.[47]

However, we should surely attempt to answer the question, and in a secular age we might properly suggest that, given the continuity between the ontic and the ontological, an obvious response is that both the diverse and changing ontic everyday world, and the Being that we experience in our own Being-in-the-world, are together the source of the givenness,[48] which would mirror both the phenomena and the intentionality of Husserl's phenomenology. Further responses to the question of who or what might be doing the giving might of course be perfectly legitimate.

A further question arises: Every being is different and is given. Does that mean that the givenness of every being is different?[49] Given the continuity between the givenness of the ontic and the givenness of our Being as Being-in-the-world, does our Being have its own kind of givenness separate from that of beings? And if so, where is the continuity? David Webb's verdict is that

> the dimension of givenness as such may not be susceptible to a final "true" account even in principle and that the variation in the dimension of givenness as such cannot therefore be treated as an improvement achieved as we drive to a more fundamental understanding. On this reading, there would be no univocal saying of Being, no ubiquitous event of the ontological difference. Moreover, the changes undergone by the dimension of givenness would be prompted not by great shifts in epochal history, but by fine-grained alterations in *what* is given and *how* it is given.[50]

Our response has to be that givenness is a diverse and changing pattern of action and is in no sense an object to be studied. It is what gives, or who gives, and not something that is itself given. Rather than being subsidiary to Being, Being and every being are subsidiary to the *es gibt*. This originary

---

47. de Beistigui, *Thinking with Heidegger*, 152.
48. Webb, *Heidegger, Ethics and the Practice of Ontology*, 5–6.
49. Webb, *Heidegger, Ethics and the Practice of Ontology*, 75.
50. Webb, *Heidegger, Ethics and the Practice of Ontology*, 78.

understanding of givenness is coherent with Steinbock's suggestion that givenness is not simply "presentation" of objects, but is itself diverse, and in particular encompasses a "revelatory givenness" of such interpersonal spheres as culture.[51]

When we study Jean-Luc Marion's philosophy we shall find multiple echoes of Heidegger's brand of phenomenology: but there is another connection. Heidegger had begun to train for the Roman Catholic priesthood before he turned to philosophy, and some of his later texts return to theological themes. Marion points out that Heidegger employs the word *Offenbarkeit*, "open manifestation," of Being, and *Offenbarung*, "revelation," of "God," and he is even able to quote Heidegger as writing that theology confronts philosophy as a "mortal enemy, a *Todfeind*."[52] But most importantly for our purposes, Heidegger has further embedded Husserl's "givenness" of phenomena in phenomenology by finding that "*Dasein is its disclosedness*,"[53] and as *Dasein* is our access to Being, this has to mean that Being is its givenness.

A SECOND PHENOMENOLOGICAL REDUCTION

In his *Réduction et donation* (*Reduction and Givenness*), published in 1989, Marion quotes Husserl as saying that "*ontology is not phenomenology*," and Heidegger that "There is no ontology *alongside* a phenomenology, but rather *ontology as a science is nothing other than phenomenology*."[54] Heidegger has returned philosophy to Aristotle's exploration of the meaning of Being—not particular beings, and not beings in general, but rather the Being of beings—and because Being is experienced in the phenomenon of *Dasein*, "being there," Being is the fundamental phenomenon, suggesting to Marion that Heidegger has contributed a second "phenomenological reduction": not only Husserl's reduction to the phenomena, to "the things themselves," but subsequently also to the phenomenon of the Being of the things themselves.

> These two rounds of the phenomenological reduction by Heidegger therefore converge toward a single goal: to receive Being itself in pure givenness and as a phenomenon.[55]

51. Steinbock, "Personal Givenness and Cultural A Prioris," 161–63.

52. Marion, *God without Being*, 62.

53. Heidegger, *Being and Time*, 171. Italics in the original.

54. Marion, *Reduction and Givenness*, 40. Italics in the original.

55. Marion, *Reduction and Givenness*, 75.

Marion goes on to ask whether there are in fact two reductions at work here: to beings, and "that of all beings to the Being of beings."[56] Heidegger defines the difference between Being and beings as the "ontological difference,"[57] but Marion finds that a second reduction to Being is not in fact what Heidegger has discussed in relation to the ontological difference, because he has granted primacy to *Dasein*, my being-in-the-world as our most immediate access to Being, rather than to Being itself.

> That primacy, because it introduces a mediating term, prohibits the question of Being from bringing out straightaway the canonical ontological difference (Being-being) and substitutes for it the "ontological difference" between two beings and their ways of Being. . . . *Sein und Zeit* owes its incompletion only to the concealment within it of the ontological difference by the "ontological difference"—namely, by *Dasein* itself.[58]

It must remain a question as to whether we can legitimately extend an understanding of Being as *Dasein* to the Being of things, whether present-at-hand or ready-to-hand: and because of this doubt, *Sein und Zeit* "was not able to stage Being directly as a phenomenon."[59] However, by 1943 Marion finds Heidegger suggesting that "Being would display itself without any ontic precondition, absolutely and as such,"[60] and so without *Dasein* as a mediator.

> If ontology completes phenomenology and if phenomenology alone renders ontology possible, it is necessary that a "phenomenon of Being" manifest itself.[61]

ES GIBT: IT GIVES

In a lecture given in 1962, in which he takes up the question of "time and Being"—a discussion that he felt unable to complete while writing *Being and Time*—Heidegger returns to the meaning of "*es gibt*."

> To think Being explicitly requires us to relinquish Being as the ground of beings in favor of the giving which prevails concealed in unconcealment, that is, in favor of the It gives. As the gift

---

56. Marion, *Reduction and Givenness*, 76.

57. Marion, *Reduction and Givenness*, 108.

58. Marion, *Reduction and Givenness*, 140.

59. Marion, *Reduction and Givenness*, 167.

60. Marion, *Reduction and Givenness*, 169.

61. Marion, *Reduction and Givenness*, 169.

of this It gives, Being belongs to giving. As a gift, Being is not
expelled from giving. Being, presencing is transmuted. As
allowing-to-presence, it belongs to unconcealing; as the gift of
unconcealing it is retained in the giving. Being *is* not. There is,
It gives Being as the unconcealing; as the gift of unconcealing it
is retained in the giving. Being *is* not. There is, It gives Being as
the unconcealing of presencing.[62]

As de Beistegui points out, *es gibt* implies the thing given, but even more
the act of giving:

In all given things, there is the thing that is actually given, the
thing given in actuality. And the destiny as well as the force of
metaphysical thought will have been relentlessly to raise the
question of the sense of such an actuality, to think the essence of
the actual. Yet in all given things there is also the giving in and
through which such things and the world that harbors them are
given. In excess of the thing in its actuality, there is the gift at the
origin of this actuality, the virtual horizon whence it unfolds.
This is a gift—a movement and an event—the sense of which
can thus not be exhausted in the actuality it opens onto. This is
an event irreducible to a sense of being as presence and of time
as present. And yet it coincides with the very event, the very
happening of being and time.[63]

The giving is ubiquitous. As Heidegger points out, "time-space . . . in the
sense of the distance measured between two time-points, is the result of
time calculation,"[64] so "true time is four-dimensional":

But the dimension which we call the fourth in our count is, in
the nature of the matter, the first, that is, the giving that determines all. In future, in past, in the present, that giving brings
about to each its own presencing . . . .[65]

And time, like Being,

remains the gift of an "It gives" whose giving preserves the realm
in which presence is extended . . . Being proves to be destiny's
gift of presence, the gift granted by the giving of time.[66]

62. Heidegger, *On Time and Being*, 6.
63. de Beistegui, "Thinking with Heidegger," 7–8.
64. Heidegger, *On Time and Being*, 14.
65. Heidegger, *On Time and Being*, 15.
66. Heidegger, *On Time and Being*, 17, 22.

Heidegger's philosophy raises the possibility of phenomenological reductions beyond that performed by Husserl, and it enables Marion to perform what he calls his "third reduction" to "the given": a third reduction prefigured by "Being itself . . . delivered in the mode of giving—from one end to the other along the path of [Heidegger's] thought, from *Sein und Zeit* to *Zeit und Sein*, from 1927 to 1962"[67]—a "delivery of Being" that Marion transformed into *"la croisée de l'être,"* "the crossing of Being":[68] a "crossing" with a cross that references Jesus' "cross," *"la croix."*

VERBS AND NOUNS

This conclusion coheres with a particular finding in relation to Heidegger's use of verbs and nouns: that verbs are used more often in the context of the "They," that is, in the context of the particularities of the world into which Dasein has fallen, but that nouns are used of the existential characteristics of Dasein: for instance, Being, Dasein, Falling, Flight, and Thrownness, suggesting an unchangeableness about Dasein as opposed to constant change in the They. Being-in-the-world seems to be a static ideal state in relation to Dasein, and a turbulent complex changing pattern of activity in relation to the world.

 This dual conceptual structure can be found all over *Being and Time*: in the distinction between the "ontological" characteristics of Dasein that are intrinsic to its Being, and those "ontical" contingent aspects of human life that are not permanent characteristics of Dasein, but that might nevertheless relate to them;[69] in the distinction between *Angst* as an existential characteristic of Dasein, and the particular fears that we experience in the world;[70] in the distinction between those "authentic" choices that are Dasein's own, and those "inauthentic" ones that are driven by the They, that is, by the world into which Dasein has fallen;[71] in the distinction between truth as an existential characteristic of Dasein, expressed by the nouns "disclosedness, uncovering, and uncoveredness,"[72] and truth as ontical, where Heidegger is happy to employ present tense active verbs;[73] and in the

---

67. Marion, *God without Being*, 102.

68. Marion, *God without Being*, 95.

69. Heidegger, *Sein und Zeit*, 11–12, 43.

70. Heidegger, *Sein und Zeit*, 182.

71. Heidegger, *Sein und Zeit*, 42–43.

72. Heidegger, *Sein und Zeit*, 226.

73. Heidegger, *Sein und Zeit*, 221.

distinction between "projection" as an existential characteristic of Dasein, and projection as experienced by the world.[74]

The nouns used for ontological characteristics of Dasein—*Verfallen, Sein, Dasein*—are nominalized verbs and so still carry some of the connotations of the verb, which means that translation by present participles is often appropriate: but there is still a difference between the grammatical constructions that we find when characteristics of Dasein's Being-in-the-world are discussed as ontological characteristics of the Being of Dasein, and when those characteristics are discussed ontically in relation to their involvement in the They: nouns for the ontological, and verbs for the ontic. The implication is that there is rather less change in the ontological patterns of action than there is in the ontic patterns of action. Ontological thrownness into the world might be regarded as a one-off and essentially unchanging event with permanent effects, whereas a constant being thrown among the They, and the resulting turbulence, can only be expressed by using verbs. As Guignon puts it, we are thrown "into an event that is always already under way, an event in which we can only let ourselves be carried on,"[75] and one that is "the inescapable givenness of one's situation."[76] The implication of our thrownness is that we are always in a particular world.[77] Dasein's givenness is ontologically a one-off event and so an unchanging pattern of action, but it is ontically a continuously changing pattern of action in the world of the They: that is, amongst Others. In the context of an actology—a conceptual framework that understands reality as action in changing patterns rather than as beings that change—it is the ontic, and so the constantly giving and the constantly given, that is the most real, and the ontological—the least giving and the least given—that is the least real.[78] Coherently with this understanding, Engelland points out that in a handwritten note in a copy of *Sein und Zeit* Heidegger had turned from regarding "transcendence as the ecstatical—timeliness—temporality" to an "event" (*Ereignis*) that Engelland interprets as an "event of appropriation."[79]

74. Torry, *Actological Readings*, chapter 4.

75. Guignon, "The History of Being," 401.

76. Borgman, "Technology," 424.

77. de Beistegui, *Thinking with Heidegger*, 64.

78. Torry, *Actological Readings*, chapter 4.

79. Engelland, "Disentangling Heidegger's Transcendental Questions," 94; Heidegger, *Sein und Zeit*, 440.

THE EVENT OF BEING

One possible Heideggerian proposal is offered by Thomas Sheehan, who suggests that *Dasein* is "drawn on by its own desired fulfillment": a fulfillment currently absent, so that our "presence-bestowing absence" gives the gift of "our imperfect presence."[80] Another possible Heideggerian proposal in an actological direction is suggested by de Beistegui when he understands being as an originary event that then withdraws.

> This is an event that always takes place as something other than itself, an origin that withdraws from the very world it discloses and effaces itself in the beings it brings to presence. Disclosing a world, it gives way to the disclosed, effacing itself behind the traces of its own event. Withdrawing from the world, the event presiding over the clearing of world abandons the world to itself, to presence and actuality, which becomes the very sense of being itself. This, then, is where metaphysical thought begins: at the point where the twofold event of being and time arrives, at the point where it has become something actual: a thing, a being, a state of affairs. Metaphysical thought does not begin at the source, with the very event of being and time, but at the end, with the very sphere of actuality onto which this twofold event opens.[81]

But perhaps the most Heideggerian suggestion that we can make is that *Dasein* is Being-in-the-world, so its Being is given by the world that is a gift, and therefore its Being is a gift. As Ruin suggests, one way of understanding Heidegger's Being is as

> a being among beings . . . exposed to the disclosure of world, in no way its agent, but rather the recipient of its gift.[82]

Being is an originary event, a foundational giving, Action itself, that gives birth to beings that are action in changing patterns, and so gives birth to time as well. Dasein, beings, and the Being of beings, *happen.*

It is in this way that an actology can offer a particular verb-intense interpretation of Heidegger's philosophy: an interpretation that understands Being-in-the-world, the present at hand, the ready to hand, the ontic, the ontological, and so on, as action in changing patterns, and thus as belonging together, and interestingly with all of their boundaries—including that

---

80. Sheehan, "*Dasein*," 204.

81. de Beistegui, *Thinking with Heidegger*, 7.

82. Ruin, "Contributions to Philosophy," 367.

between the ontic and the ontological—in principle dissolved. Conversely, Heidegger's philosophy reveals the sense in which any actology will inevitably dissolve any and every boundary, simply because everything, every event, every changing pattern of action, is action in changing patterns. Just as both *Angst* and fear are both action in changing patterns, and therefore entangled with each other, and to all intents and purposes simply different understandings of multiple related complex changing patterns of action, so an actological interpretation of reality will constantly disclose everything, every event, and every changing pattern of action, to be action in changing patterns and in principle universally related to each other and to every other changing pattern of action. Husserl might have focused on phenomena as action in changing patterns; and Heidegger might have focused on our being in the world, which we now have to understand as changing patterns of action, and never as Being in the sense of an unchanging source of being: but those two examples of foci are precisely that—they are two particular examples. To understand reality as action in changing patterns provides a framework within which we can understand both Husserl's and Heidegger's phenomenologies, and their two phenomenologies can reveal such consequences of an actological understanding of reality as the way in which it dissolves boundaries.

4

Jean-Luc Marion's conversation partners: Levinas and Derrida

INTRODUCTION

Both Emmanuel Levinas and Jacques Derrida influenced Jean-Luc Marion's philosophy, so before two chapters that discuss Marion's exploration of "the given" we shall study what both Levinas and Derrida might contribute to our understanding of an actology of the given.

Levinas was something of a bridge between Husserl and Heidegger on the one hand, and Jean-Luc Marion on the other, and his philosophy was a significant influence on Marion's: so it is in relation to those three philosophers, and also in relation to Henri Bergson and Martin Buber, that we shall study what Levinas might have to offer to our understanding of the pattern of action that constitutes giving.

Jacques Derrida, who taught Marion at the *École Normale Supérieure* in Paris between 1967 and 1971, had been exploring the meaning of "the gift" in seminars and publications since the mid-1970s, although sometimes employing different terminology: "destination, . . . the promise, . . . sacrifice, the 'yes,' or originary affirmation . . . the event, invention, the coming or the 'come.'"[1] In 1991 he published *Donner le Temps*, based on the content of a lecture earlier that year and on the content of a series of seminars given

1. Derrida, *Given Time*, x.

47

fourteen years previously. Marion was probably aware of Derrida's interest in the notion of the gift when he wrote his *Réduction et Donation*, but *Donner le Temps* would only have been available to him when he wrote his major study of the gift in *Étant Donné*.

Both Levinas and Derrida functioned as conversation partners for Marion, whose ontology of the given will form the heart of our treatment of the subject, and they will fulfil a similar function for us.

EMMANUEL LEVINAS

The Other

As far as Levinas was concerned, neither Husserl nor Heidegger had created space in their philosophies for the understanding of the Other. Both were too centered on the ego to which phenomena appeared.[2] For Levinas it was the "Other" (*autrui*) that mattered. The other's "face" "destroys the horizon of my egocentric monism"[3] and transcends any idea that I might have about them, so the "face-to-face" cannot be subsumed into any other totality, whether phenomena in general, Being, or my being in the world. Any relationship is with an Other that "cannot be resolved into 'images' or be exposed in a theme."[4] In order to express the utter otherness of the Other, Levinas describes the relationship with the Other as "a relation without relation."[5] As Peperzak puts it, Levinas "insists forcefully on the irreducible moments of heteronomy" and "supplants the overt or hidden monism of ontology by a pluralism whose basic ground model is the relation of the Same (*le Même*) and the Other (*l'Autre*)."[6]

Levinas had read Bergson, with whom he found both points of agreement and also ideas to react against, and in general found himself more in tune with the ethical implications of Bergson's writings than with the more metaphysical implications. Bergson gave primacy to both subjectivity and freedom by understanding time to be *durée*, duration, rather than a deterministic clock time; by understanding the mind as movement rather than as psychophysics; and by understanding evolution as driven by an *élan*

---

2. Davis, *Levinas*, 13–14.

3. Peperzak, *To the Other*, 19.

4. Levinas, *The Levinas Reader*, 89.

5. Levinas, *Totality and Infinity*, 79–80.

6. Peperzak, *To the Other*, 18–19.

vital (understood as creativity) rather than by biological determinism.[7] As Bergson put it

> the whole history of life until man has been . . . to create with matter . . . an instrument of freedom, to make a machine which should triumph over mechanism, and to use the determinism of nature to pass through the meshes of the net which this very determinism had spread.[8]

Similarly, Levinas regarded Being as a homogenizing of reality, and looked for "a diversity all of whose terms would maintain reciprocal relations among themselves, exhibiting thus the totality from which they proceed, and in which there would on occasion be produced a being existing for itself, an I, facing another I."[9] There is a "multiplicity in being, which refuses totalization but takes form as fraternity and discourse."[10] Levinas had read Bergson, but he then left behind the continuities that he found in his philosophy:

> The Bergsonian conception of freedom through duration . . . preserves for the present a power over the future: duration is creation . . . [but the élan vital] tends towards an impersonal pantheism, in the sense that it does not sufficiently note the crispation and isolation of subjectivity.[11]

Bergson believed that we cannot know anything or anyone other than ourselves, as we would need to know *every* element of their *durée* if we were to know someone else.[12] Levinas reaches a similar conclusion but by another route: the otherness of the Other. The other person is Other, and the future is Other in relation to the present.

There is no reciprocity between the Same and the Other, and no symmetry: and therein lies the difference between Levinas's relationship with the Other (which is not a relationship) and the relationship between I and Thou in Martin Buber's book of that name, in which he distinguishes between "I-It" and "I-Thou" relationships.

> When *Thou* is spoken, the speaker has no thing for his object. . . . he takes his stand in relation. . . .

---

7. Bergson, *Mélanges*, 495.

8. Bergson, *L'Évolution Créatrice*, 178–79; Bergson, *Creative Evolution*, 264.

9. Levinas, *Totalité et Infini*, 190–91; Levinas, *Totality and Infinity*, 215.

10. Levinas, *Totalité et Infini*, 191; Levinas, *Totality and Infinity*, 216.

11. Levinas, *Le Temps et L'Autre*, 72, 86–87; Levinas, *Time and the Other*, 80, 91–92.

12. Bergson, *Essai sur les Données Immédiates de la Conscience*, 118; Bergson, *Time and Free Will*, 185.

> First, our life with nature. . . . when we address [creatures]
> as *Thou*, our words cling to the threshold of speech.
>
> Second, our life with [people]. There the relation is open
> and in the form of speech.
>
> Third, our life with spiritual beings. There the rela-
> tion . . . discloses itself; it does not use speech, yet begets
> it. . . . we feel we are addressed and we answer.[13]

For Buber, the relationship with the *Thou* is a "meeting" that is direct and unmediated and is characterized by reciprocity and symmetry. Even in relation to those objects that we would normally describe as "it" a direct meeting of the I and the Thou is possible. "Between you and it there is mutual giving: you say *Thou* to it and give yourself to it, it says *Thou* to you and gives itself to you."[14]

Levinas uses *l'autre* ("other") to mean what can be incorporated into a relationship with us—an *autre* that encompasses both Buber's *It* and his *Thou*; whereas Levinas's *L'Autre* or *Autrui* ("Other") expresses something that cannot be incorporated into a relationship. Levinas has created a gulf between *l'Autre* and *l'autre*, rather as Heidegger located one between "Being" and "being." This suggests that the approach of the Other cannot be a phenomenon alongside other phenomena. Marion disagrees:

> For in the realm of givenness, the phenomenon of the Other,
> for the first time, no longer counts as anything like an extrater
> ritorial exception to phenomenality, but belongs to it officially,
> though with the title paradox (saturated phenomenon).[15]

de Rochechouart finds Marion's view coherent, because

> the phenomenology of givenness, understood as the last pos
> sibility of phenomenology, includes the phenomenon of the
> Other, and receives it as a saturated phenomenon. The Other no
> longer interrupts phenomenality, as for Levinas.[16]

There might or might not be a gap between phenomenology and the approach of the Other, but there is one between the self and the Other, and this is the gulf that matters to Levinas. The "Other" is one who makes a claim on us that we can only answer in terms of responsibility, and our relationship with the Other is "the invocation of a face and already speech

---

13. Buber, *I and Thou*, 16, 18–19.

14. Buber, *I and Thou*, 50.

15. Marion, *Being Given*, 323.

16. de Rochechouart, "The (Im)possibility of God's Name," 655.

[*déjà parole*]"[17] that calls us to "responsibility":[18] "the face [of the Other] imposes on me and I cannot stay deaf to its appeal, or forget it, what I mean is I cannot stop being responsible . . . . Consciousness loses its first place."[19]

> To return to exterior being . . . is to enter into the straightforwardness of the face to face. This is . . . an existence already obligated. It places the center of gravitation of a being outside of that being. The surpassing of phenomenal or inward existence does not consist in receiving the recognition of the Other, but in offering him one's being. To be in oneself is to express oneself, that is, already to serve the Other.[20]

The Work that we do as we respond to the Other—Work that Purcell terms "liturgical"[21]—is therefore not an object to be observed or controlled: it is "a movement of the Same toward the Other that never returns to the Same,"[22] and is characterized by "the total gratuity of Action":[23] that is, an unconditional pattern of action inspired by the call of the Other and constituting the response that fulfils our responsibility at least to some small extent. There is no presence of the Other, but rather an "alterity" that offers a new source of meaning that decenters phenomena by instigating a pure giving in responsibility for the Other.[24] It is because any gift that we might offer is provoked by the Other and does not have its origin in the one who gives so that the gift can be genuinely a gift.[25] In Purcell's understanding, the liturgical has become eucharistic.

> Such a seemingly utter kenosis of the self in favor of the other person is not to be understood as the annihilation of the self, but rather as the constitution of the self. "To be" is to be "for-the-other-person."[26]

---

17. Levinas, "Is Ontology Fundamental?," 128; "L'Ontologie est-elle Fondamentale?," 97.

18. Levinas, *God, Death, and Time,* 181.

19. Levinas, *Humanism of the Other,* 32.

20. Levinas, *Totality and Infinity,* 183.

21. Purcell, *Levinas and Theology,* 139.

22. Levinas, *Humanism of the Other,* 26.

23. Levinas, *Humanism of the Other,* 28.

24. Cohen, "Levinas and the Problem of Phenomenology," 363.

25. Purcell, *Levinas and Theology,* 144.

26. Purcell, *Levinas and Theology,* 152.

Whether we are relating to another human being or to God, the sheer gift of the "relation without relation" means that the relationship has no content that we can grasp and understand.

> The relation with the Other as a relation with his transcendence—the relation with the Other who puts into question the brutal spontaneity of one's immanent destiny—introduces into me what was not in me. But this "action" upon my freedom precisely puts an end to violence and contingency, and, in this sense also, founds Reason.[27]

There is no need for the inverted commas around "action." The approach of the Other cannot be understood in terms of Being or beings, and so can only be understood in terms of Action and actions: and whether we would be able to identify patterns in the action must, on the basis of Levinas's logic, remain an open question. As far as he was concerned, we are here in the realm of pure action; so not only are no quotation marks required: they must be removed.

The absolute otherness of the Other requires that the Other should not impinge on us in the ways in which things do. There is nothing to possess, and certainly no-*one* to possess. We are called to responsibility. Not only are action categories appropriate to an understanding of the Other: they are essential to it. What comes to us is pure action—a Saying—demanding action in return.

> The Other . . . reveals himself in his alterity not in a shock of negating the I, but as the primordial phenomenon of gentleness. . . . The Other is revealed in its "withdrawal" as well as in its "breaking through."[28]

A changing pattern of action impinges on us, but that pattern is not replicable, otherwise we could possess it. Immediately, it is gone, along with the actions that it patterned. And so we must respond with a pattern of action that is ours, and that will be heard as our Saying to the Other.

27. Levinas, *Totality and Infinity*, 203–4.
28. Levinas, *Totality and Infinity*, 150, 155.

The call

The section of Marion's *Prolegomena to Charity* entitled "The Intentionality of Love" is heavily influenced by Levinas, could almost have been written by Levinas, and is dedicated "In homage to Emmanuel Lévinas."[29]

> Before being conscious of myself (*Selbstbewusstsein*), I am conscious of my obligation, . . . vis-à-vis the other . . . the injunction renders me responsible *for* the other (Lévinas) . . . Even if the other did not see me and thus could not judge me, I would experience, by discovering *me* myself as an accusative dismissed of the nominative, that I owe *myself* to him: in order for him to live, I owe it to him to dedicate myself.[30]

In a dialogue with Derrida, discussed in chapter 5, Marion reveals a significant debt to phenomenology, and in particular to Levinas, for whom the Other cannot be described in terms of being, but must instead be experienced as given: and it is in this context that Marion states that "the ultimate determination of the phenomenon implies not to be, but to appear as—*given*."[31] This is true to Levinas's conviction that the Other calls out of an individuality that we can never possess in any way, and in particular cannot categorize or understand. In this sense the Other gives the Other: a situation for which the French penchant for reflexive verbs is entirely suited.[32] As we have seen, no content is transferred from the Other. "The beyond whence comes the face signifies as the trace. The face is in the trace of the absolutely completed, absolutely past Absent."[33] The trace is the mark left following an erasure, and that is all that is left to us following the call of the Other. So has there been any genuine giving at all?

In *Réduction et Donation*, Marion develops a discussion of Heidegger's concept of Being's "claim" on us into an exploration of Being experienced as a "call," in a way similar to Levinas's discussion of the claim of the Other on us and of our response in responsibility. Marion suggests that

> the passage to Being depends solely on the Being that claims. In the final instance, it is not a matter of Being but of the claim that it exerts and thanks to which it befalls man; or, if one refuses to separate Being abstractly from its claim, one would have to say that in the final instance Being intervenes as claim. . . . Being

29. Marion, *Prolegomena to Charity*, 71.
30. Marion, *Prolegomena to Charity*, 86.
31. Derrida and Marion, "On the Gift," 57.
32. Torry, *Actological Readings*, chapter 5.
33. Levinas, *Humanism of the Other*, 40.

expresses itself only by claiming, and it therefore gives itself only to a response. To hear that claim as that of Being, to give it a response according to the measure of Being, would therefore decide, finally, the "phenomenon of Being."[34]

The Other remains largely absent from Marion's philosophy, and it is only in the more theological works that we find him paying attention to Levinas's demand that we take responsibility for the Other. What Marion has found in Levinas is a means of expression not so much for the call of the Other—that is, for the other person—but rather for the call of "the given."

Ethics as first philosophy

Unlike Heidegger, for whom ontology—the study of Being as *Dasein*, "being there," being-in-the-world—was fundamental, for Levinas, ethics, not ontology, was fundamental and was "first philosophy,"[35] which coheres with our understanding that an actology rather than an ontology could provide an appropriate metaphysical basis for the Other's call to me and my response in responsibility.

For Levinas, relationship with the Other is "a relation without relation."[36] We remain "in proximity" to the Other, rather than in a relationship with them. That might risk a new route to Descartes' radical individualism, but where Levinas takes it is towards an ethical relationship, the "relation without relation," that is at the heart of philosophy, and is the basis of metaphysics, and not a consequence of it, or something needing justification. This is why ethics is first philosophy and also first theology. As Purcell recognizes,

> To state that ethics is both "first philosophy" and "first theology" is to situate the origins of philosophy and theology in praxis. It is to privilege praxis as a point of departure for both philosophy and theology. Praxis is the situation in which one finds oneself when one encounters any other person. For Levinas, as soon as one faces the other person, the situation is at once ethical, and demands response and decision. While the decision is free on the part of the subject, its provocation comes first. It is not the

34. Marion, *Reduction and Givenness*, 186.

35. Levinas, "Is Ontology Fundamental?"; "L'Ontologie est-elle Fondamentale?"; Purcell, *Levinas and Theology*, 78–79.

36. Levinas, *Totality and Infinity*, 79–80.

case of freedom then responsibility; it is rather the summons to responsibility and then the decision freely made.[37]

In his Talmudic studies, it is the doing of the Law that is central to theology for Levinas, so ethics is first theology as well as first philosophy; and liturgy is *"a movement of the Same towards the Other that never returns to the Same."*[38] Religion is ethics and liturgy: it is what we do. And for Levinas, this is the totality of both religion and theology. God is the ultimate Other, calling to us and demanding of us responsibility and decision: that is, ethics, which in the social sphere is justice; and to ensure that possibility, God withdraws.

> It is certainly a great glory for the creator to have set up a being capable of atheism, a being which without having been *causa sui*, has an independent view and word and is at home with itself.[39]

And so it is a "Man-God," "*Un Dieu Homme*," to whom Levinas refers, and not a "God-Man." "A Thou is inserted between the I and the absolute He."[40] As Purcell puts it,

> God withdraws to create the *my* time and the space for responsibility and justice. Thus, theology and the question of God arise in the context of ethics, and God arises as the counterpart of the justice rendered to others.[41]

And so for us action must be primary. For Levinas, there is both relationship and otherness, although no relationship is comprehensible in any terms other than the call of the Other and our response in responsibility. Such relationships are action in changing patterns, with nothing ever the same. Here we have radical diversity: changing patterns of action that constantly escape from those that constitute ourselves. The face is a changing pattern of action over against us, and the relationship between us is action in changing patterns; and the *autrui* is the constant changing of the other in ways that we can neither grasp nor control, it is a constant making of new demands upon us, and it is a constant calling for new responsibilities. Whether the Other is God or another person, there is constant giving and receiving from the Other to the Same, and from the Same to the Other, although never a reciprocity, which would imply a relationship rather than

---

37. Purcell, *Levinas and Theology*, 33–34.

38. Levinas, *Humanism of the Other*, 26: italics in the original.

39. Levinas, *Totality and Infinity*, 58–59.

40. Levinas, *Entre Nous: Essais sur le Penser-a-l'Autre*, 64; *Entre Nous: Thinking of the Other*, 58.

41. Purcell, *Levinas and Theology*, 72.

"a relation without relation."[42] This understanding offers the possibility of a true theology of grace[43] constituted by desire and awakening. The desire instigated by the Other and towards the Other is inextinguishable because the Other is "unanticipatable alterity";[44] and the awakening is an awakening to the intersubjective and therefore to God, in that order because the Other "is indispensable for my relation with God."[45]

All of this is much easier to understand within an "action in changing patterns" actology than within a "beings that change" ontology. It is an actology that can understand the Other as the action of the giving of the Other, and our response in responsibility as our giving of ourselves.

The three reductions

What comes to us is a Saying: an action that demands action in return.

> The Other . . . reveals himself in his alterity not in a shock of negating the I, but as the primordial phenomenon of gentleness. . . . The Other is revealed in its "withdrawal" as well as in its "breaking through."[46]

So now we have reductions to phenomena, to Being, and to the affirming and demanding "call" of the Other: "After the transcendental reduction and the existential reduction there intervenes the reduction to and of this call":[47] a call that is a phenomenon. And finally, Marion proposes the relationship "so much reduction, so much givenness," and that the

> third reduction . . . gives the gift itself: the gift of rendering oneself to *or* of eluding the claim of the call . . . According to no other horizon than that of the absolutely unconditional call and of the absolutely unconstrained response . . . it remains to be understood precisely and conceptually how the pure fact of the call can allow the most strict reduction—hence immediately the most ample givenness, before and outside of objectity and the question of Being. But to think givenness as such—as originarily

---

42. Levinas, *Totality and Infinity*, 79–80.

43. Purcell, *Levinas and Theology*, 110–34.

44. Levinas, *Totality and Infinity*, 34; Purcell, *Levinas and Theology*, 124.

45. Levinas, *Totality and Infinity*, 78; Purcell, *Levinas and Theology*, 134.

46. Levinas, *Totality and Inifinity*, 150, 155.

47. Marion, *Reduction and Givenness*, 197.

unconditional—it will be necessary to elaborate new and rigorous paradoxes.[48]

We shall pursue Marion's "elaboration" in the next chapter. It is sufficient for now to recognize that both Husserl's reduction and Heidegger's set the questions that inspired Marion's quest for a truly foundational phenomenology, beyond the things themselves, and beyond Being: a phenomenology of the given; and that as well as Husserl providing the "givenness" terminology that became so important to Marion, Levinas provided him with the concepts required for expressing both the given's call to us and our response to the given.

Levinas and Marion

There are two ways of looking at the relationship between the Levinas's and Marion's philosophies. Our treatment of that relationship so far suggests that we might interpret Marion's philosophy of the given as a generalization of Levinas's philosophy of the Other and as a way of understanding it. It is not only the other person who issues a call to responsibility, but all that is given; and for the Other to be understood in its radical individuality we need to understand the Other as given rather than as a being within Being.[49]

A very different understanding of the relationship between Levinas's and Marion's philosophies is offered by Donald Wallenfang. He sees Marion as subsuming the Other into an overarching "given," and thus as returning to the subject to whom everything is given. For Levinas, the ego is decentered by the Other, whereas for Marion the ego is recentered. This difference has consequences for the philosophers' understandings of the call and of our response to it.

> For Marion, responsibility is not a question of an ethical response to the epiphany of the face of the other, or an authentic response to one's own conscience, but a response of the gifted (l'adonné) to the pure manifestation of the phenomenon as such. . . . Instead of attending to the call of responsibility issued by the other to me, Marion displaces this call onto the givenness of phenomena in general.[50]

The result is Marion's "betrayal" of "ethics as first philosophy."[51] For Levinas,

48. Marion, *Reduction and Givenness*, 204–5.
49. Wallenfang, *Emmanuel*, 26.
50. Wallenfang, *Emmanuel*, 27.
51. Wallenfang, *Emmanuel*, 45.

> The call of the other and my ensuing responsibility for him
> precede the so-called call of givenness (*Gegebenheit*) and form
> the very anthropological structure of the perception and recep-
> tion of givenness. . . . Marion reverts back to a pre-Levinasian
> phenomenology by reducing the other to just another form of
> givenness.[52]

An alternative way of putting that is that Marion experiences the whole of
reality as both "Other" and "given," hears the call of this "given Other," and
responds with responsibility for the whole of the "given Other." In an age
in which our care for the planet is a prerequisite for any care for our neigh-
bor, Levinas's privileging of human beings over the rest of nature might
be understandable in the light of his experience of the Holocaust, but it
is no longer sufficient. Ethics as first philosophy must now go beyond the
anthropocentric.

One distinction that Wallenfang draws between Marion's and Levinas's
philosophies we can happily ignore.

> The phenomenality of announcing is other than that of appear-
> ing. Some phenomena cannot be seen but can be heard. For
> Levinas, ethical exigency is not a matter of seeing but of hearing
> the call of the other announced through the vital interstices of
> language and signification.[53]

Levinas calls the "face" that calls us to responsibility a "non-phenomenon,"[54]
which it clearly is not; and there is nothing essentially non-auditory about
what is "given." To regard the difference between hearing and seeing as
constituting a distinction between the call and the given—between "proclamation" and "manifestation"[55]—and therefore as constituting a distinction
between Levinas's and Marion's philosophies, is an entirely illegitimate logical move.

Whilst Wallenfang's sympathies are clearly with Levinas's "phenomenology of the Other," he also recognizes the value of Marion's "phenomenology of the given," and himself proposes

> a dialectical phenomenology opening onto a dialectical
> theology which harnesses the genus of both manifestation and

52. Wallenfang, *Emmanuel*, 45–46.
53. Wallenfang, *Emmanuel*, 47.
54. Wallenfang, *Emmanuel*, 48.
55. Wallenfang, *Emmanuel*, 60.

proclamation, of both contemplation and ethics, of both Marion and Levinas . . .[56]

JACQUES DERRIDA

Gift?

Derrida's book is an exploration of the meaning of "the gift" that sets off from a discussion of "giving time."[57] For there to be "giving," some "one" must give some "thing" to some "one other,"[58] but Derrida argues that immediate, eventual, or even potential, reciprocation of a gift means that no gift has been given and no gift can be given.

> Now the gift, *if there is any*, would no doubt be related to economy. . . . But is not the gift, if there is any, also that which interrupts economy? That which, in suspending economic calculation, no longer gives rise to exchange? That which opens the circle so as to defy reciprocity or symmetry, the common measure . . . It must not circulate, it must not be exchanged . . . If the figure of the circle is essential to economics, the gift must remain *aneconomic*. Not that it remains foreign to the circle, but it must *keep* a relation of foreignness. It is perhaps in this sense that the gift is the impossible. . . . For there to be a gift, *it is necessary* that the donee not give back, amortize, reimburse, acquit himself, enter into a contract, and that he never have contracted a debt. . . . It is thus necessary, at the limit, that he not *recognize* the gift as gift. Why? Because it gives back, in the place, let us say, of the thing itself, a symbolic equivalent.[59]

Derrida goes as far as to say that the gift defines impossibility: it is "*the* impossible";[60] and that it "tears time apart,"[61] because if it is in time then it belongs to an economy and is no longer a gift.

Paradoxes emerge: for instance, only if the gift is immediately forgotten can it remain a gift, but only if there is a gift can it be forgotten.[62]

56. Wallenfang, *Emmanuel*, 60.

57. Derrida, *Given Time*, 1–3.

58. Derrida, *Given Time*, 11.

59. Derrida, *Given Time*, 7, 13.

60. Derrida, *Given Time*, 7. Italics in the original.

61. Derrida, *Given Time*, 9.

62. Derrida, *Giving Time*, 16.

> Something must come about or happen, . . . in an instant that no
> doubt does not belong to the economy of time, in a time without
> time, in such a way that the forgetting forgets . . . For there to be
> forgetting in this sense, there must be gift.[63]

Particularly significant for our study of Jean-Luc Marion's "the given" in subsequent chapters, and for what Derrida's influence on it might have been, is
a dialogue between Derrida and Marion that took place in September 1997,
and so just after the publication of *Étant Donné*. Marion begins by saying
that his interest in "givenness," rather than "the gift," was sparked by Husserl's understanding of phenomena as "given," *gegeben*, and by Heidegger's
"*es gibt*," "there is," with its distinctively German connection between givenness and existence.[64] Derrida, too, distinguishes between "the gift" and
"givenness," "*Gegebenheit*," but instead of freeing the gift from the economic
circle, as he thinks Marion does, he regards the gift as an impossibility.

> If there is a gift . . . it should appear as impossible . . . A gift
> is something you do without knowing what you do, without
> knowing who gives the gift, who receives the gift, and so on.[65]

Derrida suggests that Mauss "never asks the question as to whether gifts can
remain gifts once they are exchanged,"[66] and that in Mauss's anthropological study we find

> everything but the gift. It deals with economy, exchange, con-
> tract . . . sacrifice, gift *and* counter-gift—in short, everything
> that in the thing itself impels the gift *and* the annulment of the
> gift.[67]

"Every gift is caught in the round or the contract of usury . . . The truth
of the gift is equivalent to the non-gift or to the non-truth of the gift,"[68]
even if what is given back is merely the donor thanking himself.[69] However
impossible a gift might be, Derrida finally escapes from that impossibility by
understanding that the temporal shift in the response to a gift disrupts the
economic cycle and enables the gift to retain the character of a gift.

63. Derrida, *Giving Time*, 17.
64. Derrida and Marion, "On the Gift," 56.
65. Derrida and Marion, "On the Gift," 59–60.
66. Derrida, *Given Time*, 37.
67. Derrida, *Given Time*, 24.
68. Derrida, *Given Time*, 26–27.
69. Derrida and Marion, "On the Gift," 59.

The gift is not a gift, the gift only gives to the extent it *gives time*. The difference between a gift and every other operation of pure and simple exchange is that the gift gives time. . . . but this gift of time is also a demand of time. The thing must not be restituted *immediately and right away*. There must be time, it must last, there must be waiting—without forgetting . . . It demands a de-limited time, neither an instant nor an infinite time, but a time determined by a term. . . . The thing is not *in* time; it is or it has time, or rather it demands to have, to give, or to take time—and time as . . . a rhythm that does not befall a homogeneous time but that structures it originarily.[70]

The gift's possibility?

Derrida can therefore find meaning in the "incalculability of the gift" as a definition of justice that presupposes an "irreducible excess of a disjoin-ture . . . some 'out of joint' dislocation in Being and in time itself" as the only way "to *do justice* or to *render justice* to the other as other."[71] Seung Cheol Lee makes a similar point: that the uncertainty generated by the lack of economic closure inherent in the gift, by virtue of the temporality of the gift and any response to it, is what maintains the "unconditionality of social bonds":[72] or perhaps we ought to say "at least an element of unconditional-ity in social bonds." O'Neill finds a different way of ensuring the survival of a genuine gift relationship without assuming a temporal rescue of the gift.[73] He suggests that Derrida's division between gift-giving and economic exchange is unrealistic, and points out that gifts are never precisely recip-rocated, whether a return occurs in the present of the gift or in its future, with the consequence that a gift-relationship is always maintained; and he also suggests that we receive multiple gifts from society as a whole, both past and present, that we could never repay. A genuine gift relationship can therefore be maintained without recourse to a temporal distancing of gift and response. These are all theoretical approaches to the problem of the gift, whereas Elder-Vass takes a more empirical approach by studying gift-giving in society.[74] He finds examples of genuine gift relationships in our caring

---

70. Derrida, *Given Time*, 41.

71. Derrida, *Specters of Marx*, 23, 27.

72. Lee, "The (anti-)social gift?," 644.

73. O'Neill, "What Gives (with Derrida)?"

74. Elder-Vass, "Free Goods and Positional Goods."

for children, in contributions to open source software, and in such gifts to strangers as blood donation, as does Richard Titmuss.[75]

Before the dialogue with Derrida in September 1997, Marion had already responded to his *Giving Time* in the recently published *Being Given*. He recognizes the force of Derrida's arguments, agrees that "if it appears in the present, the gift erases givenness by economy; if it does not appear, it closes any and all phenomenality to givenness,"[76] and concludes that the gift can still appear if we make "an exception to the horizon of presence and therefore of appearing . . . in thus disappearing as permanently present, the gift is not lost as given; it loses only the way of being—subsistence, exchange, economy—that contradicts its possibility of giving itself as such."[77] Such a gift occurs in the examples of "giving time" and "giving life."[78] Any gift that is "present" "economizes" on "givenness."[79] Marion proposes a phenomenological approach to the dilemma: that is, the "bracketing of . . . transcendence":[80] and in particular the transcendences of the givee, the giver, and the gift,[81] thus reducing the gift to givenness: a reduction that responds positively to Derrida's arguments, but also one that, as Marion recognizes, cannot be complete in practice, because for there to be experience of the phenomenon of the gift either the giver or the givee have "to remain in the position of the transcendental I."[82]

Givens

Rayment-Pickard suggests that what is at stake in Derrida's *Given Time* might be something deeper than the question of whether gift-giving as normally understood might or might not be possible. It is rather the question of whether there is a starting-point for philosophy: a "given"—in mathematical terms, an axiom on the basis of which we can set out on a process of reasoning. Schelling had suggested that each science is based on an axiom that cannot be conditioned by the science, and that as philosophy conditions science it cannot be conditioned by a science and its own axiom must

75. Titmuss, *The Gift Relationship*.

76. Marion, *Being Given*, 78.

77. Marion, *Being Given*, 79.

78. Marion, *Being Given*, 80.

79. Marion, *Being Given*, 81.

80. Marion, *Being Given*, 84.

81. Marion, *Being Given*, 84.

82. Marion, *Being Given*, 85.

be "absolutely unconditional."[83] For Schelling, that axiom is "the originally self-posited I,"[84] and everything else is conditioned by it.

> The I can be determined in no way except by being *uncondition-al*, for it *is* I owing to its sheer unconditionality, since it cannot become a thing at all.[85]

Marion broadens the axiom beyond the given I to all that is given:

> The question of "the gift" is the question of grounds, of a start-ing-point in philosophy, of what can be taken "as read" and from which a philosophical or religious discourse can flow.
> This is an absolutely crucial question for deconstruction which deconstructs precisely the notion that there are any grounds from which to launch philosophy or religion.[86]

The problem here is the paradox that any critique of grounds has to be a critique on the basis of some ground. The critique is assuming what it critiques. Derrida skirts the dilemma by defining language—which is the medium with which any critique must be carried out—as a field of deferred meaning. As Rayment-Pickard puts it, the gift that grounds deconstruction is both given and taken away: "*it happens.*"[87] What we are left with is con-stantly shifting philosophy and theology critiqued by a constantly shifting language. The one constant is the contingency of it all. Just as a gift ceases to be a gift because immediately it is given it becomes an element in an economy, so an *a priori*, a ground for critique, immediately becomes an ele-ment of what is critiqued. "The *a priori* is possible only as an impossibility, it can grant only what it takes away."[88] As Derrida puts it:

> There must be an event—and therefore appeal to narrative and event of narrative—for there to be gift, and there must be gift of *phenomenon of gift* for there to be narrative and history. And this event, event of condition and condition of event, must remain in a certain way unforeseeable.... The event and the gift, the event as gift, the gift as event must be irruptive, unmotivated ... They are decisive and they must therefore tear the fabric, interrupt the continuum of a narrative that nevertheless they call for, they must perturb the order of causalities: in an instant.... The gift

83. Schelling, *The Unconditional in Human Knowledge*, 41.

84. Schelling, *The Unconditional in Human Knowledge*, 45.

85. Schelling, *The Unconditional in Human Knowledge*, 83.

86. Rayment-Pickard, *Impossible God*, 113.

87. Rayment-Pickard, *Impossible God*, 113. Italics in the original.

88. Rayment-Pickard, *Impossible God*, 114.

and the event obey nothing, except perhaps principles of disor-
der, that is principles without principles. In any case, if the gift
or the event, if the event of the gift must remain unexplainable
by a system of efficient causes, it is the effect of nothing . . . .[89]

A phenomenology of the gift?

We can see that Mauss's anthropological study of "the gift" has inspired a
continuing debate since it was written; and we can also suggest that it is not
that Derrida has influenced Marion or that Marion influenced Derrida in
relation to "the gift," but rather that they were conversation partners, both in
the published dialogue and more generally in a context of widespread debate.
In that conversation, Derrida has set some important questions in relation
to the gift, and we can see that these have stimulated responses from Marion
and others that have enabled a deeper understanding of issues surrounding
the gift. While both Derrida and Marion find that they "have no access to
the gift, so long as we keep it within the horizon of economy,"[90] and both
have maintained distinctions between the gift and givenness, for Marion
both the gift and givenness are phenomena, with the distinction between
givenness and the gift suggesting that the gift is one given phenomenon
among others, whereas Derrida doubts "whether there is a phenomenology of the gift."[91] This means that for Marion, if givenness has ontological
implications, the gift will have such implications as well, whereas this might
not be the case for Derrida.

Perhaps the most significant influence that Derrida has had on Marion
is that discussion between them has enabled Marion to clarify his thought,
particularly in relation to the connection between the gift and givenness:

> In order to achieve description, if any is possible, of the gift, we
> can be led to open for the first time a new horizon, much wider
> than those of objectivity and being, the horizon of givenness.
> Through the issue of the gift . . . we may perhaps establish that a
> lot of phenomena can be explained according to the pattern of
> the gift . . . a large number of other phenomena suddenly appear
> as gifts or as given themselves, even though previously we had
> no idea that they could turn out as given. So givenness perhaps

89. Derrida, *Given Time*, 122–23.
90. Derrida and Marion, "On the Gift," 62.
91. Derrida and Marion, "On the Gift," 60.

> opens the secret, the final result and the potentially lost analysis of the gift.[92]

For Derrida, "we have the word gift in our culture . . . I am ready to give up this word at some point." Marion cannot do that, because, as Derrida suggests, Marion uses

> the word *Gegebenheit* [givenness] with gift, with the meaning of gift . . . For [Marion], everything that is given in the phenomenological sense, *gegeben, donné, Gegebenheit*, everything that is given to us in perception, in memory, in a phenomenological perception is finally a gift to a finite creature, and it is finally a gift of God.[93]

The gift, Being, and time

Before we turn to Marion's "the given," we must discuss a connection that Derrida draws between the gift, Being, and time. While it remains true for him—and we can only agree with him here—that the appearance of a gift that really is a gift in fact annuls the gift, we also have to recognize that Being does not exist in any normal sense of that word, and neither does time, because it establishes temporality and so cannot itself be temporal and so cannot exist. As Derrida puts it:

> The structure of this impossible *gift* is also that of Being—that gives itself to be thought on the condition of being nothing (no present-being, no being-present)—and of time which . . . is always defined in the paradoxia or rather the aporia of what is without being, of what is never present or what is only scarcely and dimly.[94]

If we are seeking for an ontology appropriate to the gift, then we have to ask about the characteristics of an ontology, and one vital characteristic is surely that the ontology does not exist: it is not a being, it is not temporal. Like Being, time, and the gift, it "gives itself to be thought on the condition of being nothing."[95] It would appear that the gift might have as much right to define an ontology as does Being. We find further support for this view in Derrida's suggestion that the "gap between gift and economy" is of a

---

92. Derrida and Marion, "On the Gift," 61.
93. Derrida and Marion, "On the Gift," 66.
94. Derrida, *Given Time*, 27.
95. Derrida, *Given Time*, 27.

structure "analogous to Kant's transcendental dialectic, as relation between thinking and knowing, the noumenal and the phenomenal."[96] The gift here is not itself a phenomenon, because it cannot appear. It is the economy that appears, along with its gifts that are not pure gift. It is the pure gift that cannot appear. Like Being, like time, and like any ontology, it is not, but it gives. There is only an ontology if there is a prior actology.

So yet again givenness can be far better understood within an actology than within an ontology. The converse is also true: Levinas's "Other" reveals just how radical an actology is, in the sense that action in changing patterns never gives us something to possess. By definition action moves on, and changing patterns mean that the next moment the pattern of action is different and what went before no longer exists, not even in memory: for the memory is action in changing patterns and so in the next moment that is different as well. No longer are we in the realm of the unchanging, the static, and the unitary. An actology understands reality as changing, dynamic, and diverse. There is nothing to be possessed: not the Other, and not ourselves either.

Derrida's recognition that only a time-delay can offer the possibility of a gift might not be much help in the end. In the next moment, when the gift is reciprocated, the gift, if it existed at all, no longer exists as a gift. It is now an object in someone's possession, and the act of giving that constituted it as a gift is in the past and so is now absent. All that is left is the trace: but might that be sufficient? But what is a trace? In the context of an actology it is a changing pattern of action, and a changed pattern of action is a pattern of action that is different from the previous pattern of action. However, it is also defined by the pattern of action from which it is changed. This means that there is a trace-survival of the gift, and because any reciprocation, being a different pattern of action, is not a return of the gift, there is a continuing giftedness of the gift. What this shows is that an actology can understand the givenness of the gift more thoroughly than can an ontology, because the essential unchangingness of beings within an ontology, and the unitary nature of Being that an ontology assumes, make difficult the kind of change that needs to characterize a response if the gift is to remain a gift, whereas such change is intrinsic to an actology. Conversely, Derrida's understanding of the impossibility of the gift, and his recognition that a gift is still a possibility, enables us to recognize that an actology is also both impossible and possible. On any basis of understanding other than itself, and particularly in relation to an ontology, an actology is impossible to understand. Action cannot be understood within Being categories, unless we define Being as

Action; and change cannot be understood within the unchanging. In relation to an actology of the given, only if givenness is foundational—if it is "first philosophy"—can we understand all reality in relation to it. If it is not foundational then it has to be understood within some alien conceptual context, and it is difficult to see how that could be achieved within the normal main contender, an ontology, when that is already disqualified. However, as well as an actology enabling us to understand givenness as Derrida understood it, that givenness can inform our actology and its possibility. For instance, we normally understand a trace as a unitary and unchanging mark on a page. In the light of an actology we must understand it as dynamic, changing, and diverse. This example tells us that a trace can no longer be informed by an ontology of Being, beings, the unchanging, the static, and the unitary, but must be understood as dynamic and diverse, which in fact it is, both in its physical reality and in relation to our relationships with it: and also that it must be understood within an actology of givenness. The trace is given, constantly. In the same way, an actology must be constructed out of the entirely dynamic. Everything must be on the move: and just as a gift is absent the moment it is given, so any changing pattern of action will be absent a moment after its occurrence as new changing patterns of action happen; and just as a gift remains a possibility, so the changed pattern of action forever refers back to the pattern of action that was changed, and an actology of givenness is a possibility.

For both Levinas and Derrida, givenness informs actology-building, and an actology can enable us to understand givenness. This is as we would expect, given what we know about Levinas's and Derrida's philosophies. Along with Descartes, Bergson, and a variety of others, Levinas and Derrida were significant influences on Marion's understanding of givenness. We can now see how an actology can help us to understand their philosophies, and how their philosophies can help us to develop an actology, and in particular an actology of givenness.

5

Jean-Luc Marion and "the given"

INTRODUCTION

We have studied some of those philosophers whose work has influenced Marion's philosophy—Husserl, Heidegger, Levinas, and Derrida—and later in this chapter, and also in chapter 6, we shall study Descartes' philosophy: another significant influence on Marion, but one not included in the previous chapters because it is a very different influence from that of phenomenology's engagement with givenness.

We now turn to study Jean-Luc Marion's development of phenomenology into what we might call an actology of the given, in which givenness shifts from being a characteristic of phenomena to being the very foundation of reality.

THE GIFT, THE GIVEN, AND GIVENNESS

So that we can ask about the influences on Marion's understanding of "the given," we need a brief statement of what he meant by it. First of all, it is important to understand that while "the gift," "*le don*" or "*la donation*," and "the given," "*le donné*," might be connected, they are not the same. As Derrida points out, we can use the verb "to give" in situations in which we would not use the word "gift."[1] A phenomenon can be "given" but it is not necessarily a gift. It is "the given" that is phenomenologically and therefore ontologically relevant, so that is where our focus must be; but we shall also have to discuss "the gift" because there are connections between the two concepts. When we are discussing "the gift," we shall be discussing "the given," but when we discuss "the given" we shall not necessarily be discussing "the gift."

Marion also wishes us to be clear about the relationship between "givenness" (also "*donation*") and "the given" ("*le donné*"): "The given" "leads back to" "givenness" because it "comes from it, bears its mark, or rather is identified with it. Every given manifests givenness."[2] In order to avoid ambiguity, it might be best to employ "*le don*" for "the gift," as Marion usually does:[3] in which case, we might say "*le don est le donné est la donation*," but not necessarily "*la donation est le donné est le don*."

In order to understand what Marion means by "the given," and how it fits into his philosophical project, we shall need to explore the influences on his understanding of "the given" and also the philosophies that influenced his philosophy more generally.

> The happening phenomenon happens as given—given only to consciousness if you want, given to me, but in the end always given . . . phenomena cannot appear, without appearing as given *to me*. . . . some phenomena appear as more given, or given to a larger and higher degree than others, and we may call them paradoxical or saturated phenomena.[4]

As we can already see, Marion employs "given" or "the given" in two different connected ways: of a particular given, and of givens in general—both can be "the given." Either way, it is "the given" that we experience, not "givenness":

> The given, issued from the process of givenness, appears but leaves concealed givenness itself, which becomes enigmatic.[5]

CONVERSATION PARTNERS

Hegel, Nietzsche, Bergson, and a variety of other philosophers are very occasional conversation partners for Marion, and somewhat surprisingly

1. Derrida, *Given Time*, 53–55.
2. Marion, *Being Given*, 65.
3. Marion, *Étant Donné*, 110.
4. Derrida and Marion, "On the Gift," 57.
5. Marion, *Being Given*, 68.

Maurice Blondel is almost not even that. The major influences on Marion's philosophy are the writings of Descartes, Husserl, and Heidegger, and an important but less prominent influence is Emmanuel Levinas. Marion was taught by Jacques Derrida, who remains a significant influence and conversation partner.

Marion's first major treatment of the gift and givenness was his *Réduction et Donation: Recherches sur Husserl, Heidegger et la Phénoménologie* (*Reduction and Givenness: Investigations of Husserl, Heidegger and Phenomenology*), first published in 1989. This and subsequent works reveal a significant debt to phenomenology, and particularly to Edmund Husserl. Heidegger is also a significant influence, and Levinas and Derrida as well. One influence on Marion's "the given," although less significant than Husserl and Heidegger, is Immanuel Kant, who more than anyone else gave birth to the Enlightenment, characterized by the "freedom to make public use of one's reason in all matters":[6] an Enlightenment that made subsequent continental philosophy possible. As we shall see, it is important to study Kant's philosophy here because Marion understands his own development of phenomenology as focused on a givenness more fundamental than that envisaged by Kant.

IMMANUEL KANT

There is a sense in which a search for philosophical roots is an endless task. Every modern philosopher is influenced by Plato, Aristotle, and multiple other philosophers from the past two and a half thousand years; and, in particular, no modern philosophy can escape the influence of Kant.

Kant's stated aim, as the title of his *Critique of Pure Reason* suggests, was to conduct

> the critique of our power of reason as such, in regard to all cognitions after which reason may strive independently of all experience. Hence I mean by it the decision as to whether a metaphysics as such is possible or impossible.[7]

Kant theorized that we receive intuitions of objects "by the mind's being affected by the object in a certain manner,"[8] which is "sensation"; and the result is "appearances," with the "matter" of each appearance given by sensation, and the "form" being the ordering of the appearance into a "manifold"

---

6. Kant, *What is Enlightenment?*

7. Kant, *Critique of Pure Reason*, Axii, 8

8. Kant, *Critique of Pure Reason*, A19, B33, 72.

ready to be "synthesized" into "cognition," which is knowledge that provides us with experience. Everything presented to the mind is a "presentation," with presentations being given by both "outer intuitions" and intuitions in the mind, which Kant terms "pure" or "transcendental." Among such pure presentations are the "pure forms" of the sensible intuitions ("pure sensibility," or "pure intuitions") available in the mind *a priori*: that is, logically prior to experience (and so not necessarily temporally prior to it) rather than *a posteriori*, after, or as a result of, experience.[9] Kant's conceptual framework thus assumes two examples of givenness: the givens of "outer intuitions," and the givens of the "pure intuitions." Similarly, space and time have to be given by the mind to intuitions if they are to be presented as "manifolds," that is, connected to each other;[10] so we now have layered givenness: space and time given to the mind, and then given by the mind to outer intuitions, which are then given to the understanding to be understood via pure intuitions. The pure intuitions, and also space and time, are "transcendental," by which Kant means that they are the *a priori* conditions for experience. They are givens, as are space, time, and the outer intuitions: so every stage of the cognition process functions on the basis of givens.

In the first edition of the *Critique of Pure Reason* Kant describes the process of cognition. The manifold is "gone through and gathered together" into a "unity of intuition (as, e.g., in the presentation of space)" by an "act" called the "synthesis of apprehension";[11] different presentations are then "associated" with each other by "a pure transcendental synthesis of imagination" by which a previous presentation is "reproduced" and then associated with another presentation, and so on.[12] Then follows "recognition in the concept": that is, concepts, or rules, are applied to the now apprehended and associated intuitions to "determine" them as something in particular, and thereby deliver cognition. And so, for instance,

> the concept of body serves, in terms of the unity of the manifold thought through this concept, as a rule for our cognition of external appearances.[13]

Required by this whole process is a "transcendental unity of apperception,"[14] a

9. Kant, *Critique of Pure Reason*, A20, B34, 72–73.

10. Kant, *Critique of Pure Reason*, A23, B38, 77; A30, B46, 85.

11. Kant, *Critique of Pure Reason*, A99, 153.

12. Kant, *Critique of Pure Reason*, A102, 155.

13. Kant, *Critique of Pure Reason*, A106, 158.

14. Kant, *Critique of Pure Reason*, A108, 159.

> unity of consciousness in the synthesis of the manifold of all
> our intuitions; and hence a transcendental basis also of the
> concepts of objects as such, and consequently also of all objects
> of experience.[15]

The concepts that we find in our minds are of two kinds. Concepts such
as "horse," "house," and so on, are contingent, as there might not be any
horses or houses; and they are *a posteriori* in the sense that they are given
by experience as well as enabling experience to take place. A second kind
of concept is the "pure concepts of understanding," the "categories"—for
instance, "cause" and "substance":[16]

> experience itself—i.e., empirical cognition of appearances—is
> possible only inasmuch as we subject the succession of appear-
> ances, and hence all change, to the law of causality.[17]

Similarly, "in substance alone, and as determination, can everything belonging to existence be thought."[18] The outer intuitions do not carry causality
or substantiality with them, so these pure concepts have to be applied in the
understanding if we are to experience events as causal and caused, and if we
are to experience objects as substantial. As Kant puts it, the categories are

> only rules for an understanding whose entire power consists in
> thought, i.e., in the act of bringing to the unity of apperception
> the synthesis of the manifold that has, in intuition, been given
> to it from elsewhere.[19]

The *a posteriori* concepts and the categories are all givens, the one given by
experience, and the other by the mind: and the categories must be double-
given: both to the mind, and by the mind to the manifold in order to create
experience.

The *Critique of Pure Reason* offered an understanding of how experience could be created by a mind locating given outer intuitions in a mind-
dependent and given time and space, and then by the mind giving to the
manifold thus created concepts and categories that it had been given. What
has *not* been given is "noumena," "things as such,"[20] because we cannot access them apart from phenomena, that is, apart from appearances. And in

---

15. Kant, *Critique of Pure Reason*, A106, 158.

16. Kant, *Critique of Pure Reason*, A79–80, B105, 131.

17. Kant, *Critique of Pure Reason*, A189, B234, 261.

18. Kant, *Critique of Pure Reason*, A182, B225, 253.

19. Kant, *Critique of Pure Reason*, B145, 187.

20. Kant, *Critique of Pure Reason*, A246, B303, 311.

JEAN-LUC MARION AND "THE GIVEN"   73

any case, the categories can create experience out of appearances, that is, out of "phenomena," so why would we need noumena anyway?:[21] "Objects of experience are *never* given *in themselves*, but are given only in experience and do not exist outside it at all."[22]

For Jean-Luc Marion,

> the happening phenomenon happens as given—given only to consciousness if you want, given to me, but in the end always given . . . phenomena cannot appear, without appearing as given *to me.* . . . some phenomena appear as more given, or given to a larger and higher degree than others, and we may call them paradoxical or saturated phenomena.[23]

Marion is no exception to the inescapability of Kant's conceptual construction. In *Reduction and Givenness,* he notes that phenomenology must "transgress" "the limit fixed upon intuition by Kant" because of phenomenology's "phenomenological requirement of the givenness in presence of every phenomenon with neither remainder nor reserve, the categorial not being an exception":[24] but he also recognizes that Kant operated with the same centering of the ego as we find in Descartes and in phenomenology.[25]

In Marion's *Being Given,* Kant is a frequent conversation partner. For Marion, what is "given" is a "saturated phenomenon": a phenomenon that is "exceptional by excess, not by defect," and that constitutes a "nonobjectifiable phenomenon" even if it does not meet any Kantian pre-existing "subjective condition for its experience."[26] Kant's "determination of the transcendental" is therefore "the counter-model of the gifted" ["*l'adonné*"].[27] However, once Marion leaves the world of the *Critique of Pure Reason* and enters that of the *Critique of Practical Reason,* he finds Kant's understanding of the moral law to be a "given" that decenters the ego, and to be the voice to which the ego responds.[28] We shall find Marion describing his "third reduction" in terms of a "given" that "calls" to us in much the same way as the moral law calls to Kant's free moral person:

21. Kant, *Critique of Pure Reason,* A249, 312.
22. Kant, *Critique of Pure Reason,* A492 B521, 507.
23. Derrida and Marion, "On the Gift," 57.
24. Marion, *Reduction and Givenness,* 15.
25. Marion, *Reduction and Givenness,* 204.
26. Marion, *Being Given,* 213.
27. Marion, *Étant Donné,* 453; *Being Given,* 278.
28. Marion, *Reduction and Givenness,* 279, 281.

> Practical *principles* are propositions which contain a general de-
> termination of the will, having under it several practical rules.
> They are subjective, or *Maxims*, when the condition is regarded
> by the subject as valid only for his own will, but are objective,
> or practical *laws*, when the condition is recognized as objective,
> that is, valid for the will of every rational being.[29]

While Kant might at first sight seem to be a minor influence on Marion's
"the given," he raises the questions underlying a philosophy of the given. For
Kant, the processing ego is the source of knowledge, whereas for Marion it
is "the given"; for Kant, there is no knowledge of noumena whereas there
is of phenomena, whereas for phenomenology the distinction makes no
sense—it is "the things themselves" that appear, that is, that are phenomena;
and for Marion it is "the given" of which we have knowledge: so again any
distinction between phenomena and noumena will be simply an abstract
distinction within "the given." Marion finds in Kant's *Critique of Pure Reason* a counter-model to "the given," and so a transcendental philosophy to
react against, whereas in the *Critique of Practical Reason* he finds a moral
law that is as "given" as any other "given." For Kant,

> two things fill the mind with ever new and increasing admira-
> tion and awe, the oftener and the more steadily we reflect on
> them: *the starry heavens above and the moral law within.* I have
> not to search for them and conjecture them as though they were
> veiled in darkness or were in the transcendent region beyond
> my horizon; I see them before me and connect them directly
> with the consciousness of my existence.[30]

With the moral law Kant finds himself "not in a merely contingent but in a
universal and necessary connection."[31] It is a given, inviting our obedience.

THE PHENOMENOLOGICAL AS THE GIVEN

In his *Réduction et Donation*, published in 1989, Marion finds the givenness
of the object to be constitutive of the phenomenological reduction.[32] In the
Prolégomènes à la Charité (*Prolegomena to Charity*) and in *La Croisée du
Visible* (*The Crossing of the Visible*) that followed, he picked up again the
theology that he discussed in the early *Dieu sans l'Être* (*God without Being*)

29. Kant, *Critique of Practical Reason*, 31.

30. Kant, *Critique of Practical Reason*, 191. Italics in the original.

31. Kant, *Critique of Practical Reason*, 191.

32. Ward, *Introducing Jean-Luc Marion*, 322–23.

and embarked on a more theological period that significantly aligned "the given" with love, as he had begun to do in *God without Being*.[33] He then returned to a more philosophical approach to "the given" in *Étant Donné* (*Being Given*). Here Marion is clear that "being given" does not just mean "the being is."[34] There is no article in "being given," so "being"

> must be taken for a verb, and a verb that works for an oth-
> er . . . since it puts into operation that which now proves itself
> ultimately "given." "Being given" suggests that the given is in-
> deed already and irrevocably given:[35]

so in fact we could do without the "being" entirely, and simply say "given."

> "Being given" does not reconduct the given to the status of a
> being not yet adequately named, nor does it inscribe it in sup-
> posedly normative beingness. Rather, "being given" discloses it
> as a given, owing nothing to anybody, given inasmuch as given,
> organized in terms of givenness and even employing "being"
> therein.[36]

Marion here sees himself as entirely within a phenomenology of a new phenomenological reduction:

> Only a phenomenology of givenness can return to the things
> themselves because, in order to return to them, it is necessary
> first to see them, therefore to see them as they came and, in the
> end to bear their unpredictable landing. . . . what *shows itself*
> first *gives itself*—this is my one and only theme . . . Admitting
> the phenomenality proper to the phenomenon—its right and its
> power to show *itself* on its own terms—. . . implies understand-
> ing it in terms of givenness.[37]

Marion offers the example of a painting as a phenomenon. "The painting does not appear because it is, but because it is itself exposed or exhibited":[38] that is, a reduction of the painting to an object, as Husserl might suggest, is not adequate to it as a phenomenon. Two reductions that Heidegger might have suggested—"The painting is not a being, any more than it belongs

---

33. Marion, *God without Being*, 107.
34. Marion, *Being Given*, 1.
35. Marion, *Being Given*, 2.
36. Marion, *Being Given*, 2.
37. Marion, *Being Given*, 4–5.
38. Marion, *Being Given*, 47.

among the subsisting or ready-to-hand objects"[39]—are equally inadequate to the painting as a phenomenon. It is the specific "effect" that matters: "Its phenomenality is reduced—beyond its beingness, its subsistence, and its utility—to this effect: ochre serenity."[40] The painting "lends itself spontaneously to . . . a reduction to the given."[41]

We have already studied a difficulty that relates to the concept of the gift: that any practical gift-giving immediately collapses into a non-gift, and only by separating in time the gift given and any response, or by the response leaving a remainder of a genuine gift relationship when compared with the gift, can any meaning be given to "the gift." The same now occurs with the concept of "the given": "the phenomenon can, indeed must, be reduced to a pure given in order to appear absolutely . . . It belongs to givenness to give (itself) without limit or presupposition because it gives (itself)—it alone—without conditions."[42] No longer are we securing objects, or understanding Being: we are going one step further to understand both of them as "the given." What constitutes the phenomenon is givenness: so the object, Being, *Dasein*, are all "the given," and the present is given by the future and the past, thus decentering the present as the definition of time.[43] Anything that is not "given" is epistemologically dubious.

> It belongs to the phenomenon considered in its essential phenomenality to manifest itself only as given: namely, as keeping the trace, more or less accentuated in each case, of its process of arising into appearing, in short of its givenness.[44]

And Marion is clear that such givenness lies firmly within a phenomenological approach:

> The correlation between appearing and that which appears, therefore the very definition of the phenomenon, rests entirely on givenness.[45]

It is this understanding of phenomena that means that the "essential phenomenality" of a gift is the pure givenness that is left behind after all that is not pure givenness—that is not purely gift—is extracted: so in a discussion of Marcel Mauss's *The Gift*, Marion finds that

39. Marion, *Being Given*, 48.

40. Marion, *Being Given*, 51.

41. Marion, *Being Given*, 52.

42. Marion, *Being Given*, 53.

43. Marion, *God without Being*, 176.

44. Marion, *Being Given*, 68.

45. Marion, *Being Given*, 21.

it is its very entrance into visibility that objectifies the gift, adapts it to economic exchange, and in the end removes it from givenness. Givennesss would therefore remain intact—would appear as givenness—only at the price of the disappearance or nonappearance of the gift given.[46]

This is a point that Marion emphasizes during a dialogue with Derrida, in which he describes his project as "to reduce the gift to givenness, and to establish the phenomenon as given,"[47] on the basis that description of the gift is possible and that the gift can therefore count as a phenomenon. As for the description of the gift:

> Even though the most abstract and common pattern of the gift implies a giver, an object to be given, and a receiver, you can nevertheless describe the gift, I would say the enacted phenomenon, the performative of the gift, by bracketing and putting aside, at least one and even from time to time two of those three features of the gift. And this is new: It makes clear that the gift is governed by rules that are completely different from those that are applied to the object or to the being.[48]

Heidegger had accused Western metaphysics of making foundational claims that constituted an "ontotheology,"[49] and Caputo here describes Marion's philosophy as moving "the question of the gift out of the economy of causality, out of the horizon of ontotheologic," and as a "gifting of gift . . . the emerging of a gift as what has been released from onto-theological and causal constraints, so that it becomes excess."[50] So the usual rules no longer apply. As Marion puts it, "you can describe a phenomenon as given without asking any question about the giver,"[51] and "a gracious gift appears precisely because there is no response, no answer, no gratitude back . . . because we can give without any receiver." Similarly, an inheritance can be understood as a gift without a giver. "It is within the horizon of such absences that the possible phenomenon of the gift may appear, if it appears." And not only might there be no giver or no receiver: there might be no thing that is given: for instance, "when we give time, when we give our life."[52]

---

46. Marion, *Being Given*, 78.
47. Derrida and Marion, "On the Gift," 70.
48. Derrida and Marion, "On the Gift," 62.
49. Thomson, "Ontotheology?"
50. Derrida and Marion, "On the Gift," 77.
51. Derrida and Marion, "On the Gift," 70.
52. Derrida and Marion, "On the Gift," 63.

As an example of the "new phenomenological rules" relating to the gift, "the gift or the given phenomenon has no cause and does not need any." There is no repetition, either.[53] Here, at least, "the gift" and "the given phenomenon" are aligned: a connection that Derrida deemed unlikely. As Marion puts it, Derrida "is not interested in the gift as such but in the profound structure of something which from time to time may be named the gift and appears as possible," whereas he believes "that we have to go back from the gift to givenness."[54] In *Étant Donné*, Marion recognizes the dilemma that this conclusion imposes, and wonders whether the gift might represent an exception to the conclusion that reducing the gift to givenness means that the gift must disappear.[55] Already in *God without Being* Marion had conceived of "the gift . . . as giving, and not first starting from any giver whatsoever,"[56] and in *Being Given* various ways of bracketing the givee, the giver, and the gift are discussed (for instance, respectively through anonymity, inheritance, and objectless gifts such as reconciliation). Derrida might have reduced the gift to an object, but he has not reduced it to "the given."[57] Reduced to an object, the gift is impossible, but reduced to the given it becomes a possible phenomenon. By reducing the gift to the given, it can survive the "bracketing" of the givee, the giver, or the gift, because

> the gift demands only that one give oneself over to it, by giving it or receiving it only insofar as it gives *itself* first. . . . To . . . recognize the gift implies a strict and particular phenomenological gaze: that which, faced with the fact, sees it as a gift.[58]

We have already noted how Marion's bracketing of the giver might imply that the self might find itself with only a somewhat Cartesian isolated "transcendental role as a mere screen for lived experiences." We now find this rather passive understanding of the self mitigated by the exercise of a Husserlian "*intentionality as a comprehensive name for all-inclusive phenomenological structures*"[59] that implies an active role for the self in which "an Object [is] seized upon, heeded":[60] and so for Marion "it is now a question of a gift conforming to givenness (outside economy); but it will also

53. Derrida and Marion, "On the Gift," 63, 65.

54. Derrida and Marion, "On the Gift," 68.

55. Marion, *Being Given*, 79.

56. Marion, *God without Being*, 103.

57. Marion, *Being Given*, 113–14.

58. Marion, *Being Given*, 112.

59. Husserl, *Ideas Pertaining to a Pure Phenomenology*, 199, §84. Italics in the original.

60. Husserl, *Ideas Pertaining to a Pure Phenomenology*, 76, §37.

be a matter of an immanent phenomenality, without transcendence outside consciousness":[61] "an "immanent phenomenality" constituted by "lived experiences of receivability and givability... [that] presupposes that the agent playing the role of the I exerts, each time, over and through its lived experiences, an intentionality."[62]

> The insistent power of givenness makes the gift decide *itself* as gift through the twofold consent of the givee and the giver, less actors of the gift than acted by givenness.... the gift, reduced as what decides *itself* (as receivable and givable), gets its character "given" from givenness, that is to say from itself. The gift is given intrinsically to give *itself*.[63]

Might "givenness" be understood here as a universal that itself participates in a universal Action? This is a dual question to which we shall return.

In the light of the gift treated to the third reduction:

> Givenness determines the gift as much as and in the same sense as the phenomenon because the phenomenon shows *itself* as such and on its own basis only insofar as it gives *itself*.... the gift uprooted from exchange serves... as privileged phenomenon in the attempt to win access to givenness... According to which it organizes every phenomenon as a gift giving itself... like every other phenomenon.[64]

Much of *Étant Donné* is then taken up with explorations of how Marion's understanding of phenomena as "given" relates to the history of Western philosophy in Aristotle, Descartes, Kant, Heidegger, and so on, and with discussion of the consequences of this understanding of phenomena:

> Most of the time, the intervention of the Other blocks the givenness of the gift by collapsing it into a transcendent relation and disqualifying its intrinsic character as given ... the given phenomenon arrives—crashes even—over consciousness, which receives it ... the initiative belongs in principle to the phenomenon, not the gaze ....[65]

61. Marion, *Being Given*, 115.

62. Marion, *Being Given*, 116.

63. Marion, *Being Given*, 112–13.

64. Marion, *Being Given*, 118. Italics in the original.

65. Marion, *Being Given*, 120, 151, 159.

Among the characteristics of the given that Marion explores are "anamorphosis"—the given "takes form" in its "ascent to visibility"[66] and in its contingency:[67] that is, its "unpredictable landing"[68] that "does not weaken the phenomenon but attests the arising proper to it, in short, its determination as given":[69] a given that "submits the subject to its appearing"[70] and results in a "facticity" that "renders useless the investigation into causal process supposed to have provoked it."[71] And so, for instance, Kant's moral law is a "given that arrives to me and arrives to me as a fact," a "fait accompli."[72] In this sense, necessary truths are just as much given—"having been established as necessary"[73]—as are other contingent phenomena.

SATURATED PHENOMENA

An essential characteristic of phenomena understood as "the given" is that they are "saturated": a concept introduced in book IV of *Being Given* and given a full treatment in the later *Du Surcroit* (*In Excess*), published in 2001. The idea is defined in opposition to Kant's proposal that phenomena are understood in relation to pre-existing categories that compromise "phenomenal autonomy,"[74] and Marion's point is that "given" phenomena are not restricted by these.[75] Consequences follow: "The saturated phenomenon contradicts the subjective conditions of experience precisely in that it does not admit constitution as an object,"[76] which raises the question as to what kind of experience actually occurs, as Marion recognizes when he calls "this phenomenological extremity" that "exceeds what comes forward" a "paradox" in which the self is constituted by the phenomenon rather than vice versa.[77] It is here that a conflict with Husserl's "principle of all principles"[78] arises, as the saturated phenomenon is not in any way constituted by the

66. Marion, *Being Given*, 125.

67. Marion, *Being Given*, 127.

68. Marion, *Being Given*, 132.

69. Marion, *Being Given*, 139.

70. Marion, *Being Given*, 131.

71. Marion, *Being Given*, 141.

72. Marion, *Being Given*, 143, 149.

73. Marion, *Being Given*, 149.

74. Marion, *Being Given*, 213.

75. Marion, *Being Given*, 199.

76. Marion, *Being Given*, 214.

77. Marion, *Being Given*, 216.

78. Husserl, *Ideas pertaining to a pure phenomenology*, 44 (§24).

receiver's consciousness,[79] and neither is the saturated phenomenon conditioned by a horizon of any kind. In the saturated phenomenon,

> intuition always submerges the expectation of the intention, in which givenness not only entirely invests manifestation but, surpassing it, modifies its common characteristics:[80]

and finally, the saturated phenomenon must abandon its being received in intuition, as it does in relation to the saturated phenomenon of time.[81]

The saturated phenomenon is an "auto-manifestation," in relation to which all other phenomena are lesser phenomena,[82] and, in particular, mathematics and logic experience an inversion: the more the certainty, the "poorer" the phenomena, because they offer "no accomplished phenomenality";[83] and scientific laws constitute a less poor but still poor phenomenality because they "must continually confirm the primacy of the concept over intuition, therefore the deficit of givenness."[84]

Marion then studies varieties of saturated phenomena: the event, the idol, the flesh, and the icon, saturated respectively in terms of historical quantity, the quality of bedazzlement, being torn from the category of relation, and freedom from the I:[85] although we might have to say that none of these are truly saturated phenomena because each is saturated in only one modality and not in the others, however much Marion might claim that the first three types of saturation are gathered into the fourth;[86] and we might also have to suggest that by measuring saturation in terms of these "modalities," Marion has not escaped from a set of Kantian categories that inform a Husserlian intention, therefore the intuition, and therefore the extent of givenness. Only an "excess" in all possible modalities, and not just these four, can deliver the genuinely saturated phenomenon, and Marion recognizes this when he suggests that the phenomenon as "the given" only appears in the phenomenon of revelation:

> My entire project has been directed to liberating possibility in phenomenality, to unbinding the phenomenon from the supposed equivalencies that limit its deployment . . . The maximum

79. Marion, *Being Given*, 218.

80. Marion, *Being Given*, 225.

81. Marion, *Being Given*, 245.

82. Marion, *Being Given*, 219.

83. Marion, *Being Given*, 222.

84. Marion, *Being Given*, 225.

85. Marion, *Being Given*, 228–32.

86. Marion, *Being Given*, 233.

of saturated phenomenality must remain an ultimate possibility
of the phenomenon . . . the phenomenon of *revelation*.[87]

In relation to phenomenology, revelation is phenomena characterized by a
"maximum saturation," a "saturation of saturation."[88] The conclusion that
revelation defined as phenomena of maximum saturation is a possibility is
justified by the trajectory of Marion's phenomenological explorations. This
route to the conclusion is essential because there is no feasible argument
from within phenomenology for Marion's decision that the Christian revelation is such phenomena, and in particular that the phenomenon of Jesus
Christ is saturated in all four of the modalities of historical quantity, the
quality of bedazzlement, being torn from the category of relation, and freedom from the I.[89] Although we could just as well regard the phenomenon
of Jesus Christ as constituted by unsaturated phenomena, what Marion has
achieved is a conceptual bridge between his own phenomenology and his
own Christian Faith, and in principle between phenomenology and the
Christian Faith. The argument that there is no reason not to "broaden phenomenological possibility to the measure of the possibility of manifestation
demanded by the question of God" is difficult to refute.[90]

PHILOSOPHY AND THEOLOGY

While Marion's books can generally be classified as *either* philosophy *or*
theology, we generally find philosophy in the theology and theology in
the philosophy. There is no "philosophy period" and "theological period":
simply what we might call theophilosophy and sophiatheology. In a footnote, Marion writes that "Phenomenology describes possibilities and never
considers the phenomenon of revelation except as a possibility of phenomenality . . . Revelation (as actuality) is never confounded with *revelation* (as
possible phenomenon). I will scrupulously respect this conceptual difference . . . Revelation exceeds the scope of . . . phenomenology."[91] Karl Barth's
and Hans Urs von Balthasar's theologies are represented as conforming to
this condition. However, Marion's "respect" for the "conceptual difference"

87. Marion, *Being Given*, 234–35.
88. Marion, *Being Given*, 235.
89. Marion, *Being Given*, 241.
90. Marion, *Being Given*, 242.
91. Marion, *Being Given*, 367.

is not always complete. The discussion of "an ultimate possibility of the phenomenon . . . the phenomenon of *revelation*"[92] is followed by

> The manifestation of Christ counts as paradigm of the phenom-
> enon of revelation . . . In terms of relation, Christ appears as
> an absolute phenomenon, one that annuls all relation because
> it saturates every possible horizon into which relation would
> introduce it.[93]

RECEIVING THE CALL

The final part of *Étant Donné* continues to explore some of the consequences
of understanding phenomena as "the given," and in this context the subject
becomes a "receiver":[94]

> To receive, for the receiver, . . . means nothing less than to ac-
> complish givenness by transforming it into manifestation, by
> according what gives itself that it show itself on its own ba-
> sis . . . The receiver . . . lets what gives itself through intuition
> show itself.[95]

The initiative now lies with "the given," which becomes a "self," leaving the
person receiving the given as a "witness."[96] Marion finds that Descartes
had to treat the self as a thinking object before it could be understood as a
subject; and he finds the same problem underlying Kant's and Husserl's understanding of the self.[97] Heidegger's *Dasein* dissipates the "transcendental
and empirical duality" of the Cartesian ego,[98] but only by merging them in
a self-enclosed ego with "reflective characteristics":

> To resolve *itself*, to put *itself* at stake, to precede *itself*, to agonize
> over *itself*, and each time for nothing other than itself . . . Dasein's
> "mineness" defines it so intrinsically that Dasein can neither
> multiply it nor individuate it.[99]

92. Marion, *Being Given*, 235.
93. Marion, *Being Given*, 236, 238.
94. Marion, *Being Given*, 248.
95. Marion, *Being Given*, 264.
96. Marion, *Being Given*, 249.
97. Marion, *Being Given*, 256–57.
98. Marion, *Being Given*, 258
99. Marion, *Being Given*, 261

For Marion, the I is a "receiver," so that the "I think" becomes "I am affected," and in that process the self "receives itself as a being given"[100] as a consequence of the given phenomenon:

> What gives itself shows itself, and the given phenomenon brings it about that the receiver arises by happening to him.[101]

A consequence is that "the saturated phenomenon . . . inverts intentionality and submits the receiver to the presence of the call."[102] Rather than our intentionality determining phenomena, the given phenomena determine our intentionality, so that "the subject" becomes instead a "witness" and "the gifted."[103] Marion finds anticipations of this transition in Descartes' finding that "the ego recognizes its existence only at the heart of an interlocutionary plot, in response to the originary call . . . from . . . a [God],"[104] and in the "call" represented by the I being "persuaded before exercising its own persuasion over others";[105] and also in Kant's decentering of the ego by the moral law as a "given."[106] The later Heidegger becomes a conversation partner in relation to his separation of the question of Being from *Dasein*—a Being that exerts a claim over us;[107] and Derrida's "deferring" then "stems from the gifted's strictly phenomenological conversion of what gives itself (the call) into what shows itself (the responsal)."[108] "The call . . . suffices to provoke . . . the gifted":[109] a finite gifted that "keeps within its limits" and therefore becomes "the sole master and servant of the given": that is, of the extent to which the given is received.[110] And then Levinas defines for Marion a theme for exploration:

> To receive the Other—that is equivalent first and before all to receiving a given and receiving oneself from it; no obstacle stands between the Other and the gifted. There is more: the gifted himself belongs within the phenomenality of givenness and therefore, in this sense, gives itself. . . . I reach [the Other] in

100. Marion, *Being Given*, 262.
101. Marion, *Being Given*, 262.
102. Marion, *Being Given*, 267.
103. Marion, *Being Given*, 249, 268.
104. Marion, *Being Given*, 278.
105. Marion, *Being Given*, 275.
106. Marion, *Being Given*, 279.
107. Marion, *Being Given*, 266.
108. Marion, *Being Given*, 296.
109. Marion, *Being Given*, 266.
110. Marion, *Being Given*, 219.

his unsubstitutable particularity, where he shows himself like no other Other can. This individuation has a name: love . . . Could the phenomenology of givenness finally restore to [this word] the dignity of a concept?[111]

Marion suggests that in the giftedness consequent upon receiving a given phenomenon, or an Other—another gifted—we are not speaking about a fourth reduction.

It is not added to the third reduction (to the given), nor is it confused with it; it radicalizes it by leading it to its utmost possibility.[112]

We have returned to the subject of the more theological *Prolégomènes á la Charité* published five years before *Étant Donné*.

THE GIVEN AS AN ONTOLOGY

The question now to be addressed is whether "the given" constitutes an ontology: or rather, an actology, because "being" is no longer a candidate for an ontology as it has been effectively subsumed by "the given." But perhaps the question of ontology or actology is not one that we should be discussing at all, because an ontology or an actology implies metaphysics, which Marion clearly distinguishes from phenomenology when he suggests that an ontology

devalues phenomenality . . . because it is free of a cause, the operator of objectifying intelligibility; . . . it disqualifies the phenomenon in the name of an instance without relation to appearing. On the other hand, [phenomenology] accepts all phenomenality, provided only that it appear, without reason or objectness.[113]

And in relation to the saturated phenomenon,

what metaphysics rules out as an exception . . . phenomenology takes for its norm—every phenomenon shows itself in the measure (or the lack of measure) to which it gives itself.[114]

---

111. Marion, *Being Given*, 323–24.

112. Marion, *Being Given*, xi.

113. Marion, *Being Given*, 152.

114. Marion, *Being Given*, 227.

However, there is no reason to restrict the meaning of "metaphysics" in this way. "Metaphysics" is "after physics" in relation to Aristotle's oeuvre, but "before physics" in the logic of the situation; and Aristotle himself never achieved a clear relationship between the particular phenomena studied by particular sciences and the "Being" studied by a science of Being.[115] As Pierre Aubenque has pointed out, the *Metaphysics* appears to be based on three incompatible propositions:

> a) Every science is about something in particular;
> b) Being is not something in particular;
> c) there is a science of being as being.[116]

There is therefore no reason to abandon the term "metaphysics" simply because we are now asking about phenomena. The question to be asked is "What kind of metaphysics?" and not "Should we be discussing metaphysics?." Indeed, further on in *Being Given* Marion suggests that phenomenology might be metaphysical when it thinks of the phenomenon as an object, or as a being—that is, in relation to the first and second phenomenological reductions—but not when it thinks of the phenomenon as "givens, purely."[117] Perhaps what he ought to have suggested is that phenomenology might be *ontological* when it thinks of the phenomenon as an object ("ontological" in a sense in which Aristotle might have understood the term), and also when it thinks of the phenomenon as a being ("ontological" in either Aristotle's or Heidegger's sense), but that phenomenology ceases to be ontological when it understands phenomena as "givens, purely"[118] rather than as objects or beings.

So let us stay with the possibility of a metaphysics of the given, and also for the time being with the word "ontology" understood as "the study of the basis of all reality" rather than as "a theory of being," which is too closely linked with concepts of object, being, and Being. With these understandings, it would seem reasonable to regard "the given" as both metaphysics and ontological. The question then becomes: If Marion is doing metaphysics, what is his ontology, with "ontology" understood as an understanding of the basis of all reality?

---

115. Barnes, "the Primary Sort of Science," 62, 64.

116. Aubenque, "Sens et Structure," 111–12. Translation by the author. The original French is as follows: "a) toute science porte sur un genre, b) l'Être n'est pas un genre, c) il y a une science de l'être en tant qu'être."

117. Marion, *Being Given*, 320.

118. Marion, *Being Given*, 320.

First of all we ought to ask about the ontologies that we find Marion discussing to see if any of them are candidates for his own ontology.

We have found Husserl already understanding phenomenology as givenness, although less completely so than Marion, because he understands ontology in terms of "states of affairs" constructed out of "given objects"[119] rather than understanding everything at every level as "the given." Marion has completed the process by understanding the given objects, the given self, and given connections, as stemming from a fundamental givenness. Marion's complete absorption of phenomenality in "the given" suggests that instead of saying with Husserl that "*ontology is not phenomenology*,"[120] we could say that "Marion's phenomenology is an ontology."

Heidegger offers us "ontological" and "ontic" aspects of my being in the world, with the "ontological" angst, authentic choices that belong to my *Dasein*, and so on, understood as immanent to consciousness, and the related "ontic" fear, inauthentic choices driven by "the They," and so on, as transcendent aspects of an external world.[121] Ontology is here the science of Being, with Being understood as *Dasein*, my being in the world: a Being and a world understood by Marion as given. Rather than saying with Heidegger that "There is no ontology *alongside* a phenomenology, but rather *ontology as a science is nothing other than phenomenology*,"[122] we might wish to say that "Marion's phenomenology is nothing other than an ontology."

Givenness has thus absorbed the various ontologies into a single understanding of all reality as "the given," with "the gift" as the paradigm case of givenness. It therefore seems reasonable to conclude, at least provisionally, that Marion's ontology is an "ontology of the given."

However, Marion himself raises the question as to whether reduction to "the given" is necessarily a final reduction:

> What guarantee do we have that this third reduction could not itself fall beneath the authority of another—another reduction, another authority besides the reduction—in short, that the third reduction really is the last?[123]

Marion's response is that

> in whatever way and by whatever means something can relate to us, absolutely nothing is, happens, appears to us, or affects

---

119. Husserl, *The Idea of Phenomenology*, 52.

120. Marion, *Reduction and Givenness*, 40. Italics in the original.

121. Heidegger, *Being and Time*, 42–43, 182.

122. Marion, *Reduction and Givenness*, 40. Italics in the original.

123. Marion, *Being Given*, 53.

us that is not first, always, and obligatorily accomplished in the mode of a *givenness*.[124]

Nothing escapes:

> Every negation and every denegation, every negative, every nothing, and every logical contradiction supposes a givenness . . . Deconstruction . . . remains a mode of givenness— . . . that of givenness deferred. . . . Givenness . . . fixes the horizon of the nongiven as much as of the given, precisely because one and the same horizon encircles the given with a ring of nongiven.[125]

Because nothing escapes givenness, we are even more secure in our provisional decision that "the given" constitutes Marion's ontology.

"TO GIVE" AS AN ACTOLOGY

Jean-Luc Marion has offered us a third phenomenological reduction, and we have understood his "the Given" as his ontology. However, the title of *Étant Donné* reveals a problem: Marion has not managed to escape from the verb "to be," which problematizes the idea that givenness represents a third reduction. It might in fact be better to see it as an alternative second reduction, alongside Heidegger's reduction of the phenomenon to Being and beings, with the two second reductions needing each other. This suggests a further proposal that we might make. "The given," "the Given," "givenness," and "the gift," are all nouns, whereas what is fundamental to the concept of givenness is the action of giving. Whether phenomena give themselves or are given, action is envisaged.

> The given phenomenon arrives—crashes even—over consciousness, which receives it. . . . Following the path towards its final appearing, it . . . appears only when it finishes, by falling upon what receives and then sees it. This process of the phenomenon authorizes me to think it as the incident . . . a—small—event that comes up.[126]

Marion contrasts an understanding of phenomena as events with an understanding of them as members of a causal chain, and suggests that the intelligibility of phenomena increases as we understand them as events rather

124. Marion, *Being Given*, 53.
125. Marion, *Being Given*, 56.
126. Marion, *Being Given*, 151.

than as causes and effects: "seeing as the characteristic of eventness gathers together all those previously recognized in the given phenomenon"[127]—for instance, "unrepeatability . . . excessiveness . . . possibility"[128]—and that in phenomenological terms it is the effect that is the phenomenon, and the cause an "effect of meaning."[129] Marion argues that for Aristotle, "Being should . . . be thought according to the determinations of the incident, far from the incident being ontically devalued into a marginal accident."[130] This interpretation coheres with Joseph Moreau's understanding that for Aristotle "being" refers to a "manner of being" that assumes "a subject that is"; that Being—being itself—reveals itself through "disjoined categories"; and that systematic interpretation of Aristotle's understanding of Being is impossible.[131] Marion's "incident" can be understood as both a "manner of being" and a "disjointed category." Marion argues similarly that for Descartes, "phenomenality, even that . . . of substance, is in play in the attributes, accidents, and modes which all fall under the incident";[132] and that in relation to both Aristotle and Descartes, "the phenomenological primacy of the incident over form, cause, or essence could obviously be confirmed."[133]

We have already noted the fact that Marion nowhere discusses Maurice Blondel's philosophy of action, even though he knew it (he wrote a preface to a book about Blondel's philosophy);[134] and it is even more surprising that there appears to be no treatment of action at all in Marion's oeuvre. Actions—"arriving," "coming upon," and so on—are always preparatory to "the fait accompli," the "accomplishment," of the given phenomenon:[135] but nowhere is action itself given a proper treatment. Perhaps if Marion had discussed Blondel's *L'Action* then he would have pondered on the fact that "to give" is a verb, and that without the action of giving there could be no "given," no "Given," no "givenness," and no "gift." The possibility of an alternative second reduction presents itself: a reduction of phenomena to Action and actions rather than to Being and beings, and then a third reduction to the action of giving: to "to give." But this option is not simply a parallel

127. Marion, *Being Given*, 162.

128. Marion, *Being Given*, 170–72.

129. Marion, *Being Given*, 166.

130. Marion, *Being Given*, 156.

131. Moreau, "Remarques," 246–49. Translation by the author. The original French is "une manière d'être . . . un sujet qui *est* . . . catégories disjointes. »

132. Marion, *Being Given*, 157.

133. Marion, *Being Given*, 158.

134. Coutagne and Manzano, *Maurice Blondel et la Métaphysique*.

135. Marion, *Being Given*, 151.

series of reductions to the three reductions that we find in Marion's texts, so another possibility beckons. Although "the given" can be understood as prior to the "Being" and "beings" that are given, "to give" is not prior to "action," but is rather a particular pattern of action. This suggests that what is foundational is Action, and not "to give." One can only speculate, but if Marion *had* studied Blondel's *L'Action* rather than Heidegger's *Being and Time*, then he might have found himself writing about a second reduction to "to give" and a third to "action." The books would have been very different.

Marion suggests that Husserl did not define givenness because it was givenness rather than phenomena that was foundational for his philosophy. He recognizes that Husserl's phenomenological reduction was "performed as an act," and suggests that "givenness, which the act of reduction makes manifest and by which it is ordered, must also be comprehensible as an act, no doubt the same as that of the reduction."[136] Reduction, givenness, phenomena, beings, Being: perhaps we should emphasize the active character of these actions: it reduces, it gives, it appears, it happens, it Happens . . . .

But does that not raise the same question that a "Being" ontology had raised for Marion: God is not a being among other beings, and so is not subject to Being. God is—in German, *es gibt Gott*, "there is God," "there is a God" in the same sense as "there is a universe"; but it is not true that "there is God"—in German, *dort ist Gott*, in the sense that we can indicate a being called "God." So do we not also have to say that if Marion's argument leads us towards an ontology of the given—or rather, an actology of the given—then God is not "given" in the sense that some other gives God—that is, that some other entity gives rise to God's appearing: rather, "God is given" both in the sense that God gives God to us in "the luminous darkness where God manifests (and not masks) himself . . . where he gives himself to be envisaged by us";[137] and in the sense of *es gibt Gott*, "there is God."

THE GIVEN AS A PLATONIC FORM

In *Being Given*, Marion discusses Plato's allegory of the cave, in which prisoners are chained and all they can see is a wall with shadows on it. This is the only world that they know, so for them the shadows are reality. If a prisoner is released, then they can turn round to see the fire that is causing the shadows. The prisoner is "bedazzled" and cannot see. "What forbids seeing comes from the excess of the light's intensity, be it sensible or intelligible":[138]

136. Marion, *Being Given*, 27.
137. Marion, *God without Being*, 76.
138. Marion, *Being Given*, 201–5.

a bedazzlement analogous to that experienced by the intensity of the saturated phenomenon.

> Because the saturated phenomenon cannot be borne, on account of the excess of intuition in it, by any gaze cut to its measure ("objectively"), it is perceived ("subjectively") by the gaze only in the negative mode of an impossible perception—of bedazzlement.[139]

Marion rarely mentions Plato, which is interesting because, as his discussion of the allegory of the cave rather suggests, he is in effect saying that the givenness that saturates the phenomenon is behaving like a Platonic Form. We never experience pure gift: it always immediately appears as an element in an economy, even if response might be delayed; and to bracket the givee, the giver, *and* the gift itself, leaves us with no phenomenon, and only with givenness—that is, with the Form. As the gift is the paradigm case of givenness, we have to say the same of every other instance of the given: that beings and phenomena might somehow participate in givenness, but we never experience pure givenness, just as we might experience events and objects that participate in goodness, but we never experience the Form of the Good apart from those objects and events.

Marion himself discusses the question of the universality of

> the givenness of every being and nonbeing, of every phenomenon and every inapparent, of every affection and every affective deception, etc. Should such a universal be understood as a transcendental principle of possibility?[140]

Marion's verdict is

> Certainly not, because such a principle can impose itself only prior to experience, while givenness is marked only in the very experience of the given, a posteriori more than a priori.[141]

True, givenness might appear, or "be marked," "only in the very experience of the given," but so does the object, and so does *Dasein*, and so does Being. That does not answer the question as to whether "the given" represents a Kantian transcendental category or a Platonic Form. The reduction of the phenomenon to the object, to Being, and then to the given—a givenness that is absolutely ubiquitous and that nothing escapes—suggests at least a transcendental category, and potentially a Platonic Form, however much

---

139. Marion, *Being Given*, 204.
140. Marion, *Being Given*, 60.
141. Marion, *Being Given*, 60.

Marion might object that as givenness represents a phenomenological reduction it is necessarily phenomenological and therefore cannot be either
transcendent or transcendental: that is, it cannot exist beyond the phenomenological world, neither can it be a necessary condition for experience.[142] It
is difficult to see how givenness can fail to function as a necessary condition
for experience, or how it can fail to represent something beyond phenomena, because phenomena are the given. So let us assume that the given is
a Platonic Form, as in relation to Marion's texts it makes as much sense to
think of every given as participating in the Form of the Given—or rather,
the Form of Giving—as it does to think of every given as understood as
given in relation to the category of the given.

We normally capitalize Plato's Forms. We must do the same with the
Given: and we should not only define Marion's ontology as that of Giving,
but should accordingly demote Plato's Forms in relation to it: oneness is
given, goodness is given, everything is "Giving." No longer is the Form of
the One the Form in which other Forms participate. It is the Form of Giving
in which the Forms of the One, the Good, the Just, and so on, participate.

All of this is beginning to look rather ontological. We might think that

> because givenness is never defined as a principle or ground pre-
> cisely because it delivers the given from any demand for a cause
> by letting it deliver itself, give itself,[143]

"the given" cannot be an ontology: but that is not the case. It is *precisely
because* "givenness is never defined as a principle or ground" that it can
be ontological in the sense of being foundationally explanatory. To define
givenness as a principle or ground would submit it to the conditions for
principles and grounds, and so it is those that would be explanatory, at
least to some extent, suggesting that it is *those* that would represent the ontology, and not givenness. Givenness is not a principle, not causality, not
metaphysics, except in the loosest possible sense. In theological terms it is
"revelation,"[144] and in nontheological terms it is foundational and not ac-
countable to or dependent upon any other foundation. Givenness is beginning to look distinctly ontological.

142. Marion, *Being Given*, 72–73.
143. Marion, *Being Given*, 73
144. Marion, *Being Given*, 73

MARION'S ACTOLOGY

However, as we have recognized, logically prior to givenness is the act of giving, so if we bring to our consideration of Marion's philosophy an understanding of reality as action in changing patterns—an actology—then we can make immediate sense of ubiquitous givenness: never as some kind of finished state, but always as a snapshot of a constant, diverse and changing process of giving. Conversely, Marion's philosophy of the given provides any actology that we might develop with what we might call a primary case of a changing pattern of action. "To give" is in principle a unidirectional pattern of action: but it is this that is a Platonic Form, because we never experience such a pure giving. What we experience is giving, receiving, and reciprocating: and so changing patterns of action that participate in the Form of Giving rather than the Form of Giving itself. We therefore find that an actology informed by Marion's "the given" has brought philosophy full circle to Platonic Forms.

6

Jean-Luc Marion and the God who gives

INTRODUCTION

Marion's earliest philosophical interest was René Descartes, who would not have recognized a boundary between theology and philosophy; and because Descartes, Anselm and Aquinas were continuing influences, although it is to some extent possible to divide Marion's oeuvre into the philosophical and the theological, theology constantly seeps into the philosophy and philosophy into the theology. We might define *Reduction and Givenness*, about Husserl and Heidegger, as philosophy, but the question of God regularly emerges, often in the context of discussion of Descartes' philosophy.[1] The early *God without Being* is explicitly theological throughout, as is *Cartesian Questions I: Method and metaphysics*, simply because it is about Descartes. In the later *Being Given*, Marion understands "Revelation" as an extreme givenness[2] and as a phenomenon characterized by extreme saturation.

> The hypothesis that there was historically no such revelation
> would change nothing in the phenomenological task of offering
> an account of the fact, itself incontestable, that it has been think-
> able, discussible, and even describable.[3]

1. Marion, *Reduction and Givenness*, 83, 92, 100, 131, 196–97, 200, 202, 233, 248.
2. Marion, *Reduction and Givenness*, 234–45.
3. Marion, *Being Given*, 5.

Marion hopes that Revelation so understood will build "relations . . . between phenomenology and theology" (ED2: xiv):[4] although the theologically-driven treatment of "Revelation" in fact results in a phenomenologically-expressed theology.

We have seen how Marion's philosophy might benefit from an actological reading, and how that philosophy might assist us in developing an actology. The task in this chapter is to ask the same questions of Marion's theology insofar as that can be treated separately from the philosophy.

THEOLOGICAL INFLUENCES

But what precisely are the theological influences? Marion's own Catholic Christian faith is clearly an important influence: a faith conservative in terms of the theology, exploratory in terms of its philosophical expression, and in touch with an ongoing debate as to how the Christian Faith should relate to modernity. Tracy argues that rather than attempting to "correlate the claims of reason and the disclosures of revelation," Marion regards "revelation alone [as] theology's foundation":[5]

> Revelation (I say, icon) can neither be confused with nor subjected to the philosophical thought of "God" as being (I say, idol):[6]

—and so, for instance, the "revelation" section in *Being Given* is constructed out of an uncritical approach to the biblical text, and phenomenological language is employed to express conservative Christian doctrine:

> The manifestation of Christ counts as paradigm of the phenomenon of revelation . . . the phenomenon of Christ gives itself intuitively as an event that is perfectly unforeseeable because radically heterogeneous to what it nevertheless completes (the prophecies). It arises . . . saturating the visible at one fell swoop. . . . For example, when he declines his identity and pronounces his name before those who come to arrest him, he becomes visible to them as Christ and therefore unbearable in a sense; they therefore collapse: "When he said to them: 'It is me (I am),' they recoiled and fell to the ground" (John 18:6–7). The unbearable therefore suspends perception in general, beyond

4. Marion, *Being Given*, xiv.

5. Tracy, "Foreword," xii.

6. Marion, *God without Being*, 52.

the difference between hearing and sight, because it results from
the thorough saturation of the figure of Christ.[7]

Just as Descartes meditated on his conservative Christian faith in terms of
the philosophical language available to him, so Marion has meditated on
his conservative Christian faith in the language of phenomenology. This is
not a "phenomenological philosophy of religion": it is a "phenomenological
theology."[8] Similarly, Tracy suggests that the title *God without Being* shows
that Marion "embraces . . . the revelation-based strategy for Christian
theology."[9] We might come to question this verdict.

We have discovered a wide diversity of influences on Jean-Luc
Marion's philosophy: Descartes, Husserl, Heidegger, Levinas, Derrida, and
Marion's own Christian faith. A lot of other thinkers, both philosophers
and theologians, will have influenced the ways in which those influences
will have affected Marion's philosophy and theology, but it remains true
that we can identify just a handful of major influences. If we had to choose
just three as the most significant influences on Marion's philosophy, then
it would have to be Husserl and Heidegger, who shaped the philosophical
expression, and Descartes, for whom, like Marion, there was no boundary
between the theology and the philosophy.

RENÉ DESCARTES

Jean-Luc Marion's earliest philosophical work was mainly explorations of
Descartes' philosophy, so it will be essential to study both Descartes' philosophy and what Marion wrote about it.

In his *Discourse on Method*, written in 1637, René Descartes sought
"truth" by rejecting

> as absolutely false anything which gave rise in my mind to the
> slightest doubt, with the object of finding out, once this had
> been done, whether anything remained which I could take as
> indubitable . . . But then . . . as I strove to think everything as
> false, I realized that, in the very act of thinking everything false,
> I was aware of myself as something real; and observing that the
> truth: *I think, therefore I am*, was so firm and so assured that the
> most extravagant arguments of the sceptics were incapable of
> shaking it, I concluded that I might have no scruple in taking it

7. Marion, *Being Given*, 236–38.

8. Deketelaere, "Givenness and Existence," 1.

9. Tracy, "Foreword," xii.

> as that first principle of philosophy for which I was looking. . . . I
> concluded that I was a substance whose whole essence or nature
> consists in thinking . . . .[10]

He went on to conclude that the body was distinct from this thinking being;
that "the things we conceive very clearly and distinctly are all of them true";
and that because he could conceive of a being possessing all perfections, the
idea must have been put into his mind by a being possessing all perfections,
that is, by "God,"[11] described in the later *Meditations* as

> infinite, eternal, immutable, and independent substance, all-
> knowing and all-powerful, cause and creator of myself and of
> anything else whatsoever that may exist. And these attributes
> are of such a nature that the more attentively I contemplate
> them, the less it seems that the whole conception can come from
> me. The necessary conclusion . . . is that God exists:[12]

a conclusion reiterated in a more ontological variant of the argument:

> there is no less contradiction in the conception of a God (that is
> to say, of a sovereignly perfect Being) who lacks existence (that
> is to say, who lacks a particular perfection) than in the concep-
> tion of a mountain without a valley.[13]

In relation to the first argument—"idea of a perfect God can only come
from God"—we might suggest that extrapolation from degrees of perfection
could perfectly easily generate the idea of a perfect God, and that even if the
idea of a perfect God comes from God, there is no reason why it should not
have been mediated by someone's parents or teachers.[14] And in relation to
the second, more "ontological," argument—that a perfect being must exist
necessarily—Kenny suggests that

> if what does not exist can have properties, then [Descartes] can
> perhaps prove God's existence, but he cannot prove his own.
> If what does not exist cannot have properties, he can perhaps
> prove his own existence, but he cannot prove God's existence
> from God's essence without begging the question.[15]

---

10. Descartes, *Discourse on Method*, 60–61.

11. Descartes, *Discourse on Method*, 62–63.

12. Descartes, *Discourse on Method*, 127.

13. Descartes, *Discourse on Method*, 147.

14. Kenny, *Descartes*, 145.

15. Kenny, *Descartes*, 170–71.

Having proved to his own satisfaction that God exists necessarily, Descartes then studies his own "certain passive faculty of sensing . . . the power of receiving and knowing the ideas of material things": a recognition that requires him to enquire about an "active power" capable of "forming and producing these ideas." God has given to him "a great propensity to believe that these ideas emanate from material things . . . It follows . . . that material things exist."[16]

While Descartes' own concerns are mainly epistemological—that is, he wants to know what he can know for certain—what he comes to know assumes a distinctive ontology characterized by a mind/body duality, independent existents created by God, and a God who is a being characterized by all perfections, and who functions as creator of all that is and as the guarantor of our knowledge of them.

> Whatever nature teaches us contains some truth, for by nature
> I now mean nothing else than God Himself, or the order estab-
> lished by Him among created things, as by my own nature, in
> particular, I mean nothing but the co-ordination of all that God
> has bestowed upon me.[17]

These philosophical explorations amount to the outline of an ontology that is further elaborated in the *Principles of Philosophy*, written in 1644, in which Descartes recognizes

> only two basic classes of things:
>
> 1. intellectual or thinking things, i.e. ones having to do with
>   mind or thinking substance;
> 2. material things, i.e. ones having to do with extended sub-
>   stance or body.[18]

Among the "intellectual or thinking things" are universals: "The whole source of these universals is this: we use a single idea for thinking of all individual items that resemble each other in some one respect"; and Descartes gives the examples of "two," as in "two stones"; of "triangle"; and of five universals "commonly listed: genus, species, differentia, property and accident."[19] These universals "come about," hence Chappell's claim that

---

16. Descartes, *Discourse on Method*, 159–60.
17. Descartes, *Discourse on Method*, 160.
18. Descartes, *Principles of Philosophy*, 12, §48.
19. Descartes, *Principles of Philosophy*, 15, §59.

Descartes sees them as "ideas in the objective sense and hence as objective beings":[20] and so

> we can think of the whole genus of minds or bodies, or of some species of them, in this way, in which case the idea we have, the universal that exists in our thought, just is that genus or species.[21]

Both "body"—"corporeal substance"—and "mind" are "substances": that is, "they don't depend for their existence on anything except God."[22] "Each substance has one principal attribute; (1) for mind it is the attribute of thought, (2) for body it is extension."[23] Chappell theorizes that Descartes might have understood "substance" to be a genus, and so a universal, although there is no direct evidence for that.[24]

In the *Meditations*, Descartes finds that he has

> a multitude of ideas of various things that cannot be regarded as nothing, although they may have no existence outside the mind, and which are not invented by me, even though I am free to conceive them or not, as I please, and which, finally, possess their own true and unalterable nature:[25]

and so even if there were to be no actual triangles, the triangle in his mind "possesses a nature, or form, or essence, which is immutable and eternal, which I have not invented, and which in no way depends upon my mind."[26] What unites the universals of genus, species, substance, and so on, with mathematical ideas, is that all of them are

> innate . . . born in me . . . The fact that I understand what is meant by a thing, or by a truth, or by a thought, all this seems to have no other origin than my own nature:[27]

and that the same must be true of the idea of God, "placed in me at the moment of my creation."[28] Kenny argues that these "innate ideas" underlie Descartes' entire philosophical method, including its foundational skepticism and the *cogito ergo sum*, "I think, therefore I am," that rescues him

20. Chappell, "Descartes' Ontology," 121.
21. Chappell, "Descartes' Ontology," 122.
22. Descartes, *Principles of Philosophy*, 13, §52.
23. Descartes, *Principles of Philosophy*, 13, §53.
24. Chappell, "Descartes' Ontology," 122.
25. Descartes, *Discourse on Method*, 145.
26. Descartes, *Discourse on Method*, 145.
27. Descartes, *Discourse on Method*, 120.
28. Descartes, *Discourse on Method*, 132.

from it. These "innate ideas" are all real objects in the human mind, placed there by God, and it is this innateness of the ideas that unites them all as universals, rendering unnecessary a Platonic interpretation of Descartes' passages about universals, whether mathematical or otherwise.[29] There is God, there are substances, and there are ideas: not God, substances, ideas, and Ideas. The conceptual structure might not be Platonic, but it does appear to be Aristotelian—particularly in relation to Descartes' employment of the idea of substance—in spite of the fact that one of his avowed aims was to replace Aristotle's philosophy.[30]

The centrality of God to Descartes' philosophical enterprise is no surprise: he was a committed Roman Catholic Christian, "adhering to the religion in which God had given me the grace to be instructed since childhood,"[31] and at the time of writing the *Discourse on Method* he had recently withheld from publication a treatise that contained ideas similar to those of the recently condemned Galileo because he had

> learned that certain persons to whom I defer, and whose authority governs my actions no less than my reason governs my thoughts, had expressed their disapproval of a theory in physics previously stated by someone else.[32]

It is no accident that the *Discourse on Method* is followed by six *Meditations*, and that at the end of his argument for the existence of "a sovereignly perfect being, that is to say, of God,"[33] Descartes writes:

> it seems to me fitting that I should pause for a time in the contemplation of this God, that I should ponder all His attributes, consider, admire, and adore the incomparable beauty of this immeasurable light, at least as much as my mind, dazzled by so much splendor, has the power to do. For, as in the next life the contemplation of the Divine Majesty, as our faith teaches, will be our supreme happiness, so even now we can learn from experience how a meditation of this kind, though incomparably less perfect, affords us the greatest joy we are capable of feeling in this life.[34]

29. Chappell, "Descartes' Ontology," 125; Kenny, *Descartes*, 38–39.

30. Wollaston, "Introduction," 9.

31. Descartes, *Discourse on Method*, 53.

32. Descartes, *Discourse on Method*, 83.

33. Descartes, *Discourse on Method*, 132.

34. Descartes, *Discourse on Method*, 133.

Descartes' God is both the source of all existence and a living being who can be known: a God not dissimilar to the God that we find in Aristotle's *Metaphysics*: a God who is both "final cause" and "life"—an immaterial substance that is living and thinking.[35]

> Hence it is actuality rather than potentiality that is held to be the divine possession of rational thought, and its active contemplation is that which is most pleasant and best. If, then, the happiness which God always enjoys is as great as that which we enjoy sometimes, it is marvelous; and if it is greater, this is still more marvelous. Nevertheless it is so. Moreover, life belongs to God. For the actuality of thought is life, and God is that actuality;[36] and the essential actuality of God is life most good and eternal. We hold, then, that God is a living being, eternal, most good; and therefore life and a continuous eternal existence belong to God; for that is what God is.[37]

Owens finds that "on the part of God there is no reciprocal knowledge or affection towards inferior beings,"[38] and Skemp suggests that the personal qualities that Aristotle applies to the First Mover might be incompatible with God's perfection.[39] Descartes' "incomparably beautiful" God to whom he can nevertheless relate suggests a similar incompatibility.

Jonathan Barnes finds that Aristotle illegitimately identified ontology, "a science that studies what exists insofar as it exists, and whatever holds of it in itself," with the "primary science" of theology, whereas the "primary science" is a particular science and ontology is a universal science.[40] Similarly, Marion finds that Descartes has confused the same two sciences.[41]

Whether Marion's understanding of both God and ourselves within a phenomenology of the given reduces the incompatibility, we shall be able to judge once we have studied that strategy.

Jean-Luc Marion has published several books about Descartes' philosophy and theology, with something of an emphasis on the theological

---

35. Owens, "The Relation of God to World," 211–12.

36. *enérgeia*

37. Aristotle, *Metaphysics*, XII, 1072b23–31. Perl, *Thinking Being*, 93, suggests that "divine" would be a better translation than "God." Aristotle uses the definite article with *theòs*, so it is not clear why "God" should not be the translation.

38. Owens, "The Relation of God to World," 222.

39. Skemp, "The Activity of Immobility," 231, 240–41.

40. Barnes, "The Primary Sort of Science," 64, 75.

41. Marion, *Sur l'Ontologie Grise*, §11, p. 64; *Descartes's Grey Ontology*, §11, pp. 76–77.

aspects.[42] In 1991, Marion published *Questions Cartésiennes*: a collection of essays on Descartes' metaphysics. He finds that although the 1641 *Meditations* is clearly metaphysical, arguing as it does from a deceiving God, an evil genius, and radical doubt about such intellectual objects as mathematics as well as material objects, the 1626 *Regulae ad directionem ingenii* ("Rules for the direction of the mind") contains aspects of a metaphysical argument that it does not connect together,[43] and the 1637 *Discourse on Method*, which argues only from human error to doubt about material objects, does not construct the building blocks required by a metaphysics.[44] This chronology leads Marion to the conclusion that in the *Discourse* "the method itself is equivalent to a metaphysics,"[45] a metaphysics that is an "ontotheology of the *cogitatio* . . . Here the ego thinks, therefore exists, and knows that its thoughts exist";[46] and that by the time of the *Meditations*, a "metaphysics," an "ontotheology of the *causa*,"[47] has emerged, focused on Descartes' argument that

> I should not have the idea of an infinite substance, since I am myself a finite being, if it had not been placed in me by a substance that was truly infinite.[48]

Marion points out that this is a metaphysics constructed on the basis of the individual *ego* and the individual God,[49] but with no place for other human egos. This is because "there must be at least as much reality in the efficient and total cause as in its effect,"[50] so

> whatever be the cause attributed to my being, it must itself be a thinking thing, and possess in itself the idea of all the perfections I attribute to the Divine nature,[51]

with the consequence that Descartes can only owe his continuing being to God, and not to his parents or anyone else.[52] As Marion puts it, "the *ego*

42. Garber, "Foreword."

43. Marion, *Cartesian Questions*, 51.

44. Marion, *Cartesian Questions*, 23.

45. Marion, *Cartesian Questions*, 42.

46. Marion, *Cartesian Questions*, 41.

47. Marion, *Cartesian Questions*, 41.

48. Descartes, *Discourse on Method*, 127.

49. Marion, *Sur le Prisme Métaphysique de Descartes*, 59, 136.

50. Descartes, *Discourse on Method*, 123.

51. Descartes, *Discourse on Method*, 131.

52. Descartes, *Discourse on Method*, 131.

excludes any *alter ego*"[53] by permitting other minds to be objects for the thinking being but never "another *mens* [mind]—who would function as an *ego*."[54] That conclusion is later mitigated, but only to some extent, by Descartes' understanding that because God loves people other than the self, our love for God motivates us to love others: but, as Marion points out, this is still not a relationship with another person; and his verdict is that Descartes' philosophy is "destitute of love"[55] because "the other can be loved only if the *ego* gives up trying to represent it directly and accepts aiming for it indirectly through the unobjectifiable par excellence—that is, God."[56] A *"dépassement,"* an "exceeding," is required if Descartes' philosophy is to include direct relationships with other people.[57]

Marion also suggests that where we might have hoped to find the establishment of an ontology in what might be best understood as Descartes' second argument for the existence of God (which is not a variant of the first), what we in fact find is a pre-existing theological ontology. The argument that Descartes offers here is a development of one by Anselm and that was later termed "ontological" and developed by a number of other philosophers.[58] Rather than forming an argument *for* the existence of God, it is an argument that begins with the idea of God as the supremely perfect being,[59] and thus with "a concept of the divine essence . . . accessible in the mind."[60] As Marion suggests, the argument itself is not properly ontological, because to identify existence as a perfection, and therefore to argue that a perfect being must exist, is not to identify God as necessarily existing. Because perfection is required to mediate between God and existence, the existence is not necessarily identified with God's essence, and it was only later philosophers who identified divine essence with necessary Being, and so were able to formulate a properly ontological argument:[61] an argument that unfortunately absorbed the essence of God into Being and therefore resulted in a "death of God":[62] that is, a death of God understood in terms of "being" and other

---

53. Marion, *Cartesian Questions*, 131.

54. Marion, *Cartesian Questions*, 129.

55. Marion, *Sur le Prisme Métaphysique de Descartes*, 360. Translation by the author. The original French is "destituée de la charité."

56. Marion, *Cartesian Questions*, 138.

57. Marion, *Sur le Prisme Métaphysique de Descartes*, 293.

58. Marion, *Cartesian Questions*, 139–40.

59. Descartes, *Discourse on Method*, 127, 147.

60. Marion, *Cartesian Questions*, 142.

61. Marion, *Cartesian Questions*, 142–44.

62. Marion, *Cartesian Questions*, 145.

metaphysical terms.[63] What Descartes gives to us, as Anselm already had given even more explicitly, is a theology, and not even an ontotheology,[64] because if God is the ultimate cause then God is the ultimate cause of being and is not defined by it. Any ontology here is subsidiary to the theology.

Chapter 5 of Marion's *Questions Cartésiennes 1: Méthode et métaphysique*, "Le *Cogito* s'affecte-t-il? La générosite et le dernier *cogito* suivant l'interprétation de Michel Henry" (—the English translation was published as "Does the *Cogito* affect itself? Generosity and phenomenology: Remarks on Michel Henry's interpretation of the Cartesian *Cogito*"),[65] was first published in 1988,[66] and so before *Réduction et Donation: Recherches sur Husserl, Heidegger et la phénomenologie* (*Reduction and Givenness: Investigations of Husserl, Heidegger and Phenomenology*): an early exploration of givenness, and well before *Étant Donné* (*Being Given*) was published in 1997. The chapter begins with the argument that if the *cogito, ergo sum* [I think, therefore I am] is understood phenomenologically "in terms of representation and intentionality," then

> what the *ego cogito* reaches by way of existent being immediately becomes other than that *ego*, since it amounts to the object represented by itself, but as objectivized by representation. This is therefore already no longer *ego—cogito, ergo est . . . .*[67]

This picks up Henry's understanding that the *cogito* is an example of "self-legislation": we become the "center and measure of all that is": but there is an inevitable and immediate shift to the *cogitatum*: that is, to what is thought.[68] By the reduction of the "I think" to representation of the self to the self,

> the cogito not only inserts itself into Western metaphysics; it is at one with what precedes it, with the most original truth of the *phusis* [nature], insofar as it too is constituted by the *Gegen* [the opposite; the over against].[69]

For Descartes, the "I think" appears to myself, but the world does not appear,[70] so

63. Marion, *God without Being*, xxiii.
64. Marion, *Cartesian Questions*, 160.
65. Marion, *Questions Cartésiennes*, 153; *Cartesian Questions*, 96.
66. Marion, *Questions Cartésiennes*, 259.
67. Marion, *Cartesian Questions*, 103.
68. Henry, *The Genealogy of Psychoanalysis*, 71, 83.
69. Henry, *The Genealogy of Psychoanalysis*, 101.
70. Henry, *Incarnation: A philosophy of flesh*, 65–66.

an abyss separates forever the material bodies [*les corps maté-riels*] that fill the universe, on the one hand, and the body of an "incarnate" being such as man [*un être "incarné" tel que l'homme*], on the other.[71]

Our flesh is *"none other than what feels itself, suffers itself, undergoes itself and bears itself."*[72] It can touch itself and be touched by itself, and *"our flesh alone allows us to know [connaître] . . . something like a 'body'."*[73] Karl Hefty has translated *"quelque chose comme un 'corps'"*[74] as "something like a 'body,'" whereas a better translation might be "our flesh allows us to know . . . something as a body." We do not know the other as an idea, as an appearance, or even as a given, but as an autonomous and physical object: a body—and we know it like that because we are ourselves flesh and we can touch it. And it is the *"transcendental possibility of the sensible world"* provided by our own incarnation—enfleshment—that opens the possibility of the givenness of things and *"the self-revelation of intentionality in life"*:[75] not our intentionality seeking out and appropriating phenomena, but the intentionality of givenness that gives givens. The *Gegen*, the "over against," can clearly be interpreted as an over against given to the experiencing self for whom the "transcendental performance" of the senses gives us what they give only if that is *"revealed . . . in the phenomenological completion of the givenness that it accomplishes, qua giving* [la donation qu'elle accomplit en tant que donant]."[76] Our touching reveals the givenness and can therefore interpret the giving as prior to the sensing.

We can now see why Marion finds in Henry's texts a "more radical phenomenology than one that intentionality allows," and finds that in the context of the *cogito*,

> consciousness does not at first think of itself by representation . . . but by receptivity . . . It is only on the foundation of this immediacy to itself that *cogitatio* may, at the precise moment when in doubt it challenges reflection and its intentional objects, first assure itself with certainty of itself, and then experience

71. Henry, *Incarnation: Une philosophie de la chair*, 7; *Incarnation: A philosophy of flesh*, 3.

72. Henry, *Incarnation: A philosophy of flesh*, 4. Italics in the original.

73. Henry, *Incarnation: A philosophy of flesh*, 5. Italics in the original.

74. Henry, *Incarnation: Une philosophie de la chair*, 10.

75. Henry, *Incarnation: A philosophy of flesh*, 117. Italics in the original.

76. Henry, *Incarnation: Une philosophie de la chair*, 168; *Incarnation: A philosophy of flesh*, 117. Italics in the original.

that, as long as it *experiences itself* and hence auto-affects itself,
it is, it exists.[77]

Henry, like Marion, was both a theologian and a philosopher, and, as with
Marion's books, some of his work was more philosophical, and some more
theological, but the two emphases were never divorced from each other:
but unlike Marion's phenomenology of the given, there is a sense in which
Henry's phenomenology is always theological.

> God is that pure Revelation that reveals nothing other than
> itself. God reveals Himself . . . There is only one Life, that of
> Christ, which is also that of God and men . . . The relation of Life
> to the living is the central thesis [*thème*] of Christianity . . . God
> is Life [*Dieu est Vie*].[78]

And also somewhat unlike Marion's phenomenology of the given, we
constantly find in Henry's theophilosophy a somewhat Platonic division
between a divine world (capitalized) and the world in which we live (not
capitalized).

> In the truth of the world [*Dans la vérité du monde*] any man is
> the son of man [*le fils d'un homme*], and hence also of a woman.
> In the Truth of Life [*Dans la Vérité de la Vie*] any man is the son
> of Life [*fils de la Vie*], that is to say, of God himself.[79]

We belong to an "absolute phenomenological Life"[80] as well as to the phe-
nomenological world, and that "Life" is that of God and of Jesus Christ. A
Cartesian ego as "self-givenness" is an illusion: Life gives Life to itself, and that
Life is our Life to the extent that we forget ourselves in "works of mercy."[81]

Henry knows that God is the one who gives, whereas for Marion it is
the givenness rather than the giver that is the beginning of philosophy; and
whereas for Henry there is a Platonic and Heideggerian division between
the world and Life—between inauthentic living in the They and authentic
Being-in-the-world—for Marion it is all given. However, there is a significant connection between the two philosophies. For both Henry and Marion,
the focus is firmly on the experiencing subject: in Henry's case the subject
invited to participate in Life, and in Marion's the gifted, but in both cases the
experiencing self rather than Descartes' more reasoning self.

---

77. Marion, *Cartesian Questions*, 105–7.
78. Henry, *C'est Moi la Vérité*, 68, 73; *I am the Truth*, 25, 36, 51, 54.
79. Henry, *C'est Moi la Vérité*, 91; *I am the Truth*, 70.
80. Henry, *I am the Truth*, 93.
81. Henry, *I am the Truth*, 101, 124, 140, 169–70.

Coherent with this emphasis on the individual's experience is Descartes' exploration of the "passion" of "generosity," which he regards as "born of self-satisfaction" rather than invited by an external object. "It is always the soul, alone and unique, that causes and suffers."[82] This auto-affect of the *ego* is precisely the auto-affect that Descartes requires for the *cogito, ergo sum*, so Marion can conclude that "generosity concerns the manner of the being, the survival of the being, and the perfection of the being of the *ego*, for which it thus explicitly sanctions the *sum*."[83] A true self-giving thus lays at the heart of our very existence as thinking beings: but unfortunately, given the exclusion of relationships with other *alter egos*, the self-giving can never be in the context of a relationship between two persons, with the consequence that the *ego* can receive self-giving only from God and never from anyone or anything else.

In a dialogue with Derrida, Marion describes "modern philosophy" as

> A transcendental enterprise by which something is taken for granted a priori, which is the I, ego, subjectivity, in order, starting from it, to establish the limits of the possible . . . To think amounts to foreseeing the possible, and to construct objects within the horizon of the possible. The result . . . is that some effective experiences cannot be reconstructed within the limits of the possible. . . . we do have an experience of the impossible . . . We have to deconstruct our concepts . . . At that point, mystical theology and philosophy agree with deconstruction.[84]

The starting point is Cartesian. The destination is Derridean.

Where Marion departs radically from Descartes is in his rejection of Descartes' understanding of God as causal, and so primarily understood through the concept of Being, which in Marion's view has made it impossible for Descartes

> to envisage a properly Christian name of the Gød who is revealed in Jesus Christ—a name anterior to the Being of beings (according to metaphysics), *hence* also to every thought of Being as such. For a single path can yet open: if "God is charity, *agapē*" (1 John 4:8), can *agapē* transgress Being? . . . can it no longer appear as one of the "ways" of being (even if this being has the name *Dasein*)? Can it manifest itself without passing through Being, and, if it cannot determine Being as one of its—own— "ways," can it at least mark its distance from Being? . . . One still

82. Marion, *Cartesian Questions*, 1112.

83. Marion, *Cartesian Questions*, 114, 116.

84. Derrida and Marion, "On the Gift," 74.

> must show concretely how the God who gives himself as *agapē*
> thus marks his divergence from Being, hence first from the in-
> terplay of beings as such.[85]

We shall find multiple echoes of Descartes' philosophy throughout Marion's own philosophical and theological discussions, although the causal
direction might not always be clear. Marion, like Descartes, is a Roman
Catholic theologian as well as a philosopher, and that shared faith will be
an important reason for Marion's interest in Descartes, and also for such
commonalities as the Catholic Christian theology that is integral to both of
their philosophies. A consequence of the place that theology finds in their
philosophies, but not of the theology itself, is the absence of an *alter ego*
in Descartes' philosophy, and a matching absence of the *alter ego* in *Being
Given* until the question of the Other is raised right at the end.[86] For both
Descartes and Marion, the ego and God are the two foci of the ellipses of
their philosophies.

The ontology implied by Descartes' epistemological explorations is
one characterized by a mind/body duality, independent existents created
by God, and a God who is a being characterized by all perfections, and who
functions as creator of all that is and as the guarantor of our knowledge
of them:[87] an ontology that might be better described as a theology. We
have now found Marion absorbing into an ontology of the given the mind,
the body, and all other existents, whether understood as phenomena or as
beings, and we have found God also understood as love and therefore as
givenness. "The given" has therefore absorbed Descartes' ontology.

GOD?

Jean-Luc Marion began his philosophical career as both a philosophical
theologian writing articles for a Roman Catholic journal, and as a theological philosopher studying Descartes,[88] and both Descartes and Christian
theology have remained permanent influences—hence a continuing interest
in the relationship between intentionality and revelation, and between the
ego and God. "The ambivalence of Cartesian metaphysics" that "underlies
the *Meditationes*" was constituted by "a tension between two principles—the

85. Marion, *God without Being*, 82–83.
86. Marion, *Being Given*, 322–24.
87. Descartes, *Discourse on Method*, 160.
88. Ward, "Introducing Jean-Luc Marion," 317–18.

ego and God."[89] The polarity between the *ego* as the source of knowledge and God as its revelation was one that he had found in Descartes' philosophy and that he believed should remain a tension rather than being resolved. Marion's view was that Descartes' "grey"—ambivalent—ontology, in which epistemology submerges ontology,[90] and in which the source of knowledge oscillates between the ego and God,[91] was the source of his "white" or "blank" theology, with God at its center: the ambiguity of *blanc* expressing both the presence and the absence of God.

In 1982, Marion published *Dieu sans l'Être*, the English title of which, *God Without Being*, does not capture the ambiguity of *Dieu sans l'Être*, which can mean both "God without Being" and "God without being it," that is, without being a being called God. Here, the idol—which can be a "concept that comes not from God but from the aim of the gaze"[92]—represents a phenomenology in which "the idol is seen . . . the idol presents itself to man's gaze in order that representation, and hence knowledge, can seize hold of it."[93] This is a situation in which God can function as a being and as the final cause: the God of "onto-theology." Whether "final cause," a "moral God," or any other concept: "theism and atheism bear equally upon [such an] idol."[94] In some of Heidegger's later texts Marion finds a "double idolatry": "beyond the idolatry proper to metaphysics, there functions *another* idolatry, proper to the thought of Being as such":[95] a Being "too limited . . . to pretend to offer the dimension . . . where God would become thinkable."[96] The icon, on the other hand, "does not result from a vision but provokes one. The icon is not seen, but appears":[97] that is, it gives. The icon, too, can be a concept—for instance, the idea of God—"providing at least that the concept renounce comprehending the incomprehensible, to attempt to conceive it, hence also to receive it, in its own excessiveness."[98] Both the icon and the idol are the same object: what differs is our "apprehension" and "reception" of it.[99] The idol is

---

89. Descartes, *Sur l'Ontologie Grise*, 206; *Descartes's Grey Ontology*, 269.

90. Marion, *Sur l'Ontologie Grise*, §31, p. 186; *Descartes's Grey Ontology*, §31, 238.

91. Ward, "Introducing Jean-Luc Marion," 319–20.

92. Marion, *God without Being*, 16.

93. Marion, *God without Being*, 9–10.

94. Marion, *God without Being*, 57.

95. Marion, *God without Being*, 41, 245–46.

96. Marion, *God without Being*, 45.

97. Marion, *God without Being*, 17.

98. Marion, *God without Being*, 22–23.

99. Marion, *God without Being*, 9; Ward, "Introducing Jean-Luc Marion," 319.

less a false or untrue image of the divine than a real, limited, and indefinitely variable function of *Dasein* considered in its aiming at the divine. The idol: the image of the divine that *Dasein* forms, hence that much less God than . . . a figure of the divine.[100]

To avoid idolatry, and so that "no mark of knowledge can demarcate" God, Marion crosses out Gød

with a cross . . . which demonstrates the limit of the temptation, conscious or naïve, to blaspheme the unthinkable in an idol . . . the unthinkable enters into the field of our thought only by rendering itself unthinkable there by excess, that is, by criticizing our thought.[101]

And similarly, in a meditation on the "vanity, all is vanity" in the Book of Ecclesiastes, Marion supposes the preacher as seeing

the world in distance . . . The same distance designates the same world as vain or as "beautiful and good," according to whether the gaze perceives the distance through one pole or the other: from the world, on the fringe that opens it to the excess of a distance, the totality appears to be struck by vanity; from the inaccessible point of view of Gød, at the extremes of distance, the same world can receive the blessing that characterizes it in its just dignity.[102]

But this is no ordinary distance, as the gaze that apprehends it "accedes to distance without genuinely traversing it." The only gaze that *can* traverse the distance is "the gaze of Gød . . . the gaze that can love . . . Gød loves, and from the gaze of charity comes the "goodness" of the gazed at."[103]

As we might expect, "one understands that vanity may also agree with idolatry: one and the other in fact admit an identical contrary, Gød as *agapē*."[104] But how then to speak of this Gød who is love: of God, rather than of "God"?

To free "God" from his quotation marks would require nothing less than to free him from metaphysics, hence from the Being of beings.[105]

---

100. Marion, *God without Being*, 28–29.

101. Marion, *God without Being*, 46.

102. Marion, *God without Being*, 129, 131.

103. Marion, *God without Being*, 131–32.

104. Marion, *God without Being*, 135.

105. Marion, *God without Being*, 60.

God "is," but is also free "with regard to all determinations, including, first of all, the basic condition that renders all other conditions possible and even necessary—for us, humans—the fact of Being."[106] Because "God does not fall within the domain of Being, he comes to us in and as a gift,"[107] and "the giving . . . offers the only accessible trace of He who gives":[108] and in particular of the one who gives real presence in the Eucharistic host, the "distance" of which from us, according to Marion, avoids the possibility of idolatry and permits "communion."[109]

Marion therefore takes on the task of "liberating 'God' from the question of/on Being" by finding within a selection of biblical texts

> the emergence of a certain indifference of being to Being . . . The gift crosses Being/being: it meets it, strikes it out with a mark, finally opens it, as a window casement opens, on an instance that remains unspeakable according to the language of Being . . . To open Being/being to the instance of gift implies . . . that the gift may decide Being/being. . . . Being/being is given according to the gift. *The gift delivers Being/being.* . . . Charity delivers Being/being.[110]

In this context we can understand God as the one who

> reveals himself as agape [love]: to conceive that if Gød gives, to say Gød requires receiving the gift and—since the gift occurs only in distance—returning it. To return the gift . . . this is not said, but done. Love is not spoken, . . . it is made.[111]

A "radical reversal" takes place. We "are" before we "love," whereas "only love does not have to be. And Gød loves without being";[112] and "what is peculiar to love consists in the fact that it gives itself . . . this transference of love outside of itself, without end or limit, at once prohibits fixation on a response, a representation, an idol."[113]

MacKinlay recognizes that for God to appear, or to be revealed, as God, a phenomenon "revelatory of God" is required: a phenomenon that

106. Marion, *God without Being*, xxii.
107. Marion, *God without Being*, 3.
108. Marion, *God without Being*, 105.
109. Marion, *God without Being*, 169, 171.
110. Marion, *God without Being*, 101–2. Italics in the original.
111. Marion, *God without Being*, 107.
112. Marion, *God without Being*, 138.
113. Marion, *God without Being*, 47–48.

must allow transcendence, distance, and infinite excess to appear without being reduced to concepts that are imposed by
a subject or a horizon. Such a phenomenon will be excessive,
overwhelming, ungraspable, and, indeed, saturated.[114]

This clearly requires a "hermeneutical space" in which such a revelation can
occur, which suggests that God's revelation and the believer's faith must form
a mutual and circular relationship. The saturated phenomenon "cannot be
understood apart from the existential commitment of a believer's faith."[115]
This implies that "neither the phenomena nor the recipient are described in
terms that are exclusively active or passive,"[116] and echoes Derrida's objection to Marion's concept of a gift as involving an absolute givenness. In the
real world of phenomena there is always an element of circularity, or reciprocation: it is this bidirectional pattern of action that is foundational, and
not a unidirectional gift-giving. In the context of God understood as Love,
MacKinlay's question asks whether God as Love can be a phenomenon for
us without the recipient of that love exercising love towards God: for how
can love be a phenomenon for us unless there is already an understanding
of love? Given that love is a pattern of action, there can be no understanding
of love in the absence of the practice of love, so God as Love can only be a
phenomenon for us if we are at least in principle capable of exercising love
towards God.

Calcagno asks a different question. He questions the way in which
Marion opposes God understood as Love to God understood as Being, and
suggests that to understand Being in personal terms rather than in terms of
a *causa sui* would enable God to be understood in terms of the "personal
relationality implicit in the conception of God as cause (Creator)."[117] Perhaps it was the continuing attachment to Descartes' theological philosophy
that had suggested the Being/Love polarity to Marion, and so the requirement of an absence of Being if God is to be Love. He had found in Descartes a God who is the final cause in a causal chain, *and* a God "infinite
and incomprehensible";[118] and in "the giving which constitutes the project
of phenomenology"[119] he had found a way of reconciling this ambiguous
ontology with a "blank" theology that destroys the possibility of analogy

114. MacKinlay, *Interpreting Excess*, 215.

115. MacKinlay, *Interpreting Excess*, 215.

116. MacKinlay, *Interpreting Excess*, 219.

117. Calcagno, "God and the Caducity of Being."

118. Ward, "Introducing Jean-Luc Marion," 321.

119. Ward, "Introducing Jean-Luc Marion," 322.

and so requires a "Gød" "without being,"[120] whether "being" is understood with Aristotle, Aquinas and Descartes as a "common being" shared between God and other beings, with "God" allowing itself "to be determined by the historical determinations of being,"[121] or with Heidegger as *Dasein*.[122] As Marion puts it in a discussion of Thomas Aquinas: should we "think of God starting with being or think of being starting with God?"[123]

Marion might have taken a different route and gone further than Calcagno in understanding Being in terms of Action, and so as both cause of and consistent with giving, and in that way he might have found Being and Love to be entirely compatible. He might then have been able to reinterpret the "substantial presence of Christ in the Eucharist"[124] not as related to the elements of bread and wine but instead as Christ present in the action of the Eucharist—in the taking of bread and wine, the giving thanks, the breaking of the bread, and the sharing of the bread and wine: an action in changing patterns interpretation to which giving would be integral. And he might also have found, with Prevot, that the activity of prayer could achieve the same reconciliation between Being and the given:

> Neither the God who says "I Am" nor the rigorous disclosure of given, saturated, and erotic phenomena need be forsaken in order to follow Marion's thought in the direction of a trans-ontological hymn to divine charity itself or in the direction of a vocalized and embodied desire that wants only to welcome and interpret this charity without end.[125]

As Marion sums up, "what is at stake in *God without Being*" is "to give pure giving to be thought."[126]

To continue with a theological theme: During his debate with Derrida, Marion expressed a preference for the term "mystical theology" rather than "negative theology" because "concepts . . . are put out of play only because they do not match the excess of intuition."[127] He gives the examples of Jesus meeting disciples on the road to Emmaus after the resurrection, and of the transfiguration. He recognizes that this "putting out of play" is similar to Derrida's "deconstruction . . . no concept is able to give us the

---

120. Ward, "Introducing Jean-Luc Marion," 322.

121. Marion, *God without Being*, 205.

122. Tracy, "Foreword," xv.

123. Marion, *God without Being*, 235.

124. Marion, *God without Being*, 18, 169, 171.

125. Prevot, "The Gift of Prayer," 274.

126. Marion, *God without Being*, xxvii.

127. Derrida and Marion, "On the Gift," 69.

presence of what is at stake, and that presence not only is impossible but cannot be claimed":[128] but the difference is that "deconstruction cannot say it deconstructs because of an excess of the gift," whereas "mystical theology has to claim that it is because of an excess of intuition that there could never be such a thing as a final and unified theology."[129] Clearly that is the case: but does it mean that there can be no "final and unified" ontology? Yes, it does: but that does not mean that there cannot be an ontology of the gift, an ontology of the event rather than of "the object or of being":[130] an actology.

THE GIVEN AS FOUNDATIONAL

On the basis of the discussion so far, we can conclude that "the given" has been a foundational concept both for Marion's theology and for his philosophy, from *Dieu sans l'Être* (*God without Being*) in 1982 and *Réduction et Donation* (*Reduction and Givenness*) in 1989 to the 2013 Père Marquette Lecture, *Givenness and Hermeneutics*, in which Marion explores the relationship between givenness and the hermeneutics of Husserl and Heidegger: two constant conversation partners throughout his philosophical career.

> *Hermeneutics manages the gap between what gives itself and what shows itself by interpreting the call (or intuition) by the response (concept or meaning). . . . a phenomenology of the givenness reveals phenomena as given only as far as there is in it the use of a hermeneutics of the given as shown and showing itself . . . .*[131]

There would appear to be no competitors to "the given" as a foundational concept. In the context of the theology, the terminology of *love* might be employed, but the meaning is the same as "to give." Sometimes the related "gift" might appear to be taking control of the narrative, but the gift is then understood as the paradigm case of givenness, and we are back with the primacy of "the given": primacy not in terms of the order of the argument, because that generally moves from the first reduction to the phenomenon, through the second reduction to Being, and then to "the given" as a third and subsequent reduction, but a primacy in terms of the logic of the argument.

> The phenomenon is not confined to its status as object or as being but must be characterized more originarily . . . this

---

128. Derrida and Marion, "On the Gift," 69.

129. Derrida and Marion, "On the Gift," 70.

130. Derrida and Marion, "On the Gift," 62.

131. Marion, *Givenness and Hermeneutics*, 55.

characterization can be made in terms of what Husserl . . . regularly called *Gegebenheit* [givenness].[132]

The whole of phenomenology is now wrapped up in givenness:

> The determinations of givenness—first as such, then in its conversation with the gift—confirm that it is fundamentally equivalent to phenomenality (what appears gives *itself*, what gives *itself* appears or, better, shows *itself* . . .) . . . It follows that every phenomenon falls within the given, to the point that the terms could trade places.[133]

And in book III of *Being Given*, "The Given," Marion shows how the given "translates phenomenality into the terms of givenness . . . the determinations of the given phenomenon . . . can all be transposed, term for term, into the characteristic of the reduced gift":[134] for instance,

> unpredictable landing determines the phenomenon in that it arrives to me by affecting me; that is to say, we can describe it inasmuch as it is a gift to receive, according to receivability . . . The determination of the phenomenon as incident confirms that of the unpredictable landing and refers in the same way to givenness.[135]

Book IV of *Being Given*, "The Given II: Degrees," asks about the differences between different kinds of phenomena: "mathematic idealities, logical utterances," and "material things."[136] Following a discussion of how

> the phenomenon is defined when a phenomenology (Husserl) and a metaphysics (Kant) agree to determine it within a horizon and according to an I . . . phenomena are given in and through an intuition, but this intuition remains finite—either as sensible (Kant) or as lacking or ideal (Husserl).[137]

Every phenomenon "is inscribed within a horizon" imposed by an intention that conforms to "the finitude of the conditions of experience." As we might expect, Marion asks why there should not be a phenomenon "where intuition would give *more, indeed immeasurably more*, than the intention would

132. Marion, *Being Given*, ix.
133. Marion, *Being Given*, 119.
134. Marion, *Being Given*, 173, 175.
135. Marion, *Being Given*, 174.
136. Marion, *Being Given*, 179.
137. Marion, *Being Given*, 196.

ever have aimed at or foreseen":[138] and he goes on to develop the idea of the "saturated phenomenon"[139] as a phenomenon that cannot be foreseen, that "bedazzles" when "perception crosses its tolerable maximum," that is "absolute," and therefore "evades any analogy of experience" and "does not depend on any horizon."[140]

Everything—absolutely everything—is referred back to the given: phenomena, Being, beings, the self, religion . . . . This is not to suggest that "the given" is ever all that is to be said, as each of phenomena, Being, beings, the self, religion, and so on, can be properly discussed in its own right as an instance of the "being given," as can be response to the given: but we are soon back with the givenness from which emerge phenomena, Being, beings, the self, and God.

GOD AS FOUNDATIONAL

To return to Tracy's verdict that *God without Being* aligns Marion clearly with a "revelation-based" approach to Christian Faith's relationship with modernity, as opposed to an approach that correlates "the claims of reason with the disclosures of revelation":[141] we can now understand what we might now call Marion's "given-based" approach to both theology and philosophy, or rather his "given-based" approach to what we might call his theophilosophy, as straddling the boundary between a "correlation" approach to Christian theology's relationship with modernity and a more "revelation-based" approach. As already mentioned, the French title of the book, *Dieu sans l'Être*, contains an ambiguity that is lost in the English translation, as it could mean "God without being it," that is, "God without being a being called God," just as easily as "God without Being." So can we say "God is given"? Not in the sense of God not existing and so needing to be given: although presumably we could say "God is given" in the sense that some other might bring God to appearance in relation to us. Ultimately, just as an ontology of Being has to be subject to God, and not God subject to such an ontology, so we have to say that an ontology of givenness has to be subject to God, and not God to an ontology of givenness. God is the source of the reality of which an ontology might express a fundamental reality, so God is the source of the ontology, and not the ontology the source of God: and because the God whom we have discussed in this chapter is a God who is

138. Marion, *Being Given*, 197.

139. Marion, *Being Given*, 199.

140. Marion, *Being Given*, 202, 206, 212.

141. Tracy, "Foreword," xii.

Love, and a God who gives God, the ontology, or theory of reality, of which God is the source, can only be an actology: an understanding of reality as action in changing patterns; and surely we also have to say that the God who is the source of that actology is one that can only be experienced as a saturated phenomenon that is action in changing patterns.

At the end of chapter 5 we concluded that to understand reality as action in changing patterns can make sense of the ubiquitous givenness at the heart of Marion's philosophy, and that Marion's philosophy of the given can provide any actology with a primary case of the changing pattern of action that we might characterize as giving, receiving, and reciprocating. At the end of this chapter we can draw a similar conclusion. To understand reality as action in changing patterns invites us to experience the absolutely saturated phenomenon of God as Action—the source of all action—and as the changing patterns of action of Love and Giving. Conversely, Marion's God, whom we might legitimately characterize as "God as Giving," contributes a coherent theology to any actology, and invites an identification between Action—action itself, and the source of all action—and God. Such an identification of God as *Action*, and as *action* in *changing* patterns, ensures the ungraspability of God, and ensures that we experience God as an icon and not as an idol: a primary condition for a legitimate theology as far as Marion is concerned.

7

Grace: an unconditional giving

INTRODUCTION

If reality is action in patterns, then we might define God as Action, and as the source of all action, and in relation to us as action in particular changing patterns: so we ought to try to say something about some of those particular patterns of action that characterize God.

For a Christian, the most fundamental of such patterns of action is "death and resurrection." Jesus died, and was raised to new life; and we too, through baptism, are buried with Jesus and raised to life with him, both now and in the future.[1] Another pattern of action that belongs to the definition of God, and that might be found across a greater variety of religious traditions, is that of "grace": an unconditional giving. God gives, and in that giving God is given. It is this pattern of action that I shall study in this chapter.

Theological formulation is always going to be difficult. To systematize, to create an orderly whole, is to deny the diversity of religious experience and to suggest that change can be kept within firm boundaries; but to leave everything disconnected is to deny the connectedness of life and our relationships with one another and with the past. Recent Christian theology has seen much good spirituality, pastoral theology, biblical studies, Church history, and liturgical studies, but not so much about how we might

---

1. Romans 6:3–11; 8:11–17.

understand God at the beginning of the third Christian millennium, about how we might relate Jesus Christ to our world today, and thus about how we might do Christian theology and ethics—or any theology—in a systematic fashion. I recognize that systematic formulation is always partial, never assured, always specific to its culture and its time, but still we need to do it if the Christian tradition is to develop, and if as Churches and as individuals we are to take the next steps in our pilgrimage. And we need such formulation if we are to have something to react against, for where there is no thesis there will be no antithesis and no new synthesis. As we have seen, this theological task is one to which Jean-Luc Marion has committed himself. We shall do the same.

In this context the concept of grace might be particularly fruitful because it has been a vital pivot of Christian thought and action through two thousand years; because it is a pattern of action and not a substance, and will find new life as a concept within the actology framework within which this book is written; and because grace might be a fertile concept for the future evolution of the Christian tradition, of Christian theology, and of Christian ethics, and might be an important pattern of action for connecting a variety of faith traditions with each other.

GOD'S COVENANT WITH ISRAEL

In the Hebrew Scriptures, the Christian Old Testament, we find plenty of reliance on the unmerited grace of God: "I will heal their disloyalty; I will love them freely, for my anger has turned from them."[2] God's choice of Israel was not because of any virtue on *its* part, but was an act of unmerited love: "It was not because you were more numerous than any other people that the Lord set his heart on you and chose you—for you were the fewest of all peoples. It was because the Lord loved you . . . ."[3] The covenant between God and Israel was a gift of God, and so was the Torah, the Law, which itself looked forward to a new Law: "But this is the covenant that I will make with the house of Israel after those days, says the Lord: I will put my law within them, and I will write it on their hearts; and I will be their God, and they shall be my people. No longer shall they teach one another, or say to each other, 'Know the Lord,' for they shall all know me, from the least of them to the greatest, says the Lord; for I will forgive their iniquity, and remember their sin no more."[4]

2. Hosea 14:4, NRSV.

3. Deuteronomy 7:7, 8, NRSV.

4. Jeremiah 31:33–34, NRSV.

The Hebrew Scriptures *assume* a relationship between God and Israel established by God's unconditional love, which is why they do not always mention it. The relationship was established with Abraham, with his descendants, and at the exodus from Egypt. However, the covenant was not entirely unconditional. Its granting was unconditional, but its maintenance was conditional on Israel's obedience to the Torah. In this sense we might regard God's covenant with Israel as a reciprocal giving: of the covenant by God, and of obedience by Israel. Of particular interest to the writers of the biblical wisdom tradition was the almsgiving mandated by the Torah, which they believed stored up wealth for the almsgiver in God's treasury:[5]

> Store up almsgiving in your treasury,
>   and it will rescue you from every disaster;
> better than a stout shield and a sturdy spear,
>   it will fight for you against the enemy.[6]

The Torah was not only concerned with gifts to the poor. It was also concerned with loans, which would have been an alternative and non-stigmatizing method of providing for the poorer members of society. Charging interest on a loan was illegal,[7] so a loan was always an act of generosity by the creditor to the debtor whether the debt was repaid or not; and because every seventh year debts were expunged, lending close to the seventh year might effectively have meant granting a gift rather than making a loan.[8] That did not mean that the debt would not be repaid. The debtor might not repay it, but God would. In the Torah,

> Give liberally and be ungrudging when you do so, for on this
> account the Lord your God will bless you in all your work and
> in all that you undertake.[9]

And even more explicitly in the wisdom tradition:

> Whoever is kind to the poor lends to the Lord,
> and will be repaid in full.[10]

This is a theme that we can find developing through the biblical tradition, particularly during the period during which such "apocryphal" books as

---

5. Anderson, *Charity*, 52.

6. Ecclesiasticus 29:12–13, NRSV.

7. Exodus 22:25; Deuteronomy 23:19, NRSV.

8. Deuteronomy 15:1–9, NRSV.

9. Deuteronomy 15:10, NRSV.

10. Proverbs 19:17, NRSV.

Tobit were written, and then on into the rabbinic tradition.[11] In the book of Daniel we find this promise to King Nebuchadnezzar:

> Therefore, O king, may my counsel be acceptable to you: atone for your sins with righteousness, and your iniquities with mercy to the oppressed, so that your prosperity may be prolonged.[12]

Here the word translated "mercy" carries the implication in the original Aramaic that the one who shows mercy, presumably by giving their wealth to the poor, will generate a credit for themselves.[13]

The tradition continued into the New Testament, and in the gospels we find Jesus telling a wealthy young man who has already declared his obedience to the Torah that

> You lack one thing; go, sell what you own, and give the money to the poor, and you will have treasure in heaven; then come, follow me.[14]

And we also find one of Jesus' parables explicitly stating that the consequences of *not* assisting the poor is a *lack* of wealth in God's treasury:

> The land of a rich man produced abundantly. And he thought to himself, "What should I do, for I have no place to store my crops?" Then he said, "I will do this: I will pull down my barns and build larger ones, and there I will store all my grain and my goods. And I will say to my soul, "Soul, you have ample goods laid up for many years; relax, eat, drink, be merry." But God said to him, "You fool! This very night your life is being demanded of you. And the things you have prepared, whose will they be?" So it is with those who store up treasures for themselves but are not rich towards God.[15]

An understanding of charitable activity as generating a reciprocal blessing from God continued into the Christian tradition, and ultimately transitioned into a belief that wealth stored up in God's treasury by almsgiving and the holding of Eucharists could be transferred from the almsgiver or Eucharist-sponsor to someone whose soul was in purgatory in order to shorten their time there.[16] It is easy to see how such a transaction-based

11. Anderson, *Charity*, 53–110.
12. Daniel 4:27, NRSV.
13. Anderson, *Charity*, 169.
14. Mark 10:21, NRSV.
15. Luke 12:16–21, NRSV.
16. Anderson, *Charity*, 113–81.

understanding evolved from the biblical tradition, but what was lost was the idea that the individual's almsgiving or lending was expected to be without expectation of a reward: that is, gratuitous, perhaps on the basis that all of someone's wealth was in any case a gift from God in the first place.[17] As Anderson puts it: "Almsgiving . . . allowed the individual to enact the miracle of God's grace in his own life and assume the role of an active participant in the repair of the world."[18]

The covenant with Israel had to be maintained by obedience, and so was never entirely unconditional and was not a pure gift, but its birth and constant renewal remained and still remains an act of grace: of God's unconditional generosity. And although a great deal of reciprocity appeared in the tradition during the following centuries, including in Jesus' teaching, grace remained as a thin stream through the tradition. And so the latter part of the Book of the Prophet Isaiah is first of all a promise of restoration following exile, and then a promise of a new age of peace and justice.[19] This loving God is always ready to receive back the repentant. The "waiting Father" in the parable of the Waiting Father, often called the parable of the Prodigal Son, would have been entirely familiar as an image of God to Jews of Jesus' time.[20]

Similarly, the new age for which Jesus hoped would not have been new to his hearers, and neither would the resurrection of the dead have been new (although the resurrection of an individual in the midst of the current age would have been a shock to Jesus' disciples, as indeed it was). Jesus' followers continued to hope for the dawn of a new age in which Israel would be renewed and in which all of the other nations would be welcome: but none of this was new, as the prophets had held such a hope:

> Arise, shine; for your light has come,
>   and the glory of the Lord has risen upon you.
> For darkness shall cover the earth,
>   and thick darkness the peoples;
> but the Lord will arise upon you,
>   and his glory will appear over you.
> Nations shall come to your light,
>   and kings to the brightness of your dawn.[21]

17. Anderson, *Charity*, 169.

18. Anderson, *Charity*, 170.

19. Genesis 12–17; Exodus 1–15; Isaiah 40–66; Groves, *Grace*, 11–14.

20. Luke 15:11–32; Thielicke, *The Waiting Father*, 29: "The ultimate theme of this story is not the prodigal son, but the Father who finds us. The ultimate theme is not the failures of men, but the faithfulness of God."

21. Isaiah 60:1–3, NRSV.

So there was nothing new about Jesus' attitude to God's covenant with Israel, to the unmerited love of God, or to the promise of the Kingdom of God. Was Jesus' attitude to the *Law* new? Probably not. The disputes over the meaning of the Law in which Jesus participated were within the mainstream of such debate in the Judaism of his time, and the existence of such disputes implies that the participants agreed that the Law was an integral part of God's covenant with Israel. And similarly Jesus was in the mainstream of the wisdom literature's understanding of almsgiving.[22] However, when we study in more detail a greater diversity of Jesus' actions and words, what we find is a development in his understanding of God's relationship with humanity: one that began in the reciprocity of the Torah and the wisdom tradition, and that then transformed into an understanding that God's grace really is entirely unconditional.

JESUS AND THE GRACE OF GOD

"Grace" is a noun and has often been understood to refer to something substantial, something that can be possessed, even if the substance is not like other physical substances: but here I shall take "grace" to denote the activity of generous giving that is always a self-giving activity designed to benefit the other. It would be better if the word were a verb, but as it is not we shall have to make do with the noun and constantly remind ourselves that we are discussing a pattern of action: a pattern of action that we see in the life of Jesus—a life which we might define as "grace"—and a pattern of action that we might employ as a definition of God.

Was Jesus' religion a religion of grace? And was his life a life characterized by grace in the sense in which I have defined it?

A possibility that we cannot now ignore is that we cannot be sure how much of what we find in the Gospels is what Jesus said and did and how much of it is what early Christians said he said and did but in fact he did not. We are now more aware of the Gospels as the literary creations of their authors, and we are aware that the authors had concerns of their own: moulds into which they pressed the words that came to them through the Church's oral tradition. For our purposes we need to note that in relation to Jesus' death and resurrection Mark's Gospel offers a picture of vulnerable generosity,[23] whereas Matthew's Gospel contains more of a message of sheer power that might tend to negate the "gift" nature of the Gospel:[24] but

22. Sanders, *Jesus and Judaism*, 319.
23. Mark 14:1—16:8.
24. Matthew 27:45—28:20.

as long as we are aware of the author's concerns, we shall be able to decide for ourselves how much of what we find in the Gospels is what Jesus said and did, how much is what early Christians said that he said and did, and how much it matters. The distinction between what Jesus said and did and what early Christians said he said and did does not seem to have been one in which early Christians were particularly interested. They believed the Spirit of Jesus to be present in the Church, leading them into new truth,[25] and so it was perfectly legitimate to tell a parable in which the main character was Jesus: for did not Jesus himself tell parables? So how much should it matter to *us* whether the words and actions were those of Jesus, or whether they reflect the change that Jesus brought about in the lives of early Christians? In either case we have to do with the roots of the Christian tradition, and we can ask whether there is anything distinctive about that tradition, and in particular whether an unconditional love of God is a central component.

Take the parables as an example. Are they Jesus' words? Or are the parables constructed by early Christians or by the Gospel-writer to express their own theological convictions? Take as an example the parable of the workers in the vineyard in Matthew's Gospel in which laborers who worked for different numbers of hours were all paid the same daily wage and at the end of which the vineyard owner responds to a complaint of unfairness from someone who had worked for the whole day with

> Friend, I am doing you no wrong; did you not agree with me for the usual daily wage? Take what belongs to you and go; I choose to give to this last the same as I give to you. Am I not allowed to do what I choose with what belongs to me? Or are you envious because I am generous?

Jesus, the gospel-writer, or someone else through whose hands the parable has passed, has added: "So the last will be first, and the first will be last."[26]

John Drury suggests that in this parable the Gospel-writer's message is that God's welcome of Gentiles into the Kingdom of God is not unjust to the Jews, for they receive their agreed reward.[27] Joachim Jeremias, on the other hand, suggests that the parable is Jesus' own vindication of his welcome to sinners.[28] Which interpretation is the right one? The form of the parable in the Gospel is the Gospel-writer's, but to what extent are the sentiments expressed in the parable those of Jesus? All we can be certain of is that the

---

25. John 14:25.
26. Matthew 20:1–16, NRSV.
27. Drury, *The Parables in the Gospels*, 93.
28. Jeremias, *The Parables of Jesus*, 132.

words of the parable are influenced by Jesus, by the Gospel-writer, and by other early Christians: but that is sufficient for our purposes, for what we ask when we come to this parable is whether in the early Christian tradition God's love is an active and unconditional generosity—in short, whether it is grace: and in this parable God's love *is* active and generous. It is not a universal love (as there are people who are not workers in the vineyard), and it is not fair (the complaining laborer clearly had a point): but God's love is as universal and as unconditional as the parable can make it, and we are therefore justified in finding in this parable an active, generous and universal love of God.

But let us take this conditional generosity to its unconditional extreme, and ask whether that would be new in any sense: for as we have discovered, there is a great deal in the Gospels that is *not* new. In the Hebrew Scriptures we have found an unmerited love of God, the gift of the Law, a constant welcome for the repentant, and a new order into which all of the nations will be welcomed: so Jesus' understanding of the Law would not have been entirely new to many Jews. Jesus made flour out of grain on the Sabbath[29] (thus breaking the commandment about not working on the Sabbath), and he healed a man on the Sabbath[30]—two things which other Jews who sought the deeper rather than the surface meaning of the Law might have done. Whether or not Jesus was intentionally criticizing those parts of the Law which maintained Judaism's firm boundaries against the Gentiles we do not know, but it is unlikely that by themselves these instances of Jesus' breaking of the Law would have been regarded as a complete innovation. Just as there is nothing radically new about Jesus' attitudes towards the Covenant and the Law, so his ideas about repentance were not new. If repentance *was* part of Jesus' vocabulary (that is, if the parables of the lost coin, the lost sheep and the prodigal son in Luke 15 are Jesus' words rather than Luke's exhortations to repentance) then there would have been nothing at all new about that, for the message of repentance was the message of John the Baptist whose follower at some point Jesus would appear to have been. What we cannot know is the order in which Jesus said what he said and did what he did. For instance, we might be able to theorize that Jesus was baptized by John the Baptist and became his disciple,[31] but that he then diverged from John's call for repentance and believed the Kingdom of God to be open to all, regardless of whether or not they were Jews, and regardless of their behavior. As John the Baptist was the spokesman for repentance and for righteousness,

29. Mark 2:23–27.
30. Mark 3:1–6.
31. Mark 1:1–11.

might Jesus' growing conviction that unrepentant sinners were still within the Covenant have been first of all a cause of contention between the two preachers, and then the reason for Jesus departing for Galilee?[32]

Similarly, a belief that the Gentiles would be drawn into the Kingdom of God was not new, and Jesus might have been putting this belief into action as he diverged from an early conviction that his mission and that of his disciples was only to Israel[33] and turned towards a mission to the Gentiles.[34]

So what *was* new?

One thing that was *certainly* new is that Jesus ate with "sinners" and regarded them as unconditionally welcome in the Kingdom of God. Sometimes the gospels simply tell us about the categories of sinners that Jesus mixed with, but we also hear stories about individuals such as Zacchaeus, a corrupt and no doubt hated tax-collector to whose home Jesus invited himself and who was so changed by that experience that his actions became generous giving rather than extortion.[35] We are indebted to E.P. Sanders for the clear distinction which we can now draw between "the common people" and the "sinners" or the "wicked" at the time of Jesus.[36] Very few in Jesus' time would have thought that the common people (who might not have kept all of the purity laws that the Pharisees and others worked hard to keep) were to be excluded from the salvation promised in the Covenant. In any case, purity rules were related to Temple attendance and were not particularly relevant if you lived in Galilee and did not go to the Temple.[37] But "sinners," the unrepentant wicked, were another matter—and it was the sinners with whom Jesus ate. Jesus was "a glutton and a drunkard, a friend of tax-collectors and sinners,"[38] and it was *this*, and not his occasional breaches of the Sabbath Law, that would have ensured that he was regarded as a social menace.

What seems to have been distinctive about Jesus is that he did not demand repentance from sinners and did not reject them if they did not offer it.[39] No Jew would have objected to repentant Zacchaeus being in the

32. Matthew 21:32; 11:18; and cf. Sanders, "Jesus and the Sinners," 25: "John was the spokesman for repentance and for righteousness ordinarily understood; Jesus, equally convinced that the end was at hand, proclaimed the inclusion of the wicked."

33. Matthew 10:5; 15:24.

34. Matthew 8:11–12.

35. Luke 19:1–10; Groves, *Grace*, 1–11.

36. Sanders, "Jesus and the Sinners," 10.

37. Sanders, "Jesus and the Sinners," 13.

38. Matthew 11:19, NRSV.

39. Sanders, "Jesus and the Sinners," 23–24: "Could it be that he offered them

Kingdom of God, nor to Jesus eating with him;[40] but for Jesus to eat with *unrepentant* sinners,[41] and thus to express a conviction that they too would be included in the Kingdom of God, would have been as unpopular with the average Jew as with the self-appointed defenders of the Law's minutest points of detail. Sanders concludes that "the novelty of Jesus' message was that he promised inclusion in the coming Kingdom to those who followed him, even if they did not make restitution and follow the normal procedures for gaining atonement."[42]

It is unlikely that Jesus' eating with sinners would have been invented by early Christians, who seem from the Acts of the Apostles and Paul's letters to have been deeply concerned about moral purity amongst Church members. Early Christians demanded repentance before either Jews or Gentiles could enter the new Covenant established by their Lord Jesus,[43] and in this respect they surely failed to be Jesus' followers. The early Church failed to comprehend a central point of Jesus' message—perhaps *the* central point: and ever since then the grace of God has come with conditions attached.

"Whoever does not receive the Kingdom of God as a little child will never enter it."[44] Jesus was inviting a radical new attitude to the Covenant between Israel and God: the reception of the Kingdom as a gift, a gift that remains a gift, and that is a constant giving, to be received without any sense that we have to achieve something in order to remain in the relationship that has been established by God's sheer generosity. The idea that the Covenant was a gift was not new, but the idea that nothing had to be achieved in order to *remain* in the Covenant *was* new, and the unconditional love of God at the center of Jesus' teaching, and at the center of his life, is what is distinctive about the Gospel of Jesus: the Gospel that Jesus proclaimed, and the Gospel about Jesus. Jesus' love of others was unconditional, and it remained unconditional: it was an active and life-changing love, and it

---

inclusion in the Kingdom *while they were still sinners* and *without* requiring repentance?" (Sanders' emphasis). Sanders clearly believes that Jesus did.

40. Luke 10:1–10.

41. Mark 2:15–16.

42. Sanders, "Jesus and the Sinners," 27.

43. cf. Matthew 5:20; 25:3; 18:15–17, and numerous passages in Luke and Acts. But the Matthaean passages and others might well have roots in Jesus' words. As suggested above, might Jesus have come *slowly* to his conviction that the wicked were to be welcomed unconditionally? Might some of the Gospel material have roots in his earlier convictions, which might have been closer to John the Baptist's? This would go a long way towards explaining the diversity of the Gospel material.

44. Mark 10:15, NRSV.

looked forward to a Kingdom of God in which "many who are first will be last, and the last will be first."[45]

Jesus had no quarrel with the Law, and he believed it to be God's gift to Israel, but the new age was about to dawn, and in such circumstances all that mattered was a raw, unconditional love, and a welcome with no strings attached; which is not to say that Jesus did not make substantial, if not impossible, demands. He demanded that the rich man give everything he had to the poor and then follow him;[46] he called on his followers to deny themselves, to lose their lives;[47] and he demanded perfection.[48] The Sermon on the Mount[49] is sufficiently packed with such teaching that we have to conclude that Jesus did in fact demand such perfection of his followers, presumably as an acted parable of the life of the Kingdom to come.

It is difficult for us to put ourselves inside the minds of Jesus and of his followers. They belonged to an oppressed people, and they hoped for the imminent arrival of a Kingdom of God in which Israel would be released from oppression and would be appointed as the righteous judge of the nations. It is in this context that apparently contradictory messages do in fact cohere:

1. All of Israel would be released from oppression, including the wicked, so Jesus mixed with the wicked, for they too would be welcome in the Kingdom of God that is a gift and not something in which we earn our place;

2. This Kingdom of God will be a Kingdom of righteousness, so Jesus called his followers to be righteous, with a perfection greater than that of the Pharisees, so that they might begin to live now the life of the Kingdom of God.

Thus, far from the demand for righteousness being a contradiction of the grace of God, it is its essential accompaniment, revealing the character of the Kingdom of God that is the gift of God, that is the grace of God, the center of Jesus' Gospel.

However much the early Christians philosophized or moralized this central focus of the Gospel, they could not destroy its influence entirely, and perhaps the point where its influence is most visible is the mission to the Gentiles. The Church was soon welcoming Gentiles as well as Jews, at first

45. Matthew 19:30.
46. Matthew 19:26–28.
47. Mark 8:23–24.
48. Matthew 5:48.
49. Matthew 5:1—7:29.

requiring obedience to parts of the Law, and then requiring only "faith": a transition that is surely a consequence of Jesus' life of grace, a life of unconditional welcome. As Sanders puts it: "The overwhelming impression is that Jesus started a movement which came to see the Gentile mission as a logical extension of itself."[50]

Whether Jesus' declaring of all foods clean[51] is Jesus' words or those of early Christians reflecting on the meaning of Jesus' life when they debated whether or not Gentile Christians should keep the Jewish food laws, we recognize in this saying a Jesus committed to God's covenant with Israel and to the Law, but also a Jesus who judged the Law on the basis of an all-important unconditionality. Thus Jesus opened up the traditional boundaries within the society of his time, and loosened the grip of those parts of the Law that in his view confined God's grace within tight boundaries. By doing that, Jesus opened the way for a Church in which Gentiles would eventually be accepted without having to conform to the Law—although given our ineradicable desire for boundaries, the Church has never quite believed that God's love can be totally without conditions; and he opened the way for a Christian Faith in which grace—a continual, unconditional, active giving—might be the dynamic center: a Christian Faith that might have the capacity to be rediscovered in a secular age urgently in need of a theology, a politics, and an ethics, focused on unconditional generosity.

Peter Groves correctly describes as "grace" God's relationship with his creation and with Israel, and Jesus' relationships with Zacchaeus and with other sinners of his time, whether they were repentant or not. But "grace" is not just a word that can be applied to occasional incidents and sayings: it is a word that can be applied to the whole of Jesus' life of generous giving. I make no apology for quoting at length:

> The grace of God, in scripture, is over and over gain the loving kindness of God towards those whom he has chosen to favour. This is seen in his relentless mercy towards his errant children and his unfailing love in the face of the faithless and loveless behaviour of those whom he has created. In this sense, the word "grace" describes what God is like, and what God is like is self-giving love. . . . So the grace of God characterizes all that we can say about God's revelation of himself in Jesus Christ: this is what God is like. This is the God whose revelation is witnessed by the texts that we call scripture or the Bible, and proclaimed in word and deed by the Christian Church. To say, however, that

---

50. Sanders, *Jesus and Judaism*, 220.

51. Mark 7:15.

grace can tell us about the nature of God is not to suggest that it is merely an attribute or a description. Love is not an attribute of God in the way that speed is an attribute of cheetahs. Love is what God is, something active and dynamic, and so grace is never simply a characteristic.[52]

As with the effect of Jesus' visit to Zacchaeus, we might respond to God's generously giving love with a generous giving of our own: a new generous giving that is itself a pattern of action that we might call "grace," and that is a direct result of the grace that is God. Any grace that we might exercise is itself a gift of God and so the grace of God.

> It is the gift whereby God unites human beings with his own life. Grace is the word we use to describe God's infinite love worked out in human beings by drawing those human beings into the perfect fellowship of the Trinity, the eternal selfless love of Father, Son and Holy Spirit.[53]

PAUL'S GOSPEL: SAVED BY GRACE, OR SAVED BY FAITH?

What of the Apostle Paul? Was *his* Gospel a Gospel of grace?

The most important fact about Paul is that he was converted from the strict Judaism of the Pharisees to a comparatively new sect, and that he experienced his conversion as a call to take this new religion to the Gentiles. His formative years as a Christian were spent in Damascus and Antioch, that is, among Gentiles; and the polarities characteristic of conversion experiences, combined with the needs of a Church progressively more Gentile, combined to create a distinctive theology from which Christians will never escape.

But is it a theology of *grace*?

However radical Paul's conversion, he remained a Jew, his thought-forms remained Jewish, and his convictions slowly returned from a radical rejection of the Law to a more positive evaluation of it. In an early letter he spoke of the Law as of no consequence,[54] but by the time he came to write the Letter to the Romans he had come to regard the Law as God-given and as good.[55] This is an understandable transition for someone radically converted to Christ and then having to come to terms with his own past,

52. Groves, *Grace*, 3.
53. Groves, *Grace*, 5.
54. Galatians 3:25.
55. Romans 7:22.

with the relationship between Jews and Gentiles in the Church, and with the relationship of God's choice of Israel to God's choice of Jesus Christ.

Clearly a key experience in Paul's spiritual pilgrimage was a dispute at Antioch between Paul and Peter, recorded in the Letter to the Galatians.[56] There was already a difference of view within Judaism as to whether it was right to share table-fellowship with God-fearing Gentiles. Peter had been eating with Gentiles at Antioch, but when some Jerusalem Christians visited, he ceased to do so. His motives for abandoning table-fellowship with Gentiles were probably admirable: he did not want to disturb the consciences of visiting Jewish Christians—and later on, Paul wrote to the Church in Corinth about respecting weak consciences: maybe he had learnt something from the Antioch event. But at the time, as far as Paul was concerned, Peter's action was a betrayal of the Gospel. Peter would not have disagreed with Paul that justification was by faith (for the Book of Genesis says that Abraham's faith was counted to him as righteousness),[57] or that salvation was a free gift; but he seems not to have agreed that a justification by faith common to both Jews and Gentiles was more important than the traditional distinctions resulting from God's gift of a distinctive Law to the Jews.

Paul does not record that Peter agreed with him, so we can assume that Paul lost the argument at Antioch: but that does not mean that the event had no impact on Paul, for it clearly had an enormous effect upon him, and probably focused for him the radical difference between faith in Christ and the Covenant offered by God to Israel. The event at Antioch might have been the point at which the boundaries of the Covenant were redefined for Paul to include Gentiles as well as Jews, and at which the conditions for remaining in the Covenant were equally redefined: faith in Christ rather than the keeping of the Law.[58]

What was *not* redefined in this process was the importance of grace. Grace, for Paul as for Jesus, was a given of Judaism. Certainly there was a new *channel* for the grace of God: Jesus Christ; but God's gracious character was the same when he gave the Old Covenant and the accompanying Law as when he gave Christ and the New Covenant. Paul says nothing particularly new about grace because the questions that the young churches were posing for him did not require him to do so. What Paul *was* interested in was *who* was in the new Covenant established by God's grace, and Paul's statement in the Letter to the Romans, "But if it is by grace, it is no longer on the basis

---

56. Galatians 2:11–21.

57. Genesis 15:6.

58. Dunn, *Jesus, Paul and the Law*, 122.

of works, otherwise grace would no longer be grace,"[59] is an opening up of the boundaries of the Covenant to include those who have entered by faith and have thus received grace: "Therefore, since we are justified by faith, we have peace with God through our Lord Jesus Christ, through whom we have obtained access to this grace in which we stand; and we boast in our hope of sharing the glory of God."[60]

Romans chapter 11, a discussion of the relationship between Jews and Gentiles in God's purposes, does not mention "Jesus" or "Christ" at all. It is not interested in the source or the nature of the grace that the chosen people have received. What interests Paul is where the *boundary* lies, and his conversion and subsequent experience of the Church had led him to the belief that there was now a larger chosen people, established by God's grace, and including all those with faith in Christ, a faith witnessed to in a baptism that brought both Jews and Gentiles into the same community, into a faith that Abraham had exercised, and thus into a means of maintaining membership of the chosen people older than the keeping of the Mosaic Law.[61]

Paul was not against the Law as such, and regarded it as God's gift. The parts of the Law to which the converted Paul *did* take exception were those parts that excluded Gentiles from the Covenant: circumcision, the Sabbath laws, laws regarding table fellowship, and so on; but even here Paul continued to obey the Law[62] himself because he was a Jew as well as a Christian. To declare that Paul was anti-Law because pro-grace is to read him with Reformation spectacles on. Paul held a number of basic convictions:[63] that salvation is by faith in Christ; that Jews and Gentiles are equal in the Church; and that the Law is from God. His ethical views remained essentially those of the Law. He knew that the Law was God-given, and so had continuing problems as to its current status: but he was quite clear that Jews and Gentiles alike were included in the Abrahamic Covenant through faith in Christ, and that the keeping of the Law had nothing to do with access to salvation: a salvation established by the grace of God. For Paul, Christ was the central focus, so any part of the Law that diminished the importance of faith in Christ as a means of entering the Covenant people was to be abandoned: or, as Paul later saw, was to be valued as a gift to Israel alone, a gift secondary in importance to the gift of salvation through Jesus' death and resurrection. We can certainly find God's judgement on evil-doers in Paul's

59. Romans 11:6, NRSV
60. Romans 5:1–2, NRSV.
61. Galatians 3.
62. Acts 16.
63. Sanders, *Paul, the Law and the Jewish People*, 14.

letters,[64] but punishment related to not doing God's will does not appear to deny salvation to the sinner. Both in Paul's letters,[65] and in the Letter to the Hebrews,[66] right behavior maintains the Christian in the Covenant, and wrong behavior risks putting the believer outside the Covenant: but just as the Jews believed that final salvation was possible for the Gentiles, so Paul believed that final salvation was available to Christians who had put themselves outside the Covenant by their behavior. What we do not find in Paul's letters, nor in the other New Testament documents of the early Church, is the radical welcome of unrepentant sinners as full members of the Covenant people that Jesus modelled through his table-fellowship with "the sinners." What we do find is a new corporate identity regarding itself as living at the end of time and awaiting Christ's return (although Paul's later letters envisaged something of a delay in this final event's arrival): a corporate identity entered by faith and baptism, with membership maintained by a continuing faith and by righteousness.

In the Letter to the Philippians, Paul writes this: "Therefore, my beloved, just as you have always obeyed me, not only in my presence, but much more now in my absence, work out your own salvation with fear and trembling; for it is God who is at work in you, enabling you both to will and to work for his good pleasure."[67] Here it would appear that salvation is *not* solely by God's grace: it is by our faith and our good deeds as well as by grace. We must certainly try to understand the roots of Paul's theology—perhaps he was encouraging righteousness among Gentile Christians so that Jewish Christians would be content to abandon their last ties with Judaism and join a predominantly Gentile Church—but that does not entail agreement with his solution to what might have been a difficult pastoral problem. He has substituted a faith commitment for those parts of the Law that distinguished Jews from Gentiles, and has thus turned "faith" into a work of a new Law: which is not surprising considering Paul's deep Jewish roots. He has constructed a new exclusivism based on God's choice of Jesus Christ rather than on God's election of Israel, and the mechanism for remaining within the Covenant is now "faith in Christ" rather than keeping the Law, a faith that Paul thought that Abraham had exercised[68] and that was therefore a means of including people in a covenant people that was

64. Romans 2:12–16; 2 Corinthians 5:8–10; 1 Corinthians 3:10–15; 1 Corinthians 11:29–32.

65. Romans 11:22; 1 Corinthians 6:9–10; Galatians 5:21.

66. Hebrews 10:32–39.

67. Philippians 2:12–13, NRSV.

68. Genesis 15:6; Galatians 3:6.

older than the gift of the Mosaic Law. The Christian community as a whole is kept within the Abrahamic Covenant by its faith and its behavior; and the individual is maintained within the Covenant community by her or his faith and behavior. It might be that such a theological framework was essential for the survival of a Jewish reform movement as it adapted itself to welcome Gentiles and eventually become a predominantly Gentile sect: but Paul's solution is still a betrayal of Jesus' radical grace, and raises the question as to whether Paul knew about Jesus' radical welcome of the wicked. It is surely significant that "grace" does not appear in the index of E.P. Sanders' *Paul, the Law, and the Jewish People*. Was it inevitable that grace should have been submerged by the early Church's need for boundaries in order to survive?— for "grace" as a central theological concept is not likely to be a very effective way of maintaining boundaries and an exclusive corporate identity: in fact, it would tend to demolish them. Perhaps it was simply not possible for the churches that Paul founded to remember the radical grace at the center of Jesus' religious faith and practice. But that is not to say that there are no elements of that radical grace to be found in Paul's churches.

"There is no longer Jew or Greek, there is no longer slave or free, there is no longer male and female; for all of you are one in Christ Jesus."[69] Equality between Jews and Gentiles appears to have become a reality in the early Church. They ate together, they married each other, and they regarded themselves as of equal status: for they were all of them baptized into Christ. To us this is a commonplace, but in the first century it was a colossal achievement. It was not new for Gentiles to become Jews, and it was not new for Gentiles and Jews to regard themselves as heirs of a common salvation on the basis of differing entry criteria: but for there to be equality of salvation, equality of entry criterion, and equality of status within the Covenant people, was an achievement that we might properly describe as an act of grace: an act of grace which gave birth to a community of grace. Paul's active objection to those works of the Law that marked Jews off as privileged was probably the determining factor, but the theological under-pinning of the equality practiced and experienced by Christians was "faith in Christ." In the Letter to the Romans it is Judaism that teaches salvation by grace alone (by God's choice of the Jews) and Paul who teaches salvation by one's own achievements:[70] but he writes this because he wants the Church in Rome to continue to contain Jews and Gentiles, both of whom in his view are recipients of God's grace: and it is this equality between Jews and Gentiles that appears to override every other theological consideration.

69. Galatians 3:28, NRSV.
70. Romans 2.

Francis Watson is right to ask: "Can a Paul who devotes his energies to the creation and maintaining of sectarian groups hostile to all non-members, and specially to the Jewish community from which in fact they derived, still be seen as the bearer of a message with profound universal significance?"[71] The answer can in principle be "yes" if we recognize that much of what Paul says in his letters is intended to maintain the young Church's existence and integrity, and if we understand the equality between Jews and Gentiles in the Church as a signpost towards an equal salvation for all.

Much of what Paul wrote in his letters was intended to minimize conflict within the Church (for instance, the language of "the body of Christ" was designed to persuade rich Corinthians to share their food with poorer Christians), and at the same time, and perhaps more importantly, what he wrote gave practical expression to a fundamental equality.[72] The abolition of boundaries between male and female, slave and free, Jew and Gentile, rich and poor,[73] was an obsession for Paul, although clearly we cannot expect him to have been entirely consistent, considering the strong social pressures towards inequality with which he would have had to cope. Just as Jews rarely discussed, but always assumed, God's gracious choice of Israel, so Paul assumed and comparatively rarely mentioned God's gracious choice of Jesus Christ and of all who are "in Christ" by faith and baptism. But it might have been the sometimes submerged grace-foundation of Paul's religion that had the profound effect of dismantling boundaries within the community. Paul might not have been able to envisage a Covenant community *totally* without boundaries, but the "faith" that Abraham exercised offered him a route from his own history to a Covenant community that would at least include the Gentiles to whom he had been sent by his conversion experience: an inclusion that has made it possible for us to keep alive the idea of a universal grace and the accompanying idea of a universal Covenant people.

Paul's inclusion of the Gentiles, along with Jesus' inclusion of the wicked, point unremittingly forward to the destruction of *all* boundaries: but not yet. Paul's replacement of the ritual boundary (of Sabbath, circumcision, and food laws) with a "faith" boundary sets us some connected questions that have troubled Christians throughout the centuries: If salvation is by grace alone, then why is our response by either works or faith relevant? If salvation is by grace alone, then have we not removed all human responsibility? And if faith is a requirement, then have we not denied the grace of God?

---

71. Watson, *Paul, Judaism and the Gentiles*, 181.

72. In the case of 1 Corinthians 11:17–34, equality between rich and poor.

73. Galatians 3:28.

There are clues to a possible approach to a solution to this dilemma in Paul's letters themselves. In *From Adam to Christ*,[74] Morna Hooker suggests that the phrase *pistis Christou*,[75] generally translated "faith in Christ," but perhaps better translated "faith *of* Christ," refers not to *our* faith in Christ but to *Christ's* faith or faithfulness. "If Paul appeals to his converts to be obedient on the basis of Christ's obedience (Philippians 2:8, 12), is it not likely that their faith also will be dependent on his?"[76] Christ's faith leads to our faith through our participation in him, and the righteousness which rests on faith rather than on works of the Law might best be understood as a righteousness that rests on *Jesus'* faith rather than on ours. Thus the antithesis that Paul offers is between works of the Law and the work of Christ, including Christ's faith, a faith that gives birth to our faith. If we agree with Morna Hooker, then no longer need faith and grace be pitted against one another, for the faith is primarily *Jesus Christ's* faith, and it is the generous activity of God. The "grace of our Lord Jesus Christ"[77] is the grace exercised by Jesus Christ, as well as the grace that *is* Jesus Christ, a grace from which flows the faithfulness of Jesus Christ and from which flows our faith. And perhaps we might add another step to this argument: Perhaps Paul's *pistis Christou* is purposely ambiguous. Jesus himself was not averse to employing ambiguity—for instance, his "Do not think that I have come to abolish the law or the prophets; I have come not to abolish but to fulfil,"[78] could mean either "I have come to obey the existing law and prophets" or "I have come to replace the law and the prophets"[79]—so Paul might have regarded himself as being in good company when he employed *pistou Christou* to say that Jews and Gentiles were bound together in a common faith, that Jesus' faithfulness was the source of our salvation, and that our consequent faith enabled us to enter and remain in the new covenant.

Paul's Gospel is a Gospel of grace. Yes, there are moralistic passages in his letters, because he remained a Jew and wanted his churches to survive and to grow and to exhibit that equality that a Gospel of grace implied; but such moralizing is incidental to the foundation of grace underlying Paul's theology: a grace more basic than either our faith in Christ or the faith that is Christ's faith that is itself an act of grace.

---

74. Hooker, *From Adam to Christ*.

75. Romans 3:22; Galatians 2:16; 3:22.

76. Hooker, *From Adam to Christ*, 168.

77. Romans 16:20; 1 Corinthians 16:23

78. Matthew 5:17, NRSV.

79. Torry, "Two Kinds of Ambiguity."

James Moffatt wrote *Grace in the New Testament* in 1931, but the more recent scholarship on which this discussion of Paul's theology has been based has thoroughly borne out Moffatt's thesis "that the mission of the Lord Jesus was a mission of grace, that the apostle Paul's message or what he called his 'gospel' presupposes this more seriously than some have been prepared to admit, and that a fair appreciation of the affinities and indebtedness of Christianity to its environment leaves the historical student impressed by the creative energy of the new faith mentally and morally."[80]

Does our salvation require a faith that is not Christ's but ours? Paul might not have been able to answer that question unambiguously, and his letters do contain passages that suggest salvation by works, and they certainly suggest firm boundaries around the Covenant people, though not necessarily around the people destined for final salvation: another question about which Paul might not have been able to respond unambiguously. Paul's gospel was not unambiguously a gospel of grace, but it pointed in that direction, in the direction of a gospel of unconditional, active generosity, a direction sometimes submerged by Paul himself and certainly somewhat submerged during the following centuries.

AFTER THE NEW TESTAMENT

Paul *does* talk about the grace that God has given to him[81] as well as using "grace" to express the character of a God who constantly gives, so it should come as no surprise that after the New Testament period "grace" came to be regarded more as something substantial, as a possession of the Christian, and less as a pattern of action: a process that would have been significantly assisted by a dominant "substance" and "being" conceptual framework as opposed to the weaker "action" framework that we find running parallel to it.[82] "Grace" came to mean an endowment, given by the Holy Spirit, rather than the active generosity of God in Jesus Christ.

The process of change, already latent in Paul's letters, is clearly visible in the Letter of James—"he gives all the more grace"[83]—and when T.F. Torrance surveys the second century literature of the Didache, the First Letter of Clement, the Epistles of Ignatius, the Epistle of Polycarp, the Epistle of Barnabas, the Shepherd of Hermas, and the Second Letter of Clement, he

---

80. Moffatt, *Grace in the New Testament*, xii.

81. For instance, Romans 12:3.

82. Torry, *Actology*.

83. James 4:6, NRSV.

finds a firm trend towards the pre-New Testament use of the word *charis* in which it means a character trait that a person possesses.

> The great presupposition of the Christian life [in the literature surveyed] was not a deed of decisive significance that cut across human life and set it on a wholly new basis grounded upon the self-giving of God. What took absolute precedence was God's call to a new life in obedience to revealed truth. Grace, as far as it was grasped, was subsidiary to that.[84]

Thus in the hands of these early theologians a gospel of God's grace gave way to a call to active discipleship and a handing-down of revealed truth, a call and a handing-down aided by a "grace" given to the believer by the Holy Spirit. The Gospel thus became a "new Law" and "grace" an enabling power given by the Holy Spirit to enable us to keep this new Law: a "grace" given to the Church as a possession and bestowed by the bishop at baptism and ordination. A gift was given, rather than Christians participating in the constant and generous giving activity of God.

Perhaps we should envisage a spectrum of usage, with "grace" as God's generous activity at one end, and "grace" as a substantial endowment at the other. What Torrance has identified is a shift along the spectrum from "grace" as the generous activity of God to "grace" as a spiritual substance bestowed by God on the Church. Torrance thinks that the real problem is that "grace" had become disconnected from the life and work of Jesus Christ, and had been given to the Holy Spirit to bestow:[85] but the major difference is that "grace" has become less dynamic and more static, less a generous activity and more the bestowal of a characteristic that enables us to be faithful Christians.

If we are looking for reasons for the transition of the meaning of "grace" from God's generous action to an endowment given to the elect, then we shall probably find them in the social situation of the early Christians. Particularly in urban contexts, the Christian Church was one religious institution among others, so the maintenance of boundaries was clearly an important consideration. It was probably inevitable that under these circumstances Christians should come to be defined by specific confessions of faith, by the exercise of faith, and by thinking that they had received something from God that non-Christians had not received; and what better term than "grace" to denote that "something": for to commandeer "grace" for this task meant that it could no longer express a generous activity that might

84. Torrance, *The Doctrine of Grace in the Apostolic Fathers*, 133.
85. Torrance, *The Doctrine of Grace in the Apostolic Fathers*, v.

risk dissolving the social boundaries necessary to the Church's survival in a complex society.

AUGUSTINE AND PELAGIUS

The third-century Origen recovered some of the active sense of "grace," but made it conditional on our response;[86] Tertullian used the term in a variety of ways, and generally in such a way as to deny us the exercise of free will in relation to God's grace;[87] and the fifth-century Augustine reacted against Pelagius to give us a concept of grace that made free will a difficult concept but that retained the nature of grace as a gift. For Augustine, the primary theological fact was the Fall, the first sin of Adam that implicates all of us in sin and in guilt for sin. The grace exercised towards those whom God has chosen to save is of a character that Paul would have recognized: it is an unconditional, active generosity, though also an endowment leading to a sanctified life. It is not surprising that Pelagius accused Augustine of introducing the pagan concept of "fate" when Augustine wrote passages such as this: "We must not doubt that human wills are incapable of withstanding the will of God in such a way as to prevent Him from doing what He wishes to do."[88] As far as Augustine was concerned, "grace" is irresistible, and its apparent arbitrariness is unquestionable. Whether the grace leads to faith, baptism, and membership of the Church, or to salvation sealed by a grace of final perseverance (he did not think that everybody who was given the first kind of grace was necessarily given the second), grace appears to be for some and not for others. Augustine certainly *claimed* to believe in the freedom of the will, but himself demolished the claim by saying that God creates some who will will salvation and some who will not; and by saying that "eternal life is the wages owing to the merit of righteousness,"[89] he made it clear that righteous deeds were the result of God's irresistible grace in the Christian. Such a theological position, which preserved the unconditionality of grace by making its exercise somewhat arbitrary, was no doubt a result of Augustine's sense of his own worthlessness: but its uncompromising character was the result of the dispute with Pelagius.

---

86. Drewery, *Origen and the Doctrine of Grace*, 64.

87. Williams, *The Grace of God*, 16. Williams quotes Tertullian, *De an. 21*: ". . . divine grace, which is assuredly mightier than nature, having in subjection to itself within us the faculty of free will."

88. *De corr. et grat.* xii, 38, quoted in Williams, *The Grace of God*, 26–27.

89. *Ep.* cxciv, 20, quoted in Williams, *The Grace of God*, 41.

Pelagius was a Briton who in Rome, Carthage and Palestine proclaimed a gospel of grace but one that refused Augustine's conclusion that God's grace rendered the human will impotent. A major reason for Pelagius saying what he did was that the Church was not in very good shape. Much of its activity had become conventional, and he feared that Augustine had too readily accepted the sinful world to which we belong. In a social crisis—the collapse of the Roman Empire was occurring as Pelagius and Augustine wrote their treatises—reform movements sometimes catch on because people need to feel their own dignity and that they have the ability to change their own lives and their world. Augustine was a member of the Roman establishment by education and experience, and it is not surprising that he formulated a theology that offered spiritual security to the elect and effectively left the secular world to fall apart without interference from a Christian ethic: but Pelagius was from the fringe of the Empire, and brought with him a Christianity used to a more hostile context, and thus one more dependent on the action of the Christian than on the invisible action of God.

It is a pity that Augustine and Pelagius never met to hammer out their differences, for if they had done then they might have discovered that they were both attempting to give expression to a mystery and that it was possible to live with ambiguity: something which Pelagius was better at doing than Augustine was. It is also a pity that Pelagius was not well served by his associates, one of whom, Caelestius, turned Pelagius's legitimate concern with morality into a systematic theology, thus doing for Pelagius what Augustine had done for himself. Neither was Augustine well served by those on *his* side, particularly Jerome, who branded Pelagius a heretic and rejected all attempts at reconciliation, apparently on the grounds that Pelagius believed that by God's grace some people might have remained sinless.

A Synod in CE 415 in Jerusalem agreed with Pelagius that Paul's "by the grace of God I am what I am, and his grace towards me has not been in vain. On the contrary, I worked harder than any of them—though it was not I, but the grace of God that is with me"[90] implied that if we strive to be righteous then God gives the possibility of being so. A subsequent Synod in Palestine heard Pelagius repudiate a caricature of his position (to the pleasure of Augustine and the displeasure of Jerome), and in Rome Pope Zosimus decided in favor of Pelagius. Pelagius was firmly opposed to Augustine's predestinarianism, but had not publicly questioned Augustine's orthodoxy. Augustine's allies, however, had fueled the controversy in Rome, and Zosimus' verdict had gone to Pelagius because he appeared more concerned with the peace and unity of the Church than did Augustine.

90. 1 Corinthians 15:10, NRSV.

But Augustine had not given up, and he asked the Emperor to intervene. A Synod at Carthage condemned Pelagius's views, and Zosimus caved in and excommunicated Pelagius and Caelestius for transgressing the central tenets of the Christian Faith. Thus a Christian ethicist for whom love was the highest category, and who believed in both God's grace and the freedom of the will, was condemned as a heretic.

Pelagius's concern to give equal weight to passages of Scripture that appeared to contradict each other (those about grace in Paul's letters, and Jesus' parables of the Good Samaritan and the Sheep and the Goats, both of which assume that we can choose to act righteously), lost out to Augustine's God who gives the ability to act righteously or chooses not to give that ability. Pelagius, being concerned about what it meant to be a Christian disciple, could not accept that God's grace is an irresistible power that leaves no room for human action. What is so tragic is that the Synod in Carthage found in favor of an Augustine who could so caricature his opponent's position as to say that Pelagius "under the pretence of defending the freedom of the will, disputes the grace of God and endeavours to overthrow the foundation of the Christian faith."[91] The dispute came down to different emphases—no doubt the result of differing personal experiences—polarizing themselves against each other so that in the end Augustine could not see any of his own position in that of Pelagius.

What is required now is a thorough rehabilitation of Pelagius, the theologian who spoke of God's grace of creation, God's grace of revelation, and God's grace of redemption. In Augustine's theology "grace" became a somewhat impersonal and irresistible power—a power perhaps modelled on that of the Roman Emperor, a power that Augustine wanted to see exercised in and by the Church—and it ceased to be the personal activity of a creative and saving God seeking a relationship of love with the created order. "Grace" was still a generous, self-giving activity, but it had also become arbitrary and irresistible.

The dispute need not have been so vicious, and it did not need to happen at all, for it is possible to conceive of events having multiple causes rather than single ones. Augustine's conversion was an exercise of God's grace, but it was also the result of co-operation on Augustine's part. In J.R. Lucas's view,

> St. Augustine had been right to ascribe the credit not to himself but to God, wrong to say that he himself had had no say in whether he would do God's will or not. Pelagius was right to

91. Quoted in Rees, *Pelagius*, 15.

stress man's freedom, wrong to convert autonomy into autarky, and freedom into pride.[92]

Caelestius's name should probably be where we find Pelagius's in that quotation, but the way in which Lucas's summary polarizes the two theological tendencies represents well what can happen in the heat of debate, especially when powerful institutions get involved. Perhaps in the heat of that battle neither side was a faithful ambassador for grace: an unconditional generosity.

AFTER AUGUSTINE

After Augustine, Cassian suggested that "when God sees us incline towards willing the good, he runs to meet us, directs and strengthens us."[93] This grace is "co-operant," that is, a matter of a relationship between God and humanity; and the thirteenth century Franciscans, and especially Duns Scotus, declared *all* grace to be co-operant. But the urge to tidy things up did not go away, and Anselm of Canterbury offered the Church of the twelfth century a tidy theology of the atonement. He managed to avoid making the devil the payee of Christ's ransom, but got pretty close by declaring God to be subject to a universal justice that it was his duty to uphold. Because we have sinned, there must be some righting of the balance, and this was achieved through Jesus offering himself. Anselm, and his modern-day commentator Colin Gunton, think that this is an example of grace, for God is not here a judge, and there is no compulsion on Jesus to go to his death:[94] but this is still not the grace that Jesus exercised during his ministry, for it demands that accounts be settled, that *someone puts* things right. And it is not the justification of which Paul speaks: a counting of the sinner as righteous when the sinner is *not* righteous. Paul found a complete generosity difficult, and there are roots of Anselm's atonement doctrine in Paul's ideas about Jesus' death: but Anselm has tried to make a logical system out of ideas culled from Paul's letters—letters that were never intended to be systematic theological treatises—and he thus wandered even further from Jesus' total generosity than did Paul.

---

92. Lucas, "Pelagius and St. Augustine," 737.

93. *Coll.* xiiii, 11, quoted in Williams, *The Grace of God*, 49.

94. Gunton, *The Actuality of Atonement*, 92. Gunton quotes Anselm, *Cur Deus Homo*, II, xviii: "Therefore, since he himself (Jesus Christ) is God, the Son of God, he offered himself for his own honour to himself, as he did to the Father and the Holy Spirit."

Why is it that we cannot face the idea that God's welcome of us is without condition? Why did Anselm demand that justice be satisfied? The metaphors of "justice" and "satisfaction" might have been helpful at the time if they gave to people who for some reason could not grasp an absolute generosity at least a glimpse of it: but they *are* metaphors, and if they now cloud our vision of the glory of an unconditional grace then we must abandon them and find some new way of expressing our theology of grace.

Augustine and Anselm might have done us a favor that Pelagius and Duns Scotus could not do, for to recognize and express ambiguity is not necessarily an effective way of keeping alive a vital element of the Christian tradition. However much we might question the details of Augustine's scheme, he did believe that grace is *God's* grace, and that God is gracious towards sinners. And it is Augustine whom Aquinas and Catholic theologians followed, and Augustine whom Luther and Protestant theologians followed.

Thomas Aquinas adapted Augustine's ideas to suit the rediscovered Aristotelian philosophy that he was finding so useful as a framework for expressing Christian Faith, and he found himself distinguishing between two categories of grace: *actual* grace (the movement of the soul by God) and *habitual* grace (a grace infused into the soul).[95] Actual grace wasn't too far from the grace of the New Testament, but habitual grace was a long way from it. Aquinas's scheme (and his theology in general) was determinative for Roman Catholic theology until early last century, and still possesses enormous influence.

Luther preferred to think of our wills as passive in relation to God's grace, thus returning to a scheme closer to Augustine's, and the debate between Augustine and Pelagius re-emerged as one within early Lutheranism between Luther and Melanchthon, but this time without quite so much damaging polarization. What appears to have been common ground between Luther and other Reformation theologians was the centrality of "faith," which became a new work of a new law and was the primary cause of Protestantism losing touch with grace, and thus losing touch with a gracious God, the search for whom had been the cause of Luther's Reformation. The centrality that Calvin ascribed to grace had an effect similar to Augustine's reaction against Pelagius, leaving him with a sovereign God who was generous to some but not to others.

In England, the Reformation took a different turn again, and turned grace into the kind of "substance" which the early Church Fathers and Aquinas would have recognized. The Collects of the Book of Common Prayer pray to a God "who hast given unto us thy servants grace, by a true faith,

95. Groves, *Grace*, 97–100.

to acknowledge the glory of the eternal Trinity . . ." and "who hast given us grace at this time with one accord to make our common supplications unto thee . . ." as if grace is a medicine given by God to members of the Church of England. The Book of Common Prayer appears not to have understood grace as an active, generous and unconditional love, and neither did the thirty-nine articles when they interpreted Augustine's and Calvin's ideas on predestination to mean the allocation of each human being to "life everlasting" or to "the sentence of God's predestination."[96]

One way to reconcile these different perspectives is to understand reality as action in changing patterns, and God as Action, the source of action, and the author of patterns of action, including the pattern of action that is unconditional generous giving, or grace. Jesus Christ is God living a human life among us, and so characterized by patterns of action that characterize God, and so by grace; and God's continuing action in the created order is also grace: a pattern of action that is unconditional and generous giving. We too are action in changing patterns, and so the action in changing patterns that is the grace of God impinges on the action in patterns that constitute who we are, and participates in the constant changing of who we are. We remain ourselves, and the patterns of action that we are are genuinely ourselves: but they are also to some extent the patterns of action that constitute God, and particularly the pattern of action that we call grace.

The priest and poet George Herbert clearly understood something of the nature of God's unconditional and generous giving:

> Love bade me welcome: yet my soul drew back,
> Guiltie of dust and sinne.
> But quick-ey'd Love, observing me grow slack
> From my first entrance in,
> Drew nearer to me, sweetly questioning,
> If I lack'd any thing.
>
> A guest, I answer'd, worthy to be here:
> Love said, You shall be he.
> I the unkinde, ungratefull? Ah my deare,
> I cannot look on thee.
> Love took my hand, and smiling did reply,
> Who made the eyes but I?
>
> Truth Lord, but I have marr'd them: let my shame
> Go where it doth deserve.
> And know you not, sayes Love, who bore the blame?

96. Article 17.

My deare, then I will serve.
You must sit down, sayes Love, and taste my meat:
So I did sit and eat.[97]

As Groves points out, grace is here persistent.

> As often as the poet draws back, the God of love reaches fur-
> ther and further towards him in order to draw him into fellow-
> ship . . . Throughout the poem, love answers the guest not with
> answers but with questions, enticing him to recognize the truth
> that is leading him . . . Our inclination, our half-recognition, is
> to acknowledge God by falling down on our faces and offering
> service. But the God we acknowledge is the one already serving
> us at table.[98]

What the Book of Common Prayer had understood was the ways in which
God's grace impinges on the patterns of action that constitute the reality
that is ourselves. There need be no contradiction between Herbert's poem
and the Book of Common Prayer. Grace is both a pattern of action that God
is, and it is the "practical" pattern of action of Christian discipleship.[99] In
both senses it is costly: costly to God, and costly to us.[100]

Modern Protestant thought is so diverse that it is difficult to give the
category a definition, and the diversity is nowhere as great as in the tradition's treatment of grace. Kant's concern for autonomy and responsibility
would have been recognized by Augustine as what he was attacking as Pe-
lagianism; Schleiermacher located the roots of faith in human experience,
and particularly in our feeling of dependence, and was thus in danger of
turning the story of God's generosity into a story purely about ourselves;
and Bultmann, following Paul, knew that grace is God's gracious action and,
following Kierkegaard, knew that grace is not an assured possession: but
he could not abandon the idea of a final judgment in which we are asked
whether or not we have faith in that grace. Käsemann and other followers
of Bultmann were minutely concerned with the nature of our faith, and excluded from their existentialist salvation those who boasted in their works:
although not those who boasted a right understanding of faith. And Karl
Barth's universal election of humanity in Jesus Christ, and his theology of
the Word of God, turned grace into an irresistible power: although, unlike Augustine's, a power that revealed God's sovereignty and so led to the

---

97. Herbert, "Love Bade me Welcome," in Herbert, *The Poems of George Herbert.*

98. Groves, *Grace*, 40–41.

99. Groves, *Grace*, 106.

100. Groves, *Grace*, 106–10.

universe's salvation.[101] Barth and Bultmann between them got closest to Paul's conception of grace, but Protestant theology since Luther has failed to grasp the radical nature of the grace that Jesus exercised, a grace that welcomes the wicked.

Among modern Roman Catholic theologians, Hans Küng is the nearest to Protestant thought when he describes grace as "the free personal favour of God, as His powerful and sovereign act."[102] He criticized Barth for not recognizing that grace is a personal relationship established by God, but Küng himself wrote that grace "has been given through the Holy Spirit in the Church,"[103] making it sound like an endowment rather than a continuous activity. And far from objecting to the Roman Catholic habit of dividing up grace into different kinds of grace, he approves of it.

Charles Journet, in *The Meaning of Grace*,[104] describes five "states of grace," without any recognition that a "state of grace" might be a contradiction in terms; James Burtchaell defines grace as being "favorable in complete priority to another person's behavior,"[105] but then abandons his discussion of God's grace universally active for one about the Church's ritual; Edward Yarnold[106] has attempted to relate actual and habitual grace by noting that God's active grace changes us so that our behavior changes: but he still feels it necessary to divide the "first gift" of creation from the "second gift" of grace, not realizing that creation is the activity of God's grace. Karl Rahner, in *Grace in Freedom*,[107] expresses the opinion that there is no point in discussing the causality of our actions, yet goes on to describe grace as God himself setting our freedom free from its refusal of God's self-communication: a long-winded way of being an Augustinian. On Roman Catholic theologians such as Richard Cole,[108] Teilhard de Chardin's optimistic evolutionary scheme has had an impact, an influence that has enabled Cole to recognize grace as a universal activity operating in the secular world as well as in the sacred: but he still manages to confuse "grace" and "Spirit": and because he does not grapple at all with the use of "grace" in the New Testament, he writes of an "order of grace" in which, whether we like it or not, our wills recognize the universal kingship of Christ.

101. Groves, *Grace*, 91–92.

102. Küng, *Justification*, 203.

103. Küng, *Justification*, 200.

104. Journet, *The Meaning of Grace*.

105. Burtchaell, *Living with Grace*, 21.

106. Yarnold, *The Second Gift*.

107. Rahner, *Grace in Freedom*.

108. Cole, *Universal Grace*.

It is not entirely the fault of the theologians whom I have discussed that they have wandered such a long way from the grace that we see in Jesus' life. Paul grasped something of the character of that grace when he experienced a call to take the gospel to the Gentiles and had to work out how Jews and Gentiles might be equally "in Christ": but his solution of "justification by faith" lost Jesus' unconditionality, even if at the time "faith" might have been an essential emphasis in order to maintain the Church's self-identity, and even if the faith that he discussed might be Jesus' faith in which we participate.

And so it has always been. The Church needs boundaries, and so grace has been compromised throughout the Church's history. And in the personal sphere, we have moral needs, and Pelagius's reaction to Augustine was inevitable and healthy. As John Oman puts it: "How is the personality which alike gives meaning to morality and value to religion to be preserved if not by . . . setting our religious dependence and our moral independence in antagonism?"[109] The Catholic compromise is an Augustinian Church with Pelagian members, and the Protestant compromise a Pelagian Church with Augustinian members. Oman tries to integrate religious dependence with moral independence by locating them both in a personal relationship with God, but this is at the cost of dividing morality and religion, an impossible division to maintain.

Is it simply that we are faced with a grace and a freedom that are irreconcilable because we are trying to be too literalist about language that is essentially metaphorical? Colin Gunton thinks so, believing that because we have not understood the metaphorical status of theological language we have moved the center of attention from Jesus Christ to the believer's response, because that is what we can speak about. (Perhaps this is what led to Paul's emphasis on "faith"). Gunton[110] recognizes that Wittgenstein's philosophical work on the nature of language has dissolved the absolute distinction between the metaphorical and the literal, and he urges us to treasure our metaphors, in science as much as in theology. It is true that metaphors like "victory," "justice," "sacrifice," and so on, were attempts to speak of a grace that cannot be pinned down by language: but Gunton has not told us how to discriminate between valid metaphors and invalid ones. On what basis might we decide whether we should use Augustine's predestinarian language? And when we speak of the freedom of the will, is that a metaphor? Unfortunately, the problem that Augustine and Pelagius faced, of reconciling the freedom of the will with the sovereignty of God, will not

---

109. Oman, *Grace and Personality*, 29.

110. Gunton, *The Actuality of Atonement*, 17–19.

go away quite that easily, for to appeal to metaphor does not make self-contradiction a valid use of language.

This century we have experienced some new attempts to resolve the dilemma. Albert Camus was right to conclude that an almighty God and a suffering humanity can only lead to either atheism or rebellion, and that the only other option is a suffering God:[111] so we now see the idea of a suffering God becoming a theological commonplace.[112] Perhaps this is one element of a solution to our dilemma, but it is not the whole of it. The problem is one of context: It was all very well for Jesus to eat with the wicked, but he did not have a Church to keep in one piece, he did not have a society to keep moral, and he did not have to square morality and religion with each other: for as far as he was concerned, the world as he knew it was about to end, and a whole new order of existence was about to be inaugurated.

If grace is the predominant characteristic of Jesus' ministry, the focus of Paul's theology (even if he did not always recognize this), and the primary definition of God's activity in relation to the universe and to every human being, then there are some problems that we must solve, problems with which, as we have seen, Christians have grappled for two thousand years: and an appeal to metaphor will not be sufficient to resolve the dilemma.

How are we to reconcile God's decisions with our free will?[113] How are we to reconcile morality with grace? How are we to reconcile a deciding God with a suffering humanity? How are we to conceive of God's activity in a secular world? And, perhaps more importantly than all of these questions: how are we to speak about God, and about grace, in a world in which philosophy has asked so many questions about the nature of language that we fear that we cannot speak about our *own* existence, let alone about the grace of God?

THE EUCHARIST

Throughout this book we have been assuming an actology rather than an ontology: that is, we have understood reality as action in patterns rather than as beings that change. Coherent with this understanding of reality is John Zizioulas's understanding of "being" as "communion"—that is, relationships: which means that the Church is "communion" and therefore constituted by

111. Camus, *L'Homme Révolté*, 53.

112. Doctrine Commission of the General Synod of the Church of England, *We Believe in God*, 157–58.

113. Baillie, *God was in Christ*.

active relationships.[114] There is always a sense in which the Eucharist—the commemoration of Jesus' last meal with his disciples before his death—defines the Church: but that identification between the Eucharist and the Church takes on an even deeper meaning if both are understood within an actology: an understanding of reality as action in changing patterns.

The Eucharist is constituted by the taking of bread and wine, a giving thanks, the breaking of the bread, and the sharing of the bread and the cup.[115] These actions *are* the Church, so that where there is a pattern of action that bears a family likeness to Jesus' actions as we find them recorded in the accounts of the last supper in the gospels and in Paul's letter to the church in Corinth, there is the Church, and there is the risen Christ, for Christ is his action, and if the Church is doing these actions then the Church *is* Christ's body.[116] As John Robinson puts it: the Eucharist constitutes the "body," which is "the extension of the life and person of the incarnate Christ beyond His resurrection and ascension."[117]

Jesus' fourfold action at the last supper—the taking of bread and wine, the giving thanks, the breaking of the bread, and the sharing of the bread and cup—was a pattern of action that represents an extreme grace: an absolutely generous giving. This becomes particularly clear if we understand the last supper and the Eucharist in terms of changing patterns of action rather than in terms of things that change. Within an ontology our focus might be on the bread and wine, whereas an actology focuses our attention on Jesus' actions. Quoting from what is probably the account of the last supper written closest to the event:

> And when he had given thanks, he broke it and said, "This is my body that is for you. Do this in remembrance of me." In the same way he took the cup also, after supper, saying, "This cup is the new covenant in my blood. Do this, as often as you drink it, in remembrance of me."[118]

It is as he broke the bread that he said "This is my body that is for you": so he was referring not to the bread itself, but to the breaking and sharing of the bread, and so to the coming crucifixion in which his body would be broken: a destruction that they were to understand as being for them. When it comes to the cup of wine, Mark, in the first gospel to be written, adds "which

---

114. Zizioulas, *Being as Communion*, 17.

115. Dix, *The Shape of the Liturgy*, 48.

116. Robinson, *The Body*, 47, 58.

117. Robinson, *The Body*, 57.

118. 1 Corinthians 11:24–25.

is poured out for many."[119] The pouring and sharing of the wine was the pouring out of his blood that would form a new covenant between God and a new Israel, the disciples of Jesus who awaited the coming of the Kingdom of God, just as the slaughtering of animals in the Hebrew Scriptures was one of the ways in which it was believed a covenant between Israel and God was established and maintained. It is all action. It is not about substance—that is, beings that change—but about action in patterns. Where this fourfold pattern of action is done, there the Eucharist is done, there grace is done, there the Church happens rather than is, and there unity is established with all other Christians who participate in the fourfold action of the Eucharist and who by that means become the happening of the Church.

But it is not just of the Eucharist that we can make new sense in the context of an actology. We can make sense of the entirety of the action in patterns that constitutes the Church, the continuing body of Christ. As Jürgen Moltmann has pointed out, the Church is "one, holy and apostolic" because it *does* unity, holiness, and apostolic witness.[120] Where there is apostolic activity, there is the Church; where there is action in patterns in different places and at different times, and all of it is coherent with the action in patterns that is the life, death and resurrection of Jesus Christ, and with the action in patterns that is the Eucharist, then there is the unity of the one catholic Church—that is, the one universal Church: and it is our obligation to recognize that. Where Christians do together the loving, healing and truth-telling action of Jesus, there is the unity of the Church, both the means of that unity and the fact of it. Whether we agree on the detail of Christian doctrine is irrelevant. What constitutes the Church is not ideas, but the doing of grace, Eucharist, baptism, love, healing, teaching, and hoping for the coming of the Kingdom of God. The different churches do not need to agree on what they believe before they can share in the Eucharist: it will be by sharing in the Eucharist together that the unity of the Church will be a fact. Maybe beliefs will converge as a result, but maybe not. That is not important. What matters is that together we become the risen Christ: which means the action in patterns that constitutes who we are cohering with the action in patterns that constitute the risen Christ.[121]

119. Mark 14:24.

120. Moltmann, *The Church in the Power of the Spirit*, 337–39.

121. Torry, "Action, Patterns and Religious Pluralism."

GRACE: THE ACTION WHICH IS GOD

Grace is self-giving activity, grace is the character of Jesus' activity, grace was at the heart of Paul's Christian faith, grace has been *the* focus of theological debate since the early Church, and grace has been constantly lost and rediscovered as the distinctively Christian center of Christian doctrine. In the worlds in which we live we shall never experience or exercise grace in its pure form, for our generosity shrivels in the absence of response, our motives are mixed, and human institutions need to defend themselves if they are to retain their integrity; but this makes it all the more necessary to pursue the notion of grace, to speak clearly of grace even though we know that we shall never in this life meet it in its pure form, because if we do not speak of such a grace then we shall be less able to reform our theology, our ethics, and our institutions in conformity with the grace that is the character of the God who is the absolute grace for which we seek. As Peter Groves puts it:

> Grace, the outpouring of God's love to unite our lives with his, can be "identified"... first of all in the historical individual Jesus of Nazareth, and subsequently in all events that we acknowledge as part of our Christian experience. The act of believing in Christ is the result of the grace of God in the gift of faith. Acknowledging God as creator is responding to the grace of God in all that has been made. These actions are unequivocally my actions, freely performed by me because they are not constrained or coerced by anything else. But, since God is the creator of all things, it is also true that they depend on God. Were it not for the creative act of God that is sustaining everything at every moment in its existence, there would be no freedom and no action at all.[122]

An actology—an understanding that reality is action in changing patterns—is clearly the right conceptual framework for expressing grace as the center of Christian faith: a means whereby, possibly for the first time, grace can be spoken of as grace, as self-giving *activity*, and a means whereby God can be spoken of in terms of the activity that is self-giving love. Here we encounter the possibility that we have been seeking: a genuine gift—or rather, a genuine giving—that is a pattern of generous and unconditional love of such infinite extent that reciprocation is impossible. So here we encounter the only absolute gift-giving and givenness: in the grace of God.

In previous chapters we have asked how an actology might enable us to interpret Husserl's, Heidegger's and Marion's philosophies, particularly

---

122. Groves, *Grace*, 83–84.

in relation to the givenness of phenomena; and we have asked what those philosophies might have to offer to the development of an actology. In this chapter we have asked the same questions, but about theology: How does an actology enable us to interpret theology, particularly in relation to grace? And what does that theology have to contribute to the development of an actology? We have found that to understand grace in the context of an understanding of reality as action in changing patterns can offer us a reading of grace more faithful to Jesus' exercise of grace than would be possible within an ontology that understands reality as beings that change. Conversely, we might say that to understand God as Action, the source of all action, and as particular changing patterns of action—and particularly that of grace—contributes a theological dimension, and perhaps even a theological foundation, to any actology.

8

A giving polity

INTRODUCTION

In chapter 1 we studied Marcel Mauss's *The Gift*. In her introduction to the English translation, Mary Douglas suggests that the practices that Mauss discussed were more about politics and economics than they were about religion, and that Mauss himself had drawn conclusions relating to social policy, particularly in relation to healthcare and unemployment insurance: but as she also points out, modern social policy bears very little relation to the tribal gift-giving that Mauss records.[1]

> Social democracy's redistributions are legislated for in elected bodies and the sums are drawn from tax revenues. They utterly lack any power mutually to obligate persons in a contest of honour.[2]

Douglas recognized that "voluntary cycles of exchange"[3] do take place in society, but also that when she was writing her foreword to *The Gift* in 1990 there was little census or survey evidence available.[4] (This situation was

1. Douglas, "Foreword," xiii.
2. Douglas, "Foreword," xix.
3. Douglas, "Foreword," xx.
4. Douglas, "Foreword," xx.

soon to change. A particularly interesting survey of financial, employment, childcare and various other practices was already being undertaken on an Exeter local authority housing estate, the results of which were published in 1992.[5]) What she might have recognized but did not is that "social democracy's redistributions" were often encumbered with obligations and with opportunities for stigma and shame: it was just that the obligations and stigma were imposed on individuals by governments and various media rather than on tribes by other tribes. So in this chapter we shall study a variety of social policies, particularly in relation to tax and benefits, and we shall ask about the extents of gift-giving, obligation, shame, stigma, reciprocity, and so on.

STIGMA AND SHAME IN A BENEFITS SYSTEM

Stigma is the consequence of the pattern of action denoted by the verb "to stigmatize": an active process, afflicted on an individual or institution by another institution or individual. Erving Goffman lists three types of stigma: "physical deformities," "blemishes of individual character," and "the tribal stigma of race, nation, and religion."[6] It is the second of these that is generated by means-tested benefits: that is, government-provided incomes that are reduced as earned and other incomes rise, that vary with household structure, and the receipt of which depend on the claimant seeking employment or additional employment. Such systems divide a country's population into claimants and non-claimants, so non-claimants can come to assume that other people are having to claim means-tested benefits because of their own character flaws: but it is the detailed regulations as well as the overall structure that communicate society's valuation of claimants.[7] A particularly relevant aspect of those regulations is the level of bureaucratic interference in the lives of claimants that the rules require, and particularly the face to face interviews during which people who might be younger than ourselves seek information about our households, our living arrangements, and the sources of our income; the requirement to provide evidence, which suggests that we are not trustworthy; decisions made by often obscure processes during which "discretion" is exercised within "relationships of domination and subordination, within which supplication becomes a standard mode of conduct";[8] perfunctory "work-related" interviews designed to incentivize employment but that assume that the

5. Jordan et al., *Trapped in Poverty?*

6. Goffman, *Stigma*, 13–14.

7. Tonkens et al., "Introduction."

8. Hill, *Social Security Policy in Britain*, 110; Wagner, *Fiscal Sociology*, 196.

claimant possesses no employment incentive of their own;[9] and complex benefits rules and onerous sanctions regimes in the context of which it is irrational for someone to change their employment market status because they might end up without an income if they do.[10] All of this results in both the stigmatization of benefits claimants by the general public, politicians, and the media, and self-stigmatization if we find ourselves on means-tested benefits. The stigmatizing of households that receive means-tested benefits, and the stigmatizing of the benefits themselves, generate a circular process in which it is easy for governments to reduce the adequacy of the benefits concerned and to make more onerous the process of receiving them,[11] to the point where the regulations represent "cruel, inhuman or degrading treatment."[12] The psychological effect is shame, which appears to be a global phenomenon among the economically disadvantaged.[13]

It is no surprise that research has shown that means-tested benefits experience a more negative image than either contributory benefits or universal and unconditional benefits. Receipt of contributory benefits depends on contributions having been made to a fund administered either by a government or by some other agency such as an employer or trade union, and Mauss finds the mechanism to be informed by the same "to give, to receive, to reciprocate" as tribal reciprocal gift-giving. In

> our social insurance legislation . . . the worker has given his life and his labour, on the one hand to the collectivity, and on the other hand, to his employers. Although the worker has to contribute to his insurance, those who have benefited from his services have not discharged their debt to him through the payment of wages. The state itself, representing the community, owes him, as do his employers, together with some assistance from himself, a certain security in life, against unemployment, sickness, old age, and death.[14]

Universal benefits, which generally means unconditional rather than simply universal incomes, are paid equally to everyone of the same age, without conditions being imposed, and so represent the nearest that it is possible to get to the pure gift declared impossible by Derrida. A good example is the

---

9. Handler, "Myth and Ceremony in Workfare," 117.

10. Welfare Reform Team, Oxford City Council, 2016: 51; Patrick, 2017b: 123–44

11. Hirsch, Could a "Citizen's Income" Work? 4–5.

12. Adler, Cruel, Inhuman or Degrading Treatment?

13. Walker et al., "Poverty in Global Perspective."

14. Mauss, The Gift, 86.

UK's Child Benefit,[15] paid equally to every family with the same number of children, whatever their incomes, household structure, or employment status. No stigma is attached to Child Benefit simply because everyone with the same number of children receives the same amount of money every month.[16] The same is true of such public services as the UK's National Health Service, free at the point of use for every legal resident—a "unique . . . instrument of social policy"[17]—and free public education up to the age of eighteen. An unconditional income for every adult—a Basic Income, Universal Basic Income, or Citizen's Income—would be equally free of stigma and shame.

UNCONDITIONALITIES

There are at least two kinds of unconditional social policy: unconditional provision, such as an income paid equally for every child every week or every month; and unconditional access, such as a public health service in which hospital treatment and visits to a family doctor are free to every legal resident. The differences mean that both kinds are required, and that one kind cannot substitute for another, as is sometimes suggested.[18] An unconditional income could not substitute for healthcare free at the point of need because some individuals require multiple instances of expensive healthcare whereas others require minimal amounts. A further reason for not thinking that free tax-funded healthcare could be replaced by a market in healthcare and an unconditional income is the multiple market failures experienced by a market in healthcare resulting from information asymmetries between patients, doctors, and insurance companies.[19] The research by Schneider et al. that reveals that markets for healthcare, whether the patient or an insurance company pays, are less efficient and less effective than tax-funded healthcare that is freely available at the point of need, shows that the way

15. Larsen, *The Institutional Logic of Welfare Attitudes*, 141; Baumberg et al., *Benefits Stigma in Britain*, 4, 11.

16. In 2010 a proposal was made to withdraw Child Benefit from the highest earners, but that proved impossible to implement so an additional tax charge was imposed on high earners living in households that received Child Benefit. Significant injustices have been the result. (Torry, *Why we Need a Citizen's Basic Income*, 19–20)

17. Titmuss, *The Gift Relationship*, 225.

18. Murray, *Losing Ground*, 227, 230; Murray, *Charles Murray and the Underclass*, 50; Murray, *In our Hands*.

19. Matsaganis and Leventi, "Pathways to a Universal Basic Pension in Greece"; Schneider et al., *Mirror, Mirror 2021*; Torry, "Primary Care, the Basic Necessity: Part I"; Torry, "Primary Care, the Basic Necessity: Part II."

in which a public service is delivered is an essential dimension of public service provision;[20] and that same research suggests that a reasonable hypothesis would be that if we are looking for both efficiency and effectiveness then unconditionality should be the default option unless proved otherwise. Clearly with any public service, some kind of rationing mechanism is required. In some cases, such as leisure centers and transport, subsidized payment might be the best option; but other methods are also available. In the UK, the patient's General Practitioner functions as a gatekeeper who ensures that relevant healthcare is provided rather than healthcare that will make the most profit for the provider.[21] This, along with monopsony (monopoly purchasing power) and the absence of the market failures suffered by insurance company healthcare funding, is the root of the UK's ability to outdo other wealthy nation healthcare systems in terms of effectiveness and efficiency. Similar considerations apply in relation to publicly funded education systems.[22]

Parallel to the difference between free at the point of need healthcare and a market in healthcare is the difference between blood donated for a fee and paid for by the recipient, as in the US, and blood freely given by donors and freely given to patients, as in the US and the UK. Commercial operators in the blood and organ donation field might say that they "wish to set people free from the conscience of obligation"[23] implied by the kind of unpaid donation practiced in the UK, but some of the questions about the advisability of paid-for blood donation raised by Richard Titmuss in his 1970 *The Gift Relationship*[24]—for instance, that in a market in which blood donation is paid for those who donate because they need the money might not tell the truth about infections[25]—proved to be prescient during the 1980s when blood products derived from commercially provided blood from the US infected UK patients with AIDS and hepatitis viruses. Titmuss compares unpaid donation with the gift exchanges discussed by Mauss (Chapter 1), defines the relationship established by unpaid donation as a "stranger relationship,"[26] and finds

20. Schneider et al., *Mirror, Mirror 2021*; Torry, "An Essential Dimension of the Social Minimum."

21. Torry, "Primary Care, the Basic Necessity: Part I."

22. Schneider et al., *Mirror, Mirror 2021*.

23. Titmuss, *The Gift Relationship*, 159.

24. Titmuss, *The Gift Relationship*, 157.

25. Titmuss, *The Gift Relationship*, 240.

26. Titmuss, *The Gift Relationship*, 215.

social gifts and actions carrying no explicit or implicit individual right to a return gift of action are forms of "creative altruism"... creative in the sense that the self is realized with the help
of anonymous others; they allow the biological need to help to
express itself.[27]

This is the kind of reflexive return, to the self from the self, discussed by
Derrida as an argument for the impossibility of a genuine gift; and it is also

an act of freedom in the twentieth century which, compared
with the emphasis on consumer choice in material acquisitive-
ness, is insufficiently recognized.[28]

Titmuss emphasizes the importance of such freely chosen, unremunerated
social contributions in a context of

few opportunities for ordinary people to articulate giving in
morally practical terms outside their own network of family and
personal relationships[29]

and demands the "right and freedom to give."[30] (It is unfortunately the case
that the withdrawal of governments from increasing numbers of areas of
social provision—evidenced by growth in demand at increasing numbers
of foodbanks—is making available more of the kinds of "giving in morally practical terms outside [one's] own network of family and personal
relationships."[31])

At the end of his study of blood donation in a variety of different countries, Titmuss concludes

that the commercialization of blood and donor relationships
represses the expression of altruism, erodes the sense of community, lowers scientific standards, limits both personal and
professional freedoms, sanctions the making of profits in hospi-
tals and clinical laboratories, legalizes hostility between doctor
and patient, subjects critical areas of medicine to the laws of the
marketplace, places immense social costs on those least able to
bear them—the poor, the sick and the inept—increases the danger of unethical behaviour in various sectors of medical science
and practice, and result in situations in which proportionately

27. Titmuss, *The Gift Relationship*, 212.
28. Titmuss, *The Gift Relationship*, 225.
29. Titmuss, *The Gift Relationship*, 226.
30. Titmuss, *The Gift Relationship*, 242.
31. Titmuss, *The Gift Relationship*, 226.

> more and more blood is supplied by . . . exploited human popu-
> lations . . . Redistribution in terms of blood and blood products
> from the poor to the rich appears to be one of the dominant
> effects of the American blood banking systems.[32]

Unpaid contributions to a society's healthcare in the form of blood and organs ought not to be replaced by markets in organs and blood; public services free at the point of use cannot be replaced by an unconditional income; and an unconditional income cannot be replaced by additional public services. The unconditionalities are all different, and they achieve different objectives: unpaid contributions of blood and organs to avoid multiple problems related to markets in organs and blood and to enable donors to exercise moral responsibility; unconditional public services to provide for needs when they arise; and unconditional incomes to provide a secure ability to purchase goods and services. Just as proposals are made for Basic Income schemes, so proposals are made for adding to the list of public services currently provided unconditionally such as the UK's National Health Service. Some such proposals are for genuinely unconditional public services, such as extensions of the currently often free public transport at certain times of day for individuals over state retirement age: but care must be taken when reading "Universal Basic Services" proposals to ensure that what is being proposed is genuinely universal. For instance, free transport, housing or food for households with low incomes would be a service that was neither unconditional nor universal, whereas free school lunches for every child would be both unconditional and universal.[33]

It is sometimes suggested that Basic Income and Universal Basic Services are mutually exclusive social policies.[34] They are not. Genuine unconditional and therefore universal services, and genuine unconditional and therefore universal incomes, would both offer considerable benefits to society and the economy, both could reduce poverty,[35] and they would be entirely compatible if a feasible revenue neutral Basic Income scheme and additional public services that required limited additional public expenditure were both to be implemented.[36]

---

32. Titmuss, *The Gift Relationship*, 245–46.

33. Coote and Percy, *The Case for Universal Basic Services*, 51–56, 125–26; Portes et al., *Social Prosperity for the Future*; Statham et al., *Universal Basic Services*, 4.

34. Gough, "Move the Debate from Universal Basic Income to Universal Basic Services."

35. Matsaganis, "Benefits in Kind and in Cash," 91.

36. Percy, "Universal Basic Services," 222.

UNCONDITIONAL INCOMES

As far as this author can tell, the first writer to propose an equal and unconditional income for every adult in a community was Thomas Spence. In 1796 he proposed that all of the land in a parish should be made "the property of the corporation or parish," that the land should be let to tenants, and that the rents should be applied to a variety of purposes, among which was a distribution to all members of the community: "each, without respect of person, is sent home with an equal share": and by each he meant everyone, "male and female, married and single . . . from the infant of a day old to the second infantage of hoary hairs."[37] A year later, Spence offered more detail on the effects that he expected his equal dividends to deliver. Everyone experiencing financial difficulties would be able to "start again," and "as both young and old [would] share equally alike of the parish revenues, children and aged relatives will . . . be accounted as blessings."[38]

> The people will receive, without deduction, the whole produce of their common inheritance . . . will be vigilant and watchful over the public expenditure, knowing that the more there is saved their dividends will be the larger . . . Universal suffrage will be inseparably attached to the people both in parochial and national affairs, because the revenues, both parochial and national, will be derived immediately from their common landed property. The government must of necessity be democratic. . . . There will exist only the robust spirit of independence mellowed and tempered by the preference and checks of equally independent fellow citizens.[39]

During the following two centuries the idea of unconditional incomes for every member of the community came and went, but since the early 1980s a continuous and diverse debate has taken place in multiple countries and now globally; pilot projects and related experiments have been held; and research has been conducted.[40] Spence has been shown to have been prescient in relation to the effects that unconditional incomes have delivered during pilot projects. Take, for example, the results of a two year pilot project in Namibia:

---

37. Spence, *The Meridian Sun of Liberty*, 8, 12; Torry, *Basic Income: A History*, 36–43.

38. Spence, *The Rights of Infants*, 13.

39. Spence, *The Rights of Infants*, 11–12.

40. Torry, *Basic Income: A History*.

- The villages of their own volition elected an advisory committee of eighteen residents, and among its achievements were the opening of a post office, the establishment of savings accounts, and the closure of shebeens (drinking houses) on the day of the monthly distribution of the grants;

- New shops were opened;

- The number of people experiencing daily food shortages fell from 30 per cent to 12 per cent of the population in just six months;

- The number of people who rarely experienced food shortages rose from 20 per cent to 60 per cent of the population;

- Economic activity rose fastest among women;

- Average income rose in every earnings quintile, and proportionately more for lower quintiles;

- Average income rose a staggering 200 per cent in the lowest quintile *excluding* the N$100 (US$12) Basic Income, because people could now purchase the means for making an income, and they did;

- Low-wage employment was in many cases replaced by better-paid self-employment.

- The Basic Income was not inflationary;

- Women's economic status rose relative to men's; and

- The Basic Income was more effective than conditional transfers partly because it could not be removed by a local bureaucrat if someone had fallen out with them, as a conditional cash transfer could be; and also because there was almost no opportunity for bureaucratic skimming of Basic Incomes, whereas conditional services and cash transfers require administration and therefore risk being skimmed.[41]

In any country, a Basic Income would provide a secure layer of income for every individual and household; improve social cohesion; and increase employment incentives for any household taken off means-tested benefits by their Basic Incomes. Basic Income schemes—that is, Basic Incomes, along with the funding method fully specified, and with changes to existing tax and benefits systems fully specified—could be constructed that would leave no funding gap and would reduce both poverty and inequality.[42] Above all in relation to the discussion above, a Basic Income would require no

41. Torry, *Basic Income: A History*, 206.

42. Torry, "Do we Need Basic Income Experiments?"; Torry, *Two Feasible Basic Income Schemes for the UK.*

intrusive bureaucratic inquiry; would be radically simple to administer; and would attract no stigma or shame, simply because everyone would receive the same amount unconditionally.[43]

There is still much debate: about the definition of Basic Income and how to interpret it; how much the Basic Income should be; precisely who within a country should receive it; and so on:[44] but much is now fairly settled, particularly in relation to the different feasibility tests that would need to be passed for a Basic Income to be implemented.[45] The global Basic Income debate is now a significant social fact, and at some point, whether by accident or by mainstream social policy planning, a country will implement a Basic Income and will reap the benefits.

As Richard Titmuss has suggested, "poor quality selective services for poor people were the product of a society that saw 'welfare' as a residual, as a public burden."[46] Unconditional public services and incomes, on the other hand, are provided for everyone, and so are more likely to remain of high quality[47] (unless significant inequality enables a high proportion of the population to abdicate from both public provision and from paying for it). Because unconditional incomes and public services benefit everyone, they turn "welfare" into a shared experience to which everyone contributes according to their means. The most efficient way to assist the poor is to make proper unconditional provision for everyone and to ensure that the wealthy pay more in tax than they receive in unconditional incomes and public services.[48]

To return to the route by which we arrived at a consideration of unconditional incomes and services: selective schemes generate stigma, whereas unconditional services and incomes do not.[49] If we want to be rid of stigma, then we need additional public services free at the point of use, and unconditional incomes to provide a secure layer of income for every individual in society.

43. Torry, *101 Reasons*; Torry, *A Modern Guide to Citizen's Basic Income*; Torry, *Static Microsimulation Research on Citizen's Basic Income*; Torry, *Two Feasible Basic Income Schemes for the UK*.

44. Torry, *Basic Income—What, Why, and How?*

45. Torry, *The Feasibility of Citizen's Income*.

46. Titmuss, *Commitment to Welfare*, 134.

47. Walker, "For Universalism," 149–50.

48. Spicker, *The Idea of Poverty*, 136.

49. Baumberg, "The Stigma of Claiming Benefits," 196.

RECIPROCITY

Throughout this book we have encountered the concept and practice of reciprocity: in Chapter 1 we found tribes responding to gifts with further gifts in order to maintain a hierarchy of honor; and in Chapter 4 we read Derrida's argument for the impossibility of the gift: that either there will be an expectation that the one receiving the gift will reciprocate, or the donor will self-reciprocate in the sense of a psychological return of some kind.

It is difficult to escape reciprocity, that is,

> the quality, state, or condition of being reciprocal; reciprocal action or relation, esp. reciprocation of cooperative or altruistic behaviour; an instance of this,

where "reciprocal" means

> Of the nature of, or relating to, a return (in kind); made, given, etc., in response; answering, corresponding. . . . Relating to, or of the nature of, a mutual or simultaneous exchange; given and received mutually; traded, exchanged. . . . Of a person or thing: sent or given by each party to the other, esp. as a formal exchange.[50]

Reciprocity is a social norm, or "moral repertoire," by which any transfer from one person or institution to another comes with an expectation of some kind of return.[51] So, for instance, an individual who does a good turn for someone might expect a good turn in response at some point; or a government might expect a benefits claimant to do something either after or before a benefit is paid. Such reciprocity might be either expected or required, and might be expected or required before the benefit is paid, or might be expected or required after it is paid, with the implication that further benefit will not be paid if a reciprocity expectation or requirement is not met. The four varieties of reciprocity would therefore be

- ante/required;
- ante/expected;
- post/required; and
- post/expected.

Means-tested benefits to which sanctions are applied if specified work tests and maybe other conditions are not met would be an example of ante/

50. Oxford English Dictionary.

51. Dean, "Popular Paradigms and Welfare Values," 150; Svallfors, "Welfare States and Welfare Attitudes," 10.

required reciprocity;[52] a further and far less stigmatizing example of ante/ required reciprocity would be contributory benefits, paid out on the bases of contributions previously paid into a fund and of the claimant suffering some such contingency as unemployment, illness, or retirement; and an example of post/expected reciprocity would be the expectation that someone in receipt of a Basic Income might choose to contribute to society in some positive practical way.

Stuart White suggests that in a social context reciprocity should be expected to fulfil a "fair-dues" condition:

> Where institutions governing economic life are otherwise sufficiently just, e.g., in terms of the availability of opportunities for productive participation and the rewards attached to these opportunities, then those who claim the generous share of the social product available to them under these institutions have an obligation to make a decent productive contribution, suitably proportional and fitting for ability and circumstances, to the community in return. I term this the fair-dues conception of reciprocity.[53]

If it is post/expected reciprocity that White is describing then it will be different from the ante/required reciprocity constituted by the work test and sanctions regimes now experienced by recipients of means-tested benefits, and it will be the kind of reciprocity that we might expect to see operating in the context of a Basic Income.

White offers a number of arguments for the importance of reciprocity as a social norm. Reciprocal activity can generate self-esteem, which is both a public and a private good; non-reciprocation burdens other people with providing for society's needs; to expect not to reciprocate carries an implication of superiority; to expect others not to reciprocate implies servility; and a welfare state is more likely to remain politically acceptable and survive if it is founded on reciprocity. White suggests fair-dues reciprocity can be exercised in a variety of ways—by paid labor, care work, and voluntary community activity—all of which are the kind of "civic labor" that generates the "civic minimum" of income, healthcare, and so on, needed to constitute the kind of society in which "institutions governing economic life are . . . sufficiently just" and so in which reciprocity can be legitimately expected.[54]

---

52. Dean, *Social Policy*, 51.

53. White, *The Civic Minimum*, 59.

54. White, *The Civic Minimum*, 59, 99, 131, 132.

White's proposal, that "in a context of otherwise sufficiently fair economic arrangements, everyone should do their bit,"[55] implies that if "economic arrangements" become *not* "sufficiently fair," then the obligation to reciprocate must lapse. And so, for instance, if obligations apply to some but not to others, and particularly if there is not a sufficient "civic minimum" because some sections of a society are not meeting their obligations, then we might legitimately decide that "economic arrangements" are not "sufficiently fair." This might occur in a context in which wealthier members of society are not making a sufficient contribution to the "civic minimum." As White suggests, only if everyone in a society is contributing work can any kind of work test "be defended as a necessary device for protecting citizens against the unfair resource claims of those who are unwilling to meet the contributive obligations they have to the community."[56] A somewhat different failure of "economic arrangements" to be "sufficiently just" would be if opportunities for gainful employment were to disappear from a community. It could legitimately be argued that only if relevant opportunities for making a contribution were to be available could "economic arrangements" be regarded as "sufficiently just" for a contribution to be expected.[57]

However, an assumption underlying this discussion of reciprocity is that the "civic minimum" is created solely by current effort. This is not entirely true, as a significant proportion of the resources available to a society are the gifts of nature or creation, and a further significant proportion are the product of the work of past generations. These are genuine gifts to us, although it might be added that the gifts of creation will only remain gifts if some kind of covenant or contract with nature enables nature to continue to make resources available to us.[58] As White puts it in an article published three years after *The Civic Minimum*:

> Some resources are properly seen as belonging to a common citizens' inheritance fund, and it is implausible that the individual's entitlement to a share of this fund is entirely dependent on a willingness to work.[59]

White goes on to argue for the legitimacy of an unconditional income on the basis that

---

55. White, *The Civic Minimum*, 18.
56. White, *The Civic Minimum*, 152.
57. De Wispelaere, *Universal Basic Income*.
58. Serres, *The Natural Contract*.
59. White, "Reconsidering the Exploitation Objection to Basic Income," 13.

1. "Even if basic income is bad for reciprocity, this is outweighed by its positive effects on other concerns of fairness, such as the prevention of market vulnerability.

2. "Even if basic income is bad for reciprocity in one way, it is also likely to have positive effects in terms of this same value."[60]

Any household lifted off means-tested benefits by its Basic Incomes would experience an increased incentive to seek paid employment because additional income would no longer suffer from the high withdrawal rates typically associated with means-tested benefits; for the same reason we could expect a greater incentive to learn and use new skills; we could legitimately expect the existence of a solid financial floor on which to build to encourage the formation of new businesses, social enterprises, and co-operatives, as we saw in the Namibian pilot project, referenced above; we could expect an improvement in employment terms and conditions; and we could also expect households to experience more freedom in relation to their employment patterns and so more opportunities for caring and voluntary community work of various kinds. All of this would contribute to the "civic minimum" required to establish the conditions for a just fair-dues reciprocity of a post/ expected variety.[61]

A SOCIAL POLICY ACTOLOGY

The fundamental difference between a pure gift and a reciprocated gift is that the former is a pattern of action that follows a trajectory from one person or institution to another, whereas the latter pattern of action is circular, with the original pattern of action generating a further pattern of action that impacts the source of the original pattern of action, and thereby giving birth to a constantly changing spiral of action. A variant is the single-direction trajectory with a subsidiary loop back to the origin: the situation in which the return to the gift is a psychological benefit to the donor.

As we have seen throughout this book, the changing spiral of action is typical of tribal gift-giving and also of social policy that is characterized by reciprocity of some kind. The genuinely unidirectional gift that is the givenness explored by Husserl, Heidegger and Marion, and the possibility of which is questioned and then recognized by Derrida, finds its closest social policy parallel in such unconditional incomes and public services as

60. White, "Reconsidering the Exploitation Objection to Basic Income," 14.

61. Torry, *Why we Need a Citizen's Basic Income*, 41–49; White, *The Civic Minimum*, 168.

Basic Income and the UK's Child Benefit and National Health Service, and particularly that proportion of those incomes and services constituted by a common inheritance made up of the gifts of nature and the product of the work of previous generations. Post/expected reciprocity might result from such a gift polity, and such reciprocal action would contribute to the civic minimum on which further gift-giving would be possible: but there is no obligation to reciprocate.

AN ACTOLOGY OF MONEY

Money is action in changing patterns. It is not the paper banknotes or the numbers in ledgers, although those represent it to us. It is the patterns of action of buyers and vendors. Money is created by civil servants writing entries in the government's own ledgers and in those of the country's population, and by commercial banks writing entries in their own ledgers and in those of its customers. A means-tested benefit is the complex of patterns of actions constituted by attending appointments, submitting to interviews, filling in forms, purchasing goods and services, and experiencing the anxiety generated by the knowledge that that entry might not appear next month. A Basic Income is the simple pattern of action constituted by the same entry appearing on a bank statement every month, and the spending of that money on goods and services.

The way in which our economy funds social policy can be understood in two different ways. The more intuitive way is to understand public services, social security benefits, and so on, to be funded by the various taxes that governments collect from individuals and businesses. The less intuitive, but ultimately more useful, way is to understand public services, benefits, and so on, to be funded by governments creating money, and then extracting some or all of that money from the economy by charging taxes to individuals and businesses.[62] The reason for employing this less intuitive understanding is that it makes it easier to understand both the possibilities for funding such policies as unconditional incomes, and the difficulties that might be encountered.

---

62. Jackson and Dyson, *Modernising Money*, 47–80; Mellor, *Money*; Weeks, *The Debt Delusion*, 52–81.

FUNDING MECHANISMS FOR BASIC INCOME

Take the proposal that governments should fund a Basic Income by creating new money. What this means is that a government might create more money than it plans to extract through taxation, thus increasing the total amount of money circulating in the economy. If the "velocity" of money remains the same—that is, the frequency with which the same money is spent in transactions remains the same—then the Basic Incomes will enable households to buy additional goods and services without taking on additional debt, which is how rather too much consumption is currently funded. (Debt is simply another means of creating new money, this time by commercial banks writing entries on their customers' bank statements: the money is then repaid with interest, which destroys the new money and adds to the banks' profits.) If the additional new money fills an existing gap between labor income and the value of goods and services produced in the economy, then there would be no risk of adding to inflation, and there could be efficiency benefits for the economy.[63] It is only if there is more money in the economy than the value of goods and services to be purchased that the value of money will fall and inflation will be the result, and, in the open global economy to which most countries belong, an additional effect of too much money in the economy will be that the value of the currency will fall relative to other currencies, exports will become more competitive, and imports will become more expensive. What this means is that new money should be added to the economy until the total stock of money equals the value of goods and services produced, and then no more should be added: so although money creation might be a useful means of kick-starting a Basic Income, the mechanism could not be used to fund it permanently.[64] A revenue neutral method would then be required: that is, additional taxation and reductions in the costs of existing benefits would have to equal the total cost of the Basic Incomes.[65]

A Basic Income does not necessarily mean that on average individuals would receive additional money. Particular Basic Income schemes might mean that some households would gain, and others might lose, with preferably poorer households gaining and households with higher incomes contributing more in additional taxation than they would receive in their Basic Incomes: but overall there would be no additional money. A Basic Income is not a means of providing people with additional money: it is a means of

63. Kőműves et al., *Macroeconomic Implications of a Basic Income*, 33.

64. Crocker, *Basic Income and Sovereign Money*, 3–52; Crocker, "Funding Basic Income by Money Creation."

65. Torry, *Two Feasible Basic Income Schemes for the UK.*

providing every individual with a secure layer of income on which they can build in the knowledge that their Basic Incomes will never be taken away from them. It is that secure layer of income that would provide the economic, social and employment advantages that a Basic Income would deliver.

TOWARDS UNCONDITIONALITY

Unconditional and universal benefits and public services represent a new direction for social policy, currently visible only in free education, free at the point of need healthcare, and unconditional benefits, currently restricted to people at both the young and the elderly extremities of the age range. Given the efficiency and effectiveness of unconditional provision, the lack of stigma and shame, the social cohesion, and a variety of other employment market, social and economic advantages, the question ought not to be "Should we do this?" but "To what extent can we do this, and how can we fund it?" Funding by a mixture of progressive income, wealth, business, and consumption taxes would seem to be obvious answers, along with a carbon tax, a land value tax, a financial transaction tax, and an element of money creation.[66]

We have seen a Keynesian paradigm come and go, and we are now immersed in a neoliberal paradigm that is significantly failing to solve the major problems facing societies, economies, and the planet. Unconditional giving would be an obvious candidate for the next social policy paradigm.

The Mont Pelerin Society, established after the Second World War, gave birth to think tanks that promoted neoliberal economics. Think tank staff became legislators and public servants, so that when the Keynesian paradigm collapsed at the end of the 1970s there were enough people in relevant positions to establish neoliberalism as a new economic paradigm, particularly in the US and the UK, but elsewhere too.[67] We need a new strategy, not just in relation to Basic Income, which already has its global network, but in relation to the unconditionality paradigm. Both Keynesian and neoliberal ideas were thought outlandish at the time, but they established themselves as fertile generators of social and economic policy. There is no reason why an unconditionality paradigm should not be able to do the same. Such a paradigm would represent an ante/expected variant of reciprocity, but above all it would represent, even if imperfectly, the perfect giving explored by Jean-Luc Marion and instantiated in Jesus as the grace of God.

66. Torry, *The Palgrave International Handbook of Basic Income*, 157–90.
67. Torry, *A Modern Guide to Citizen's Basic Income*, 234, 246–49.

The obvious philosophical foundation for such an unconditionality paradigm would be an actology: an understanding of reality as action in changing patterns, because such an actology would enable us to see unconditional giving as a changing pattern of action relating to human life, society, and the economy as changing patterns of action, and to reality as a whole understood as action in changing patterns, and might enable us to see unconditional giving as the pattern of action closest to the heart of reality because everything is given.

A GIVING SOCIAL POLICY

In his book *The Gift*, discussed in Chapter 1, Marcel Mauss describes multiple contexts in which gifts are exchanged between tribes, and discusses the fact that a variant of tribe-to-tribe gift-exchange, that is, exchange between tribes and their gods, has frequently transitioned into almsgiving:

> the fruits of a moral notion of the gift and of fortune on the one hand, and of a notion of sacrifice, on the other. . . . The gods and the spirits accept that the share of wealth and happiness that has been offered to them and had been hitherto destroyed in useless sacrifices should serve the poor and children.[68]

However, such "charity," which might still be regarded as religious rather than economic, is "wounding" for anyone who accepts it.[69] Raventós and Wark, in their *Against Charity*, list a multitude of other things that are wrong with charity: that the wealthy can gain more from their giving than the people to whom they give; charity can embed inequality; the wealth that makes charity possible is often the proceeds of exploitation; and charity categorizes and cheapens human life.[70] Things can be no better when the giving requires reciprocation, because where reciprocation of gifts remains a significant social custom, poor families can find themselves financially ruined by social expectations of generosity.[71] But however difficult this and other downsides related to reciprocal gift-giving might be, Mauss concludes that gift and reciprocal gift have for millennia created social bonds between tribes that might otherwise have been at war,[72] and he offers a moral exhortation to maintain, and where necessary reintroduce, the

68. Mauss, *The Gift*, 23.

69. Mauss, *The Gift*, 33, 83.

70. Raventós and Wark, *Against Charity*.

71. Mauss, *The Gift*, 84.

72. Mauss, *The Gift*, 104.

"give, receive, reciprocate" principle in social policy.[73] In his *Giving Time,* Derrida remarks on the stream of imperatives that appear towards the end of Mauss's book: imperatives to give, and also "to limit the excess of the gift and of generosity . . . by economy, profitability, work, exchange."[74] Wealth must be shared, *and* the individual must rely on their own hard work.[75] Mauss has understood that "give, receive, reciprocate" requires mitigation, but all he can suggest is that we should tone it down a bit.

We have found in Husserl, Heidegger, and Levinas, variations on givenness, in Derrida the perfect gift that is impossible, and in Marion reality as the given. That journey was also taken in both Judaism and the Christian Faith. What we now require is a social policy that takes that same journey towards the gift and does not stop with the "to give, to receive, to reciprocate" model, however mitigated. As Raventós and Wark suggest, an unconditional income is not charity: it is justice.[76] This is precisely the point that Thomas Spence made. We might not regard his solution to the occupation of land for individual profit—that the community should take possession of it, rent it out, and employ the proceeds for the benefit of the public and to supply unconditional incomes to every individual—to be realistic politics, but that is no reason to give up on the idea that a common inheritance of nature and the product of the work of previous generations belongs to everyone, so some way must be found to extract at least a proportion of the profit to distribute to everyone.

It is the continuing salience of "to give, to receive, to reciprocate" in social policy that makes any new unconditional incomes or public services, or any significant extension of such unconditional incomes and public services as the UK's Child Benefit and National Health Service, initially unpopular, and also that makes such unconditional incomes and services generally popular *after* their implementation. Such post-implementation popularity does not suggest that the reciprocity principle has been circumvented: rather it suggests that implementation alters the direction of reciprocation, so that the unconditional income or service constitutes the initial gift, inviting a reciprocal response from those who receive it.

Mauss calls for "reciprocating generosity."[77] It is not that we should abandon reciprocity: it is rather that we should recognize that the perfect gift is a possibility, both philosophically and in social policy, and it is that

73. Mauss, *The Gift*, 87–89.

74. Derrida, *Giving Time*, 62–63.

75. Derrida, *Giving Time*, 63–64; Mauss, *The Gift*, 87–88.

76. Raventós and Wark, *Against Charity*, 193.

77. Mauss, *The Gift*, 106.

perfect gift that makes space for and inspires a "post" reciprocity that is not even expected, let alone required, but is itself a gift. For such a paradigm to be possible the initial gift must be utterly unconditional, with no requirement or expectation of any kind of return. A gift might then be given in return.

Most of this book has been about the ways in which a handful of philosophers have understood giving and the gift, and it has suggested that an actology can provide a useful basis for the interpretation of their philosophies and that their philosophies can provide useful resources as we develop an actology. The previous chapter asked the same questions in relation to the Judaeo-Christian tradition. This chapter has asked about unconditional giving in social policy: a changing pattern of action that might suggest that we should employ an actological framework as we study further social policy fields, and that invites us to regard unconditional giving as a primary pattern of action and thus as actologically primary.

9

Givens

INTRODUCTION

Is everything given, or do we create some of it? And is anything given once and for all, or is the giving always a continuous process of new giving? Before we turn to more general considerations, we shall explore these questions by studying the works of three philosophers: Edmund Husserl, Gaston Bachelard, and Georges Canguilhem, in order to ask whether an actology might contribute towards an understanding of the givens that they explore, and whether their explorations might contribute to the development of an actology.

EDMUND HUSSERL AND THE GIVENNESS OF MATHEMATICS AND LOGIC[1]

As we would expect from the originator of phenomenology, Husserl's treatment of mathematics and logic begins with phenomena:

> We are concerned with discussions of a most general sort which cover the wider sphere of an objective theory of knowledge and, closely linked with this . . . the *pure phenomenology of the*

1. Torry, *Actological Readings in Continental Philosophy*, chapter 3.

173

experiences of thinking and knowing. This phenomenology, like the more inclusive *pure phenomenology of experiences in general,* has, as its exclusive concern, experiences intuitively seizable and analyzable in the pure generality of their essence, not experiences empirically perceived and treated as real facts, as experiences of human or animal experients in the phenomenal world that we posit as an empirical fact. . . . Phenomenology . . . lays bare the "sources" from which the basic concepts and ideal laws of *pure* logic "flow," and back to which they must once more be traced, so as to give them all the "clearness and distinctness" needed for an understanding, and for an epistemological critique, of pure logic.[2]

Logic and mathematics are just as much phenomena as are the phenomena of the world around us, and so are just as objective. They are phenomena to which we relate rather than being constructions of our own minds.

We are concerned with a *phenomenological origin* . . . we are concerned with *insight into the essence* of the concepts involved, looking methodologically to the fixation of unambiguous, sharply distinct verbal meanings.[3]

In relation to mathematics and logic, it is concepts, "the ideal," or "abstractly apprehended universals,"[4] of which we experience phenomena, rather than what is "real" in our worlds,[5] which interestingly inverts Plato's view that it is universals rather than the contingent things that we experience as "objects" that are the most real. However, although they are clearly different, logic, mathematics and real objects are all experienced phenomena, and that includes logic and mathematics in their pure ideal forms rather than intimately connected to real-world objects. "There is mathematics," and "There is logic."

The problem is that the phenomenological basis for mathematics and logic is Husserl's own insight (*Einsicht*) or intuition (*Anschauung*)—"intuition" is "an act of insight"[6]—and any insight must be somebody's insight. It is difficult to see how transition might be possible from the individual's contingent insight to the kind of universal insight that might deliver logic and mathematics as objective and phenomenological rather than as

2. Husserl, *Logical Investigations*, I, §1, 166: italics in the original.

3. Husserl, *Logical Investigations*, §67, 153–54.

4. Husserl, *Logical Investigations*, I, §2, 167.

5. Husserl, *Logical Investigations*, §62, 145.

6. Husserl, *Logical Investigations*, 7, §39, 86; Findlay, "Translator's Introduction," lxxxvi.

mind-constructed by individual logicians and mathematicians. Husserl understood the problem: "How can the ideal be introduced into the real, how can suprasubectivity enter into subjective act?"[7] He knew that "thinking subjects must be in general able to perform, e.g., all the sorts of acts in which theoretical knowledge is made real,"[8] because it is in such acts that we experience the phenomena of logic and mathematics: but he still believed that somehow mathematics, logic, and theory generally, "are what they are . . . whether we have insight into them or not."[9] The "insight" and "intuition"—"*Einsicht*" and "*Anschauung*"—by which we experience phenomena are clearly cognitive functions and so are psychological realities, so we certainly relate to logic and mathematics psychologically, which Husserl recognizes: "each truth . . . belongs to the realm of the absolutely valid, into which we fit all cases of validity into which we have insight or at least *well-founded surmises* . . ."[10] If insight and intuition that experience logic and mathematics were not cognitive functions then they would not be in the real world and logic and mathematics would not be phenomena in the normal sense: they really would be in a world of their own. As Husserl himself suggests, there really is "an unbridgeable difference between sciences of the ideal and sciences of the real."[11] Husserl ends up either treating logic, mathematics, theories and so on as contingent and to some extent mind-dependent entities accessed via phenomena no different in essence from other phenomena, or, more often, finding that his versions of logic, mathematics and so on are floating free from the real world as (mere) ideas with little or no relationship with the real world.

Perhaps Husserl ought to have been content with this outcome. Perhaps there is not a problem, and mathematics and logic can be understood in two very different ways that might nevertheless be relatable within an actology of givenness. What is given is phenomena of a real world—a world apparently ordered in mathematical and logical ways; and also what is given is ideal mathematics and ideal logic. An actology understands reality as action in changing patterns, but those changing patterns will necessarily exhibit some kind of temporary order, possibly over vast terrains of time and space (which are themselves ideal givens). It should be no surprise that we experience relationships between the orderings represented by ideal mathematics and logic and the orderings of the changing patterns of action

7. Quoted in Bouckaert, "The Puzzling Case of Alterity," 197.

8. Husserl, *Logical Investigations*, §65, 150.

9. Husserl, *Logical Investigations*, §65, 150.

10. Husserl, *Logical Investigations*, 7, §39, 86. Italics not in the original.

11. Husserl, *Logical Investigations*, 8, §48, 113.

in the real world. All of it is phenomena; the ideal mathematics and logic are pure pattern and are not themselves action so in that sense they are ideal and not real; and phenomena of the real world are action in changing patterns, and so real and often mathematically and logically patterned. That is how the gulf between the ideal and the real is bridged. And all of it is given: ideal mathematics, ideal logic, and the action in changing patterns of the real universe.

GASTON BACHELARD AND NON-GIVENNESS[12]

"Nothing is given. Everything is constructed":[13] so "everyday" thinking about "substance," atoms as particles, and so on, must be discarded; and any "homogeneous systems" need to experience a "total reorganization of the system of knowledge" informed by "dynamic ways of thinking that escape from certainty and unity" and directed towards "specifying, rectifying, diversifying."[14] It is this process that has led to such scientific advances as an understanding of substance as structured energy.[15] However much thinking might be "dynamic," Bachelard envisaged scientific change as always exhibiting the same structure: "epistemological obstacles" such as changes in the context, less understood experimental results, and so on, lead to a search for new mathematics; new mathematics and "epistemological acts" then stimulate new theories and enable new experimental methods to be developed to test them; and then the process starts again as new epistemological obstacles inspire "better questions."[16]

> Through technical progress, the reality studied by the scholar changes appearance, thus losing that character of permanence which forms the basis of philosophical realism. For example "the reality of electricity" of the nineteenth century is very different from "the reality of electricity" of the eighteenth.[17]

12. Torry, *Actological Readings in Continental Philosophy*, chapter 9.

13. Bachelard, "The Idea of the Epistemological Obstacle," 25.

14. Bachelard, "The Idea of the Epistemological Obstacle," 26.

15. Kotowicz, *Gaston Bachelard*, 61–65.

16. Bachelard, "The Idea of the Epistemological Obstacle," 26, 30; Kotowicz, *Gaston Bachelard*, 47.

17. Bachelard, "Le Philosophie Dialoguée," 18. Translation by the author. The original French is as follows: Par les progrès techniques, la réalité étudiée par le savant change d'aspect, perdant ainsi ce caractère de permanence qui fond le réalisme philosophique. Par exemple «la réalité électrique» au dix-neuvième siècle est bien différente de «la réalité électrique» au dix-huitième.

"Rectification,"[18] perhaps better termed "critique," is a continuous process in which error "gives rise to more precise tasks and drives knowledge on . . . to make a whole."[19] But that "whole" is not some kind of objective reality: it remains a limit that is never reached, and such "objects themselves" as atoms "appear to us as functions of relations."[20] Here everything is action in an "open" "field of action":[21]

> As thinking has no means to stop its own minimal becoming, it can no longer measure the vertiginous and multiple becoming of atoms.[22]

But what of the mathematics that Bachelard believed to be at the heart of the process of change? Is science simply "applied mathematics"?[23] Newly invented mathematics—or is it newly discovered mathematics?—has certainly been instrumental in the development of new theories: for instance, Albert Einstein found new geometries to be useful as he developed his theory of General Relativity. His theories have been tested and found to relate closely to what happens in the real world: and because it is new theory that generates new experiments—"materialized theories"[24]—and perhaps new experimental methods as well, and therefore it is theory that discovers new aspects of how the universe works, we might legitimately be able to say that reality is an "objectification of theoretical assumptions."[25] Because science has a "wholly mathematical constructivist nature,"[26] Bachelard is able to use the term "noumenal" to describe the mathematics that gives birth to new theories, and thus to new experiments and new reality. What is discovered by the theory-defined experiments is local and contingent: but the mathematics is not, although unlike Kant's noumena—that is, things in themselves—mathematics is entirely accessible[27] and we can "speak of the structure of [the mathematical] noumenon."[28]

18. Bachelard, "Objectivity and Rectification," 243.

19. Bachelard, "Objectivity and Rectification," 249.

20. Bachelard, "Objectivity and Rectification," 252.

21. Bachelard, "Objectivity and Rectification," 254.

22. Bachelard, "Objectivity and Rectification," 257.

23. Tiles, "Technology, Science, and Inexact Knowledge," 24.

24. Castelao-Lawless, "Phenomenotechnique in Historical Perspective," 44, 50, 57.

25. Privitera, *Problems of Style*, 9.

26. McArthur, "Why Bachelard is not a Scientific Realist," 172.

27. Bachelard, "Noumenon and Microphysics," 78.

28. Bachelard, "Noumenon and Microphysics," 83.

> Mathematics is the originator of many subtleties, which, though still in need of confirmation through experimentation, irresistibly attract the physicist, not because of the seductiveness of an unstitched novelty, but because of the noumenal coordination of those subtleties.[29]

Because it is mathematics that determines theory and experiment and thus reality, there is no room for a prior ontology to do so. We can therefore find novel science emerging: hence the disruptions given birth as scientific communities develop new theories, new experiments, new results,[30] and "new phenomena" that are

> made up . . . from scratch. . . . In the beginning was the Relation, and that is why mathematics governs reality.[31]

Consistency is neither obtained nor required, and what emerges is "complementary realities"[32] in multiple domains and with multiple possibilities for explanation, particularly in relation to the "essentially mathematical . . . hidden world which modern physics describes."[33]

> In the unknown world of the atom, could there be a kind of fusion between the act and the being, or between the wave and the corpuscle?[34]

The process of scientific change might deliver no universal, eternal or necessary laws, but what of the mathematics itself? Euclid's theorems—for instance, that the angles of a triangle in a Euclidean plane add up to 180°— would appear to be necessarily, universally, and eternally true. Mathematics evolves—for instance, Riemannian geometry can handle more types of space than Euclid's can: but once invented—or discovered?—Riemannian geometry will always deliver the same results in relation to the same surfaces, just as Euclidean geometry does in relation to Euclidean planes. So even if mathematics evolves, any particular mathematics, once discovered or invented, does not in fact change, and is universal, necessary, and eternal from the point in time at which it was invented or discovered. So is mathematics contingent? It would appear that any particular mathematics is not, but that mathematics as it relates to science is. Bachelard suggests that the

29. Bachelard, "Noumenon and Microphysics," 79.

30. Kotowicz, *Gaston Bachelard*, 71–72; Privitera, *Problems of Style*, 11–13.

31. Bachelard, "Noumenon and Microphysics," 80–81.

32. Bachelard, "Noumenon and Microphysics," 76.

33. Bachelard, "Noumenon and Microphysics," 80.

34. Bachelard, "Noumenon and Microphysics," 76.

"structure of the noumenon" can change,[35] which suggests that here he has in mind the varieties of mathematics that generate theories, experiments, and new reality: and as he recognizes,

> a mathematician can be led—through experiments as well as through reason—to start new constructions based on both a novel axiomatic and a new noumenal intuition. . . . it is through similar steps that the mathematician will change his axioms of mathematics and the physicist will change his operational definitions.[36]

It is here that Bachelard's mathematically-constructed theories, experiments, and realities cohere with Cartwright's recognition that scientific laws are local and contingent.[37] It is in the *practice* of mathematics, theory construction, and experiment, that change and diversity are ubiquitous.[38] It is also here that Bachelard's understanding of scientific change coheres with Thomas Kuhn's theory of the paradigm shift: a theory influenced by Bachelard.[39] Kuhn's understanding of a paradigm is of a way of understanding reality within which a scientific community constructs and tests theories. As evidence mounts against a paradigm and its theories, turbulence breaks out as thought experiments are conducted and new paradigms are sought and tested, and eventually a new paradigm will emerge along with its accompanying tested theories.[40] For Kuhn, the entire process is contingent, whereas for Bachelard, for whom it is newly invented or discovered mathematics that precedes new theory, there is at least an element of non-contingency, even if the choice and application of the mathematics are contingent. In practice, of course, scientific change can take off from anywhere in the process: from mathematics, an experimental result, flaws discovered in a theory, a new understanding of how the universe might work, and so on. To suppose that mathematics fulfils a privileged role is itself a contingent choice. As Lee Smolin points out:

> Mathematics is one language of science, and it is a powerful and important method. But its application to science is based on an identification between results on mathematical calculations

35. Bachelard, "Noumenon and Microphysics," 83.

36. Bachelard, "Noumenon and Microphysics," 81–82.

37. Cartwright, *The Dappled World.*

38. Privitera, *Problems of Style,* 13–14.

39. Simons, "The Many Encounters of Thomas Kuhn and French Epistemology."

40. Kuhn, "A Function for Thought Experiments," 6, 26; Kuhn, *The Structure of Scientific Revolutions.*

and experimental results, and since the experiments take place
outside mathematics, in the real world, the link between the two
must be stated in ordinary language. Mathematics is a great tool,
but the ultimate governing language of science is language.[41]

Bachelard's understanding of the importance of the imagination is in fact
a recognition that mathematics is not necessarily where scientific understanding begins:

> Contrary to a universe where masses are stable, where the events
> are lazy and chained up, imagine a world that is multiple, discon-
> tinuous and of a perfect mobility, without friction and kinetic
> wear. Just make sure that all this is rationally possible, that is that
> no intimate contradiction slips into your first suppositions. Make
> also sure that nothing superfluous is added, in other words, that
> the system of postulates is complete and close[d]. Once these pre-
> liminaries are established, close your eyes on the real and entrust
> yourself to intellectual intuitions. That way you will construct a
> rational world and you will produce unknown phenomena.[42]

Mathematics has certainly aided our understanding of the atom, but here
Bachelard is aware that it is imaginative leaps that have inspired the search
for the mathematics that study of atoms requires. Whether mathematics is
contingent or somehow eternal and unchanging is not at issue here: what
is given is the process of change and the reality revealed, which is itself
dynamic.[43] There might be a certain stability about a scientific process
normally comprised of mathematics, theory, and experiment, and that constantly "rectifies" knowledge: but that stability will itself constantly change,
and it might not always include mathematics. "Rationalism is a capacity to transcend reality as it presents itself, it is an open-ended quest that
creates new realities."[44] As Bachelard puts it, science offers us a "working
phenomenology,"[45] and not access to objects existing independently of our
discovery of them: so presumably the same has to be said of mathematics.

Mary Tiles summarizes the image of science that emerges as "of
something dynamic, something in process, not finalized . . . a multidimensional portrayal of the dynamics of scientific progress."[46] Knowledge is

41. Smolin, *Time Reborn*, 247.

42. Bachelard, *Les Intuitions Atomistiques*, 150–51, quoted in Kotowicz, *Gaston Bachelard*, 173–74.

43. Kotowicz, *Gaston Bachelard*, 181.

44. Kotowicz, *Gaston Bachelard*, 50–51, 54.

45. Bachelard, "Noumenon and Microphysics," 77.

46. Tiles, "Technology, Science, and Inexact Knowledge," 158, 160.

always "incomplete" and "approximate," rather than an approximation to knowledge:[47] so everything about the scientific method and its discoveries is characterized by change, and often radical change:[48] but the paradox is that what does not change is the ubiquity of change.

So what is given? The ubiquity of change: a given entirely coherent with an understanding of reality as action in changing patterns, that is, an actology. And what Bachelard's work contributes to the development of an actology is that it locates the scientific process as a primary case of action in changing patterns, as long as we recognize with Smolin that the role of mathematics in scientific fields is entirely contingent.

GEORGES CANGUILHEM AND THE UBIQUITY OF DIVERSITY AND CHANGE

In the real world, diversity and change are ubiquitous. Take, for example, Canguilhem's studies in the medical sciences. For Canguilhem, life does not conform to laws, but is what he calls an "order of properties":

> By "order of properties" we mean an organization of forces and a hierarchy of functions whose stability is necessarily precarious, for it is the solution to a problem of equilibrium, compensation, and compromise between different and competing powers. From such a perspective, irregularity and anomaly are conceived not as accidents affecting an individual but as its very existence.[49]

This suggests that any "order" of properties is a changing order and therefore only ambiguously an order; and we might seriously question Canguilhem's verdict that although "the obstacle to biology and experimental medicine resides in individuality: one does not encounter this sort of difficulty when experimenting on purely physical entities."[50] The physical sciences, such as physics and chemistry, might discover some regularities, but we now know that laws are only ever approximations, and that a law that applies in one set of circumstances will not necessarily apply in another.[51] Divergence is not an aberration: it is essential to life, and to everything else as well. In every field of knowledge, "individual singularity" is "an adventure."[52]

47. Tiles, "Technology, Science, and Inexact Knowledge," 171, 161–63.

48. Tiles, "Technology, Science, and Inexact Knowledge," 160.

49. Canguilhem, *Knowledge of Life*, 125.

50. Canguilhem, *Knowledge of Life*, 124.

51. Cartwright, *The Dappled World*.

52. Canguilhem, *Knowledge of Life*, 125.

Because medical science has human beings as its field of study, and each human being is a unique person, "normal" "has no properly absolute or essential meaning,"[53] and all that it can ever refer to is the mean of some quantifiable characteristic: and then only when we are discussing a single individual, because quantities between different individuals are incommensurable.[54] "Health" will be different for each individual, and can only be evaluated by that individual; and conversely, pathology will also relate to the individual. The physical functioning of a person's organs will no doubt affect their health, and if organs are not functioning efficiently then a pathology might be experienced: but in the context of a failing organ it would be perfectly legitimate for someone to decide that they are in health and are not suffering from a pathology. Canguilhem has reasons for asking whether "health" can have any scientific status.[55] "Health, the body's truth, does not arise out of an explanation of theorems. There is no health for a mechanism."[56]

Health and pathology change from person to person, and they also change for each individual as their self-chosen norms change,[57] because

> health, as the expression of the *produced* body, the body as product, is lived assurance . . . it is the feeling of a capacity to surpass initial capacities, a capacity to make the body do what initially seemed beyond its means. . . . Let us call this health free, unconditioned, unaccountable. This health is not an object for those who believe themselves to be specialists in it.[58]

The body is "produced" all the time by its changing context, and because the body's context and the physical functioning of the body change all the time, I might experience myself as being less or more healthy.

However, not everything is entirely individual. We live in societies within which norms evolve, and we cannot avoid being influenced by them. Social norms relating to health will to some extent influence each individual's experience of health and pathology, and each individual's sense of health, and each individual experience that someone might label as a pathology, will influence social norms, which will in turn influence individual norms, which might change in order to enhance someone's sense of their health. But still we have found nothing unchanging, because although social norms might change slowly, they do change. For instance:

53. Canguilhem, *Knowledge of Life*, 127.
54. Canguilhem, *Knowledge of Life*, 129.
55. Canguilhem, *Writings on Medicine*, 46.
56. Canguilhem, *Writings on Medicine*, 47.
57. Canguilhem, *Knowledge of Life*, 130–31.
58. Canguilhem, *Writings on Medicine*, 49.

attitudes to smoking have changed radically during the past fifty years, and the increasing stigma attached to smoking, as well as a more widespread understanding of the damage that smoking does to someone's lungs, along with the invention of vaping—the ingestion of nicotine via inhalation of a vapor—have resulted in fewer people smoking, and therefore in an increase in health: both in relation to the functioning of lungs, and in relation to people self-identifying as healthier. However, such developments are contingent—they are not necessary, eternal, or universal—and so they change constantly. Whilst social norms might change more slowly than individual norms (although not always), they change nonetheless.

Might we find extreme cases to exhibit elements of unchangingness? If someone's heart stops beating and it cannot be restarted, then that person will die. If they were conscious during that process then we might be able to say that they did not feel healthy, and would not have identified as healthy. They and everyone around them would have agreed that they were experiencing a pathology. Once they were dead, of course, there would be no question of health or of pathology, because they would not be there to experience and express health or pathology: but perhaps in relation to what we might call the limit condition as death was approached, we might have been able to say that they were not healthy and were experiencing a pathology. But even this limit scenario does not offer us an example of unchangingness. It would only take one individual to identify the coming of death as health for them—either because they were tired of life, or out of religious conviction—to plunge us back into the ubiquity of contingency in relation to health and pathology.

So is there anything that does not change and that is unitary rather than diverse? Might the fact that health, pathology, and normativity, are entirely individual and contingent, be something that does not change? For in general, to say that change and diversity are ubiquitous is always to say something that by definition does not change and that is unitary and not diverse: except, of course, that what is meant by "unchanging" and "unitary" at one moment and one place will not be the same as what is meant by "unchanging" and "unitary at another time and in another place because everything will be different and everything will have changed and will still be changing.

We might also suggest that Canguilhem should know that as well as the individual deciding whether or not they are healthy, a person with tar-covered lungs and who therefore coughs constantly is necessarily unhealthy and has a pathology. Norms are individual and social, but might they not also be related to the states of organs? Yes, they will be so related: but how they relate will always be socially constructed and will be radically individual. Someone might regard themselves as healthy in spite of the tar and the cough simply because they are still alive. It would appear that any normativity relating to health, pathology, or the normal more generally, can only be that of "regulative ideals that guide the life sciences."[59] Chimisso suggests that philosophy's task is to study "the space and relation between life and science."[60] This might again be a mistake based on the idea that there is a boundary between the subject matter of science and the diverse and changing reality of life, whereas in fact science is just as diverse and changing, as is the whole of what it studies, the methods that it uses, and the content of its findings. Anything that is real is action in changing patterns, and because both life and science are in practice action in changing patterns, they are both real. Foucault might be closer to Canguilhem's insights than Chimisso when he understands the history of science as one of evolution and discontinuities.

> The history of the sciences is not the history of the true, of its slow epiphany; it cannot hope to recount the gradual discovery of a truth that has always been inscribed in things or in the intellect, except by imagining that today's knowledge finally possesses it in such a complete and definitive way that it can use that truth as a standard for measuring the past. And yet the history of the sciences is not a pure and simple history of ideas and of the conditions under which they appeared before they faded away. In the history of the sciences one cannot grant oneself the truth as an assumption, but neither can one dispense with a relation to truth and to the opposition of the true and the untrue.[61]

The task is "discourses that rectify and correct themselves, and that carry out a whole labor of self-development governed by the task of "truth-telling."[62] It is new ways of truth-telling that change the sciences so that "science is always making and remaking its own history,"[63] and any normativity relates to particular sciences in the particular ways in which they are carried out.[64]

Here nothing unchanging and unitary is given. What is given is diverse and changes constantly: so the pattern of action that we might identify as giving is diverse and changes constantly. Our life is given: but that life is never the same from one moment to the next, even if we are dead. Giving is

59. Chimisso, "The Tribunal of Philosophy and its Norms," 321.

60. Chimisso, "The Tribunal of Philosophy and its Norms," 322.

61. Foucault, "Life: Experience and Science," 471.

62. Foucault, "Life: Experience and Science," 471.

63. Foucault, "Life: Experience and Science," 472.

64. Foucault, "Life: Experience and Science," 473.

action in *changing* patterns: so what we mean by "giving" changes from time to time and from place to place.

GIVENS

Es gibt in German means "there is," but literally translated into English it means "it gives." German is thus able to express far better than English can the fact that everything that is is given. As Heidegger puts it:

> *Es gibt* numbers, *es gibt* triangles, *es gibt* paintings by Rembrandt, *es gibt* U-boats; I say *es gibt* rain today, *es gibt* roast veal tomorrow. A great variety of *es gibt*, and each time it has a different meaning and yet in each one it has an identical element of significance . . . Again: the question asks whether *es gibt* something. The question is not whether *es gibt* chairs or tables, or houses or trees, or sonatas by Mozart or religious powers, but whether *es gibt* anything whatsoever. What does anything whatsoever mean? Something universal, indeed, one might say, the most universal, that applies to every possible object. To say of something that it is something is the smallest assertion I can make of it. I face it without presupposition.[65]

We might write this in two different versions:

> There are numbers, there are triangles, there are paintings by Rembrandt, there are U-boats; I say there is rain today, there is roast veal tomorrow. A great variety of there is, and each time it has a different meaning and yet in each one it has an identical element of significance . . .

> It gives numbers, it gives triangles, it gives paintings by Rembrandt, it gives U-boats; I say it gives rain today, it gives roast veal tomorrow. A great variety of it gives, and each time it has a different meaning and yet in each one it has an identical element of significance . . .

We shall leave to one side for the time being what the "it" that gives is. What we can say on the strength of the content of this and preceding chapters is that if we understand reality as action in changing patterns, then the fundamental patterned action is that of giving, which must be the basis of all other action in changing patterns. There is no action without it being given, whether the action be chaotic and unpatterned or ordered in some way.

65. Heidegger, "Die Idee der Philosophie," 67–68.

There is no action in changing patterns without the action and the changing patterns being given; and there is no pure pattern, such as mathematics and logic, without that being given.

In relation to mathematics, take the example of the triangle. Its definition is pure pattern, as is the space that we need in order to define the triangle. There is no action and no change, so no reality. What we have is a pure pattern that we might describe as a tautology, in the sense that the fundamental theorem related to the triangle is that its angles add up to a straight line. What is real is individual triangles, whether drawn, constructed, or imagined. These are changing patterns of action, and so constitute a family of relatively stable changing patterns of action, with family resemblances. There is no real triangle that is not a member of this diverse family of different realities of which the ideal triangle is not a member. In relation to this family of triangles we can make predictions, and they will be approximately accurate: but it is only of the ideal triangle that any theorems will be universally and absolutely true.

The universe and everything else—whatever that is—is given. Mathematics, logic, space, and time, are given; and God is given because God gives God. All of this is action in changing patterns, and it is unconditionally given.

> Knowledge and research bears on self-evidently existing nature,
> on the human world, on the self-evident givenness of the series
> of numbers, self-evident givenness of geometrical constructive
> formations and the like.[66]

Our research and knowledge must be like that: and it would appear that there might be no better way to achieve that than to understand reality as action in changing patterns, and to understand Action, action, every conceivable changing pattern of action, and every conceivable pure pattern, as given.

---

66. Husserl, *Analyses Concerning Passive and Active Synthesis*, 371.

10

An actological journey

INTRODUCTION

In this short final chapter we shall summarize some of the conclusions to which the different chapters have come, and will also ask whether we might be able to draw some general conclusions. But before we do that, we shall ask about the actological journey so far as a reader might find it in the three previous books in the "Actological Explorations" series; and after we have summarized this book's conclusions we shall ask about the journey still to be travelled.

THE JOURNEY SO FAR

In *Actology: Action, change and diversity in the western philosophical tradition*, we traced a thin actological thread from Parmenides and Heraclitus two and a half thousand years ago to John Boys Smith in the twentieth century. We found that only a metaphysic constructed at the change end of the change/unchanging spectrum, and on the diversity side of the diversity/ unity distinction, such as Hesiod's chaos, enables us to speak of both Action and Being, both actions and beings, both change and the unchanging, both diversity and unity, in Parmenides' poem; and that in Heraclitus's fragments, fire and everything else is active and diverse. We found that both Plato's and

Aristotle's philosophies lie in a variety of positions on the change/unchanging, diversity/unitary and dynamic/static spectrums. In Hegel's and Marx's philosophies we found ubiquitous change in particular patterns; in Blondel's *L'Action* we found an action-based conceptual structure unique in its consistency and breadth; and we hypothesized that if Bergson and Blondel had worked together then they might have developed understandings of both space and time as action in layered and changing patterns, thus creating the kind of framework required for a coherent understanding of reality. In Teilhard de Chardin's writing we discovered a theocosmology characterized by action in changing patterns; in Whitehead's process philosophy an action in changing patterns conceptual structure compromised by undynamic elements; in Geoffrey Studdert Kennedy's theology a God who suffers with the world; in Wittgenstein's philosophy language as action in changing patterns; and in John Boys Smith's booklet an evolution that evolves.[1]

We come to the end of *Actology* understanding that

> everything—or rather, every action, and every bundle of actions in patterns that we experience as a stable reality of some kind—is action, with its source in Action. All of it is action in changing patterns: and the meaning of "actions in patterns," and of "action in changing patterns," changes along with everything else. There is no still point where we can stand to survey the shifting landscape.[2]

And also by the end of *Actology*

> we have found among the writings of early Greek philosophers and Aquinas the building blocks for an action-in-patterns metaphysic; in Hegel and Marx we have found an understanding of history as actions in patterns (especially if we go on to understand dialectic as itself a changing pattern); in Blondel, we have found that reality—including being—is understood in terms of action; we have found that if we remove his remaining rigidities, then Bergson can offer us an understanding of space and time as actions in patterns; we have found that although he did not get this far himself, Teilhard de Chardin invites us to contemplate God, the cosmos, and everything else, in terms of actions in patterns; we have found that Whitehead and the other process theologians invite a more consistent treatment of reality than they achieved, and also invite an understanding of God in terms of Action; in Studdert Kennedy we have found a suffering

---

1. Torry, *Actology*, 210–15.
2. Torry, *Actology*, 216.

God active in the midst of the world's suffering; in Wittgenstein we have found an understanding of language in terms of actions in patterns connected to other actions in patterns; and we have found that John Boys Smith invites an understanding of changing patterns of changing language, and changing patterns of other actions in patterns too.[3]

It is the actology developed by the end of *Actology* that was then employed to interpret Mark's Gospel in the second book in the "Actological Explorations" series, *Mark's Gospel: An actological reading.* Mark's Gospel is full of action, change and diversity and so invites an actological interpretation that focused on the action, change and diversity and that by doing that delivers a distinctive theology.

The third book in the "Actological Explorations" series might be regarded as a sequel to the first volume in that it employs an actology to interpret a variety of continental philosophers, and also asks how their philosophies might help us to continue to develop an actology.

We found that "action" can function as an additional category and regulative principle in Kant's epistemological project and might at the same time bridge the gulf between phenomena and things in themselves, and securely bond knowledge, objects, events, freedom, God, the cosmos, and everything else in a single conception. We found an actology to be the ideal conceptual framework within which to study the action, change and diversity all over Nietzsche's texts; that his work reveals an ontology to be an inadequate conceptual framework within which to study contemporary philosophy and culture; and that an actology reveals inconsistencies in his writings. We found that an actology can provide a basis for a Husserlian phenomenology, and that it reveals mathematics and logic to be pure pattern and so actologically empty; and that it can bridge the Heideggerian divide between Dasein's ontological existential characteristics and its ontic Being-in-the-world. An actology reveals Levinas's "Other" to be a universal and so nonexistent and at the same time able to express the radical otherness of every human person in ways that an ontology cannot. We decided that an actology would provide a better basis for Deleuze's *différence* and *répétition* than a "univocity of Being" ontology could provide; that an actology would provide both Gadamer's hermeneutics and Merleau-Ponty's perception with the conceptual basis that they require; that an actology can handle the radical contingency and locality that we find in Bachelard and Foucault more easily than an ontology can; and that Michel Serres' diverse philosophy demands diverse actologies.

3. Torry, *Actology*, 216.

MICHEL SERRES AND THE GIVEN

One particular actology through which we found ourselves reading Serres'
The Natural Contract was the kind of actology of the given that we have
explored in this volume.[4]

The Natural Contract tackles the relationship between human beings
and nature, with a view to implementing a "natural contract" between nature and humanity. The reason for such a contract now being an urgent
necessity is that human beings now

> take up the entire chain of beings, spiritual, living, and inani-
> mate: . . . our collectivities are becoming as powerful as seas and
> share the same destiny. We have invaded not only the space of
> the world, but, if I dare say so, ontology.[5]

Pollution is now a matter of "philosophy, even of metaphysics,"[6] so the
natural contract must be

> the precisely metaphysical recognition, by each collectivity, that
> it lives and works in the same global world as all the others . . . I
> call the natural contract metaphysical because it goes beyond
> the ordinary limitations of the various local specialties, physics
> in particular. It is as global as the social contract and in a way
> makes the social contract enter the world . . . .[7]

Serres discusses how law, that is, human decision-making, has managed
to control science, and how science has polluted nature, so now human
decision-making, that is, law, must establish a natural contract in order to
reshape the relationship between nature and humanity.[8] We must

> Make peace by a new contract between the sciences, which deal
> relevantly with the things of the world and their relations, and
> judgment, which decides on men and their relations. It is better
> to make peace between the two types of reason in conflict today,
> because their fates are henceforth crossed and blended, and be-
> cause our own fate depends on their alliance.[9]

4. Torry, *Actological Readings in Continental Philosophy*, chapter 10.

5. Serres, *Natural Contract*, 20.

6. Serres, *Natural Contract*, 24.

7. Serres, *Natural Contract*, 46.

8. Serres, *Natural Contract*, 86, 93.

9. Serres, *Natural Contract*, 93.

As Serres here recognizes, science and law need each other, so what is required is "a single reason"[10] within which they can both belong. In this context he refers to Leibniz's principle of sufficient reason: the requirement that everything should have a reason—"*principium reddendae rationis*"—and he emphasizes the *reddendae* here. "Not only does each thing have its sufficient reason, but also reasons must be given back or *rendered*."[11] Reciprocity is required, which implies that a contract exists. According to the principle of sufficient reason, everything requires a reason, so reason must be given back to everything, that is, to "the given."[12] The world of nature and humanity is given to us, and we must give reason in return. "The principle of reason thus consists in the establishment of a fair contract . . . This rational contract . . . balances the given with reason."[13] The problem is that

> the given itself is disappearing under the weight and power of reason's productions. . . . Today, we ourselves, reasonable men, are brought to plead on the side of the given, which, for some time, has been laying down its arms.[14]

In order to preserve "the given," we need a natural contract: but such a contract is "metaphysical" because "global," which suggests that it would be best understood and constructed in the context of an actology of the given, and that a natural contract would be at the heart of such a metaphysics.

Serres wrote *Le Contrat Naturel* (*The Natural Contract*) before Derrida published *Donner le Temps*, but he would have known Mauss's *Essai sur le Don* (*The Gift*), published seventy years previously,[15] and would probably have known Jean-Luc Marion's recently published *Réduction et Donation: Recherches sur Husserl, Heidegger et la phénoménologie*: an early exploration of the givenness that would later be explored more fully in *Étant Donné*. Jean-Luc Marion was Director of Philosophy at Paris University X: Nanterre, so Marion and Serres might well have known each other by the time Serres published *Le Contrat Naturel* in 1990. The important difference between these different understandings of the given is that both Mauss and Marion recognised the complexity of gift-giving, and discussed the reciprocity inevitably attached to it: a concept underlying Serres' own treatment of the

10. Serres, *Natural Contract*, 89.
11. Serres, *Natural Contract*, 89.
12. Serres, *Natural Contract*, 90.
13. Serres, *Natural Contract*, 90.
14. Serres, *Natural Contract*, 91.
15. Marion, *Étant Donné*, 126.

obligation to "render reason" to "the given,"[16] whereas Derrida understood "the gift" to be entirely unidirectional and so impossible.[17] Unfortunately Serres rarely referenced the sources of his allusions, so we cannot know with any precision how he understood "the given," and neither can we know whether he might have regarded givenness as an ontology in the way that Marion does.

THE CONCLUSIONS OF THIS BOOK

Just as *Actological Readings in Continental Philosophy* might be regarded as a sequel to *Actology*, so this volume might be regarded as a sequel to both of them. Readers might wish to revisit the final section of each chapter for more detailed conclusions relating to the gift, giving, the given, and givenness: but here it might be worth drawing together summary versions of the conclusions of each chapter.

In chapter 1 an actological reading finds that it is the action in patterns of the giving that constitutes the gift-giving, and that it is a complex pattern of changing patterns of action that constitutes reciprocity. Because every pattern of action will change multiple other patterns of action, and potentially every other pattern of action, a pure giving and a pure gift are impossibilities. There will always be repercussions for the giver, the recipient, the reciprocity, the act of giving, and anyone or anything else related in any way to the initial giving. Reciprocity is ubiquitous. The pure gift is a limit that is never reached; the point at the end of a spectrum of infinite length. So an actology can facilitate a creative reading of human gift-giving, and equally the social activity of reciprocal gift-giving invites us to understand the whole of reality as constituted by changing patterns of action, and so the gift as well as the giving, the reciprocating, and all of the participants in the complex social activity. There are no unchanging beings here: everything is action in changing patterns.

In chapter 2 we have found that the phenomenon can only be both a relationship between the action in changing patterns that constitutes the subject's transcendental and intentional "acts of consciousness"[18] and the action in changing patterns that constitutes the given phenomena. Equally, phenomenology offers us multiple examples of action in changing patterns: the individual person, society, and the appearing of phenomena. In Husserl's

16. Serres, *Natural Contract*, 89.

17. O'Neill, "What Gives (with Derrida)?"

18. Husserl, *Cartesian Meditations*, 36.

phenomenological world there is no Being and there are no beings: there is Action, and action in changing patterns.

At the end of chapter 3 we concluded that as *Dasein* is Being-in-the-world, its Being is given by the world, so its Being is a foundational giving, and Action itself as it gives birth to action in changing patterns, and so to temporality. Dasein, beings, and the Being of beings, are all action in changing patterns: they *happen*. An actology can therefore offer a verb-intense interpretation of Heidegger's philosophy that understands Being-in-the-world, the present at hand, the ready to hand, the ontic, and the ontological, as action in changing patterns, and thus as belonging together. The boundary between ontic and the ontological is dissolved. Such a reading of Heidegger's philosophy suggests that any actology will dissolve the many boundaries that we find in western philosophy, because everything is action in changing patterns.

In chapter 4 we understood that Being, time, and the gift all suffer from non-existence: Being because it is not a being, time because it is not temporal, and the gift because its appearance negates it as a gift.[19] The gift is not, but it gives: so the only possible ontology is an actology, just as any relationship with an Other can only be action in changing patterns and never some kind of possession. We are left with a "trace," which in the context of an actology is a changing pattern of action, which means that an actology can understand the call of the Other and our response, and the givenness of the gift and its reciprocation, more thoroughly than can an ontology. Conversely, Derrida's understanding of the impossibility of the gift, and his recognition that a gift is still a possibility, enables us to recognize that an actology is also both impossible and possible if understood on any basis other than itself. So only if givenness is foundational—if it is "first philosophy"—can we understand all reality in relation to it. As well as an actology enabling us to understand givenness as Derrida understood it, and the Other as Levinas understood that, givenness can inform our actology and its possibility. For instance, within an actology we can understand a trace as dynamic, unchanging, and diverse. The trace is given, constantly. And just as the gift is gone as soon as it is given, and the Other can never be possessed, so *any* changing pattern of action will be absent a moment after it has occurred and new changing patterns of action will be happening. Equally, just as a gift remains a possibility, and the Other continues to call us, so the changed pattern of action forever refers back to the pattern of action that was changed, and an actology of givenness is a possibility. As with Mauss, Husserl, and Heidegger, we have found that for both Levinas

19. Derrida, *Given Time*, 27.

and Derrida, givenness can inform the construction of an actology, and an actology can enable us to understand givenness.

In chapter 5 we have found that if we read Marion's philosophy through an actological lens then it can make immediate sense of ubiquitous givenness, which is never a finished state, but always a constant, diverse and changing process of giving. Conversely, Marion's philosophy of the given provides us with a consistent example of a foundational changing pattern of action constituted by giving, receiving, and reciprocating.

In chapter 6 we studied Marion's more theological texts, and concluded that because God is Love, and is a God who gives God, the theory of reality of which God is the source can only be an actology. We have also concluded that to understand reality as action in changing patterns is to experience God as Action—the source of all action—and as the changing patterns of action of Love and Giving. Conversely, Marion's God—"God as Giving"— offers to any actology a consistent theology, and invites an identification between Action and God. Such an identification of God as *Action*, and as *action* in *changing* patterns, ensures that we experience God as an icon and not as an idol, which is a primary condition for a legitimate theology.

Chapter 7 finds in the Judaeo-Christian tradition a pattern of action that we denote as "grace": self-giving activity. Grace is to be found in the Hebrew Scriptures, it is the character of Jesus' activity, grace was at the heart of Paul's Christian faith, grace has been *the* focus of theological debate since the early Church, and grace has been constantly lost and rediscovered as the distinctively Christian center of Christian doctrine. We never experience or exercise grace in its pure form, because our motives are mixed, and human institutions need to defend themselves if they are to retain their integrity: but this makes it all the more necessary to emphasize the place of grace at the heart of the Christian tradition, because God is the absolute grace for which we seek. Grace is a changing pattern of action, so an actology rather than an ontology is needed: for only if we understand reality as action in changing patterns will we be able to understand grace as a pattern of action that is con- stitutive of God, and that this pattern of generous and unconditional love is of such infinite extent that reciprocation is impossible. So here we encounter the absolute gift-giving and givenness that we have sought and have so far failed to find. We have found it in the grace of God. To understand God as Action, as the source of all action, and as particular changing patterns of action—and particularly that of grace—contributes a theological dimension, and perhaps even a theological foundation, to any actology.

In chapter 8 we find the pattern of action "to give, to receive, to re- ciprocate" alive and well in social policy, and then ask whether the way in which reciprocation is often understood as required of citizens *before* the

State provides for them might be reversed into an understanding that unconditional incomes and services can *generate* reciprocation. Perhaps the perfect gift is a possibility, both philosophically and in social policy, and it is that perfect gift that makes space for and inspires a "post" reciprocity that is not even expected, let alone required, but is itself a gift. Such a new social policy paradigm requires the initial gift to be utterly unconditional, with no requirement or expectation of any kind of return. A gift might then be given in return. All of this suggests that we should employ an actological framework as we study social policy, and that we might regard unconditional giving as a primary pattern of action and thus as actologically primary.

In chapter 9 we have explored a variety of "givens." The German *es gibt* means "there is," but literally translated into English it means "it gives." Everything that is is given. This provides yet one more encouragement to regard giving as a fundamental pattern of action, and it encourages us to understand Being as Action and being as action. There is no action without it being given; there is no action in changing patterns without the action and the changing patterns being given; and there is no pure pattern, such as mathematics and logic, without that being given. The universe and everything else—whatever that is—is given. Mathematics, logic, space, and time, are given; and God is given because God gives God. All of this is action in changing patterns, and it is unconditionally given. Only an understanding of reality as action in changing patterns can make sense of this.

A consistent message has emerged as we have surveyed the conclusions of the different chapters of this book: that an actology concentrates attention on the act of giving rather than on the object given; that the "giving, receiving, reciprocating" pattern of action is ubiquitous; that pure giving is an ideal and a universal; and that "giving" might be regarded as an actology's primary pattern of action.

And as we have surveyed the conclusions of the chapters of all four of the volumes in the "Actological Explorations" series we can appreciate the importance of constructing and employing an actology. It is to that task that our future actological explorations will be dedicated.

THE ACTOLOGICAL JOURNEY
STILL TO BE TRAVELLED

We have explored some of the ways in which an actology can enable us to read significant philosophical and theological texts in new ways, and how those philosophical and theological sources can help us to develop an actology, giving depth to the simple idea that reality is action in changing patterns. The question now to be addressed is where our actological explorations should go next: in practical terms, what should the next volume in the "Actological Explorations" series be about?

One possibility is to reverse the process that we have followed so far. Instead of starting with some philosophical or theological text and asking how an actology might relate to it, perhaps we should begin with an actology and employ the philosophical and theological texts that we have read, and perhaps others as well, to work out in a systematic fashion some of the consequences of an actology for philosophy and theology.

To take an example: If reality is action in changing patterns, then how should we understand time? Time is not itself action in changing patterns, and to that extent is not real. Perhaps like the mathematics and logic that we studied with Husserl, time is pure pattern. Take an object existing through time. An object is always action in changing patterns, and one of the patterns of its action might be unidirectional and might relate to a similar unidirectional pattern to be found in multiple other examples of action in changing patterns. The pattern, like all patterns, changes, and in this case it patterns all other changing patterns of action in relatively predictable ways. This way of understanding time coheres with what we know about time, and particularly that it is a framework within which all other action in changing patterns takes place, and that at the same it is local and contingent. We might say similar things of space, except that it is multidimensional and that objects can retrace their steps, which they cannot do in the context of time.

Such discussion of time and space mirrors to some extent what we might say about mathematics and logic in the context of an actology: Time, space, mathematics and logic are ideal and universal as ideal pure patterns, and they are action in changing patterns when relating to the action in changing patterns that constitute the world in which we live. Every action in changing patterns that we experience exhibits to some extent patterns that we might identify as time and space. Like mathematics and logic, time and space are given, just as action is given and action in changing patterns is given: and like mathematics and logic, time and space are aspects of action in multiple many-layered changing patterns.

In the context of midrange distances and time intervals the patterns that constitute time and space will change relatively little, but in the contexts of the micro and the macro, stability can break down and new time-patterns and space-patterns can emerge. So action in changing patterns, time and space relating to it, and logic and mathematics related to it, will generate a new reality: reality as action in changing patterns. As Henri Bergson put it, everything is in motion[20]—"There are changes, but there are underneath the change no things which change"[21]—and the human person is

> neither a rigid immovable substratum nor distinct states pass-
> ing over it like actors on a stage. There is simply the continuous
> melody of our inner life . . . a melody which is going on and will
> go on, indivisible, from the beginning to the end of our continu-
> ous existence.[22]

And when we turn to Bergson's theology, God "has nothing of the already made; he is unceasing life, action, freedom."[23]

We have explored action in changing patterns, time, space, logic, and math-ematics, and we have begun to ponder on the relationships between them. The task of doing philosophy and theology in the context of an actology has only just begun. Much work is ahead of us.

20. Papanicolaon and Gunter, *Bergson and Modern Thought*, 356.
21. Bergson, *The Creative Mind*, 173.
22. Bergson, *The Creative Mind*, 176.
23. Bergson, *Creative Evolution*, 262; Carr, *The Philosophy of Change*, 160.

Bibliography

Adler, Michael. *Cruel, Inhuman or Degrading Treatment? Benefit Sanctions in the UK.* Cham: Palgrave Macmillan, 2018.

Anderson, Gary A. *Charity: The Place of the Poor in Biblical Tradition.* New Haven and London: Yale University Press, 2013.

Appadurai, Arjun. "Introduction: Commodities and the Politics of Value." In *The Social Life of Things: Commodities in Cultural Perspective*, edited by Arjun Appadurai, 3–63. Cambridge: Cambridge University Press, 1986.

Aubenque, Pierre. "Sens et Structure de la Métaphysique Aristotélicienne." In *Études Aristotéliciennes: Métaphysique et Théologie*, edited by Pierre Aubenque et al., 111–52. Paris: Librairie Philosophique J. Vrin, 1985.

Bachelard, Gaston. *The Formation of the Scientific Mind: A Contribution to a Psychoanalysis of Objective Knowledge.* Translated by Mary McAllester Jones. Manchester: Clinamen, 2002. First published in French in 1938.

———. "The Idea of the Epistemological Obstacle." Translated by Mary McAllester Jones. In Gaston Bachelard, *The Formation of the Scientific Mind: A Contribution to a Psychoanalysis of Objective Knowledge*, 24–32. Manchester: Clinamen, 2002. Originally published in 1934 as 'La formation de l'esprit scientifique'.

———. *Les Intuitions Atomistiques (Essai de classification).* Paris: Boivin, 1933.

———. "Noumenon and Microphysics." *The Philosophical Forum*, 27 (1) (2006), 75–84. https://doi.org/10.1111/j.1467-9191.2006.00230.x. Translated from Gaston Bachelard, "Noumène et Microphysique," in *Études*, Paris: J. Vrin, first published in *Recherches Philosophiques* (1931–32) 55–65.

———. "Objectivity and Rectification: The role of detail the objective." Translated by David Webb in 2021 from chapter 14 of Gaston Bachelard, *Essai sur la Connaissance Approchée*, Paris: La Librairie Philosophique Vrin, 1928.

———. "Le Philosophie Dialoguée." *Dialectica*, 1 (1) (1947), *What is Dialectic/ L'Idée de Dialectique/Die Dialektische Denkweise*, 11–20. https://www.jstor.org/stable/42963796

Baillie, D.M. *God was in Christ.* London: Faber and Faber, 1948.

Barnes, Jonathan. "The Primary Sort of Science." In *Aristotle: Metaphysics and Practical Philosophy: Essays in Honour of Enrico Berti*, edited by Carlo Natali, 61–76. Louvain-la-Neuve: Editions Peeters, 2011.

Baumberg, Ben. "The Stigma of Claiming Benefits: A Quantitative Study." *Journal of Social Policy*, 45 (2) (2016) 181–99.

Baumberg, Ben, et al. *Benefits Stigma in Britain*. Canterbury: University of Kent/ Elizabeth Finn Care, 2013. www.turn2us.org.uk/About Us/Research-and-Insights/Benefits-Stigma-in-Britain.

Berghofer, Philipp. "Husserl's Conception of Experiential Justification. What it is and Why it Matters." *Husserl Studies*, 34 (2) (2018) 145–70.

Bergson, Henri. *Creative Evolution*. Translated by Arthur Mitchell. Paris: Presses Universitaires de France, 1911.

———. *The Creative Mind*. Translated by M. L. Andison. Westport CT: Greenwood, 1946.

———. *Essai sur les Données Immédiates de la Conscience*. First published in 1888. Paris: Presses Universitaires de France, 1970.

———. *L'Évolution Créatrice*. First published in 1907. Paris: Les Presses Universitaires de France, 1959.

———. *Mélanges*. Edited by André Robinet. Paris: Presses Universitaires de France, 1972.

———. *Time and Free Will: An Essay on the Immediate Data of Consciousness*. Translated by F.L. Pogson. London: George Allen and Unwin, 1910.

Boedeker, Edgar C., Jr. "Phenomenology." In *A Companion to Heidegger*, edited by Hubert L. Dreyfus and Mark Wrathall, 156–72. Malden, MA: Blackwell, 2005.

Borgmann, Albert. "Technology." In *A Companion to Heidegger*, edited by Hubert L. Dreyfus and Mark Wrathall, 420–32. Malden, MA: Blackwell, 2005.

Buber, Martin. *I and Thou*. Translated by Ronald Gregor Smith. Second edition. Edinburgh: T & T Clark, 1958. First published in German in 1923.

Burtchaell, James. *Living with Grace*. London: Sheed and Ward, 1973.

Caillé, Alain. "Marcel Mauss et le paradigme du don." *Sociologie et sociétés* 36 (2) (2004) 141–76. https://doi.org/10.7202/011053ar.

Calcagno, Antonio. "God and the Caducity of Being: Jean-Luc Marion and Edith Stein on Thinking God." *Paideia*, 1998. https://www.bu.edu/wcp/Papers/Reli/ReliCalc. htm.

Camus, Albert. *L'Homme Révolté*. Paris: Gallimard, 1951.

Canguilhem, Georges. *Knowledge of Life*. Translated by Stefanos Geroulanos and Daniela Ginsburg. New York: Fordham University Press, 2008.

———. *Writings on Medicine*. Translated by Stefanos Geroulanos and Todd Meyers. New York: Fordham University Press, 2012.

Caputo, John D. and Michael J. Scanlon, eds. *God, the Gift, and Postmodernism*. Bloomington: Indiana University Press, 1999.

Carman, Taylor. "Authenticity." In *A Companion to Heidegger*, edited by Hubert L. Dreyfus and Mark Wrathall, 285–96. Malden, MA: Blackwell, 2005.

Cartwright, Nancy. *The Dappled World: A Study of the Boundaries of Science*. Cambridge: Cambridge University Press, 1999.

Castelao-Lawless, Teresa. "Phenomenotechnique in Historical Perspective: Its origins and implications for philosophy of science." *Philosophy of Science* 62 (1) (1995) 44–59.

Cedrini, Mario Aldo, Angela Ambrosino, Roberto Marchionatti and Alain Caillé. "Mauss's *The Gift*, or the necessity of an institutional perspective in economics." *Journal of Institutional Economics* 16 (2020) 687–701.

Cerbone, David R. "Realism and Truth." In *A Companion to Heidegger*, edited by Hubert L. Dreyfus and Mark Wrathall, 248–64. Malden, MA: Blackwell, 2005.

Chappell, Vere. "Descartes' Ontology." *Topoi* 16 (2) (1986) 111–27.

Chimisso, Cristina. "The Tribunal of Philosophy and its Norms: History and philosophy in Georges Canguilhem's historical epistemology." *Studies in History and Philosophy of Biological and Biomedical Sciences* 34 (2003) 297–327.

Clair, Jean, Axel Kahn, Julia Kristeva and Jean-Luc Marion, *Lumières, Religions et Raison Commune*. Montrouge: Bayard, 2012.

Cohen, Joseph. "Levinas and the Problem of Phenomenology." *International Journal of Philosophical Studies* 20 (3) (2012) 363–74.

Cole, Richard G. *Universal Grace: Myth or Reality?* New York: Orbis, 1977.

Coleman, Simon. "On Mauss, Masks, and Gifts: Christianities, (In-)dividualities, Modernities." *Hau: Journal of Ethnographic Theory* 5 (1) (2015) 295–315.

Coote, Anna and Andrew Percy. *The Case for Universal Basic Services*, Cambridge: Polity, 2020.

Crocker, Geoff. *Basic Income and Sovereign Money: The Alternative to Economic Crisis and Austerity Policy*. Cham: Palgrave Macmillan, 2020.

———. "Funding Basic Income by Money Creation." In Julio Andrade, Geoff Crocker and Stewart Lansley, "Alternative Funding Methods," in *The Palgrave International Handbook of Basic Income*, edited by Malcolm Torry, 180–85. Cham: Palgrave Macmillan, 2019.

Crowell, Steven Galt. "Heidegger and Husserl: The Matter and Method of Philosophy." In *A Companion to Heidegger*, edited by Hubert L. Dreyfus and Mark Wrathall, 49–64. Malden, MA: Blackwell, 2005.

Davis, Colin. *Levinas: An Introduction*. Cambridge: Polity, 1996.

Dean, Hartley. "Popular Paradigms and Welfare Values." *Critical Social Policy* 18 (55) (1998) 131–56.

———. *Social Policy*. Second edition. Cambridge: Polity, 2012.

de Beistegui, Miguel. *Thinking with Heidegger: Displacements*. Bloomington and Indianapolis: Indiana University Press, 2003.

Deketelaere, Nikolaas. "Givenness and Existence: On the Possibility of a Phenomenological Philosophy of Religion." *Palgrave Communications*, 127, 2018. https://www.nature.com/articles/s41599-18-0184-87.pdf.

de Rochechouart, Alice. "The (Im)possibility of God's Name. Levinas, Derrida, Marion." *Revista Portuguesa de Filosofia* 76 (2–3) 639–60.

Derrida, Jacques. *Donner le Temps, I: Fausse Monnaie*. Paris: Éditions Galilée, 1991.

———. "Given Time: The Time of the King." Translated by Peggy Kamuf. *Critical Inquiry* 18 (2) (1992) 161–87.

———. *Given Time, I: Counterfeit Money*. Translated by Peggy Kamuf. Chicago: Chicago University Press, 1992.

———. *Specters of Marx*. Translated by Peggy Kamuf. New York: Routledge, 2006.

Derrida, Jacques and Jean-Luc Marion. "On the Gift: A Discussion between Jacques Derrida and Jean-Luc Marion, moderated by Richard Kearney." In *God, the Gift, and Postmodernism*, edited by John D. Caputo and Michael J. Scanlon, 54–57. Bloomington: Indiana University Press, 1999.

Descartes, René. *Discourse on Method and Other Writings*. Translated by Arthur Wollaston. Harmondsworth: Penguin, 1960.

———. *Principles of Philosophy*. Translated by Jonathan Bennett, 2017. https://www.earlymoderntexts.com/assets/pdfs/descartes1644part1.pdf. (References give both page and paragraph numbers.)

De Wispelaere, Jurgen. *Universal Basic Income: Reciprocity and the Right to Non-exclusion*. London: Citizen's Income Trust, undated.

Dix, Gregory. *The Shape of the Liturgy*. London: Dacre, Adam and Charles Black, 1945.

Doctrine Commission of the General Synod of the Church of England. *We Believe in God: A Report by the Doctrine Commission of the General Synod of the Church of England*. London: Church House, 1987.

Douglas, Mary. "Foreword: No Free Gifts." In Marcel Mauss, *The Gift: The Form and Reason for Exchange in Archaic Societies,* translated by W.D. Halls, ix–xx. London: Routledge, 1990.

Drewery, Benjamin. *Origen and the Doctrine of Grace*. London: Epworth, 1960.

Drury, John. *The Parables in the Gospels*. London: SPCK, 1985.

Dunn, James D.G. *Jesus, Paul and the Law*. London: SPCK, 1990.

Elder-Vass, Dave. "Free Gifts and Positional Gifts: Beyond Exchangism." *European Journal of Social Theory* 18 (4) (2015) 451–68.

Engelland, Chad. "Disentangling Heidegger's Transcendental Questions." *Continental Philosophy Review* 45 (2012) 77–100.

Findlay, J.N. "Translator's Introduction." In Edmund Husserl, *Logical Investigations*, volume 1, lxxvii–lxxxvii. Abingdon: Routledge, 2001. First published in 1970.

Foucault, Michel. "Life: Experience and Science." In Michel Foucault, *Aesthetics, Method and Epistemology: The Essential Works of Michel Foucault, 1954–1984*, volume 2, edited by James D. Faubion, translated by Robert Hurley and others, 465–78. London: Penguin, 2000.

Frank, Stephanie. "The 'Force in the Thing': Mauss' Nonauthoritarian Sociality in *The Gift*." *Hau: Journal of Ethnographic Theory* 6 (2) (2016) 255–77.

Garber, Daniel. "Foreword." In Jean-Luc Marion, *Cartesian Questions: Method and Metaphysics*, translated by John Cottingham, Jeffrey L. Kosky and Stephen Voss, ix–xiii, Chicago: Chicago University Press, 1999.

Goffman, Erving. *Stigma: Notes on the Management of Spoiled Identity*. London: Penguin, 1990

Gough, Ian. "Move the Debate from Universal Basic Income to Universal Basic Services." In *Basic Income—On data and policy*, edited by Iulia Sevciuc, pp. 26–28. Paris: UNESCO, 2021. https://unesdoc.unesco.org/ark:/48223/pf0000380169.

Graeber, David and David Wengrow. *The Dawn of Everything: A New History of Humanity*. London: Penguin, 2022.

Groves, Peter. *Grace*. Norwich: Canterbury Press, 2012.

Guignon, Charles. "The History of Being." In *A Companion to Heidegger*, edited by Hubert L. Dreyfus and Mark Wrathall, 392–406. Malden, MA: Blackwell, 2005.

Gunton, Colin   *The Actuality of Atonement,* Edinburgh: T. and T. Clark, 1985.

Handler, Joel. F. "Myth and Ceremony in Workfare: Rights, Contracts, and Client Satisfaction." *The Journal of Socioeconomics* 34 (1) (2005) 101–24.

Hardy, Lee. "Translator's Introduction." In Edmund Husserl, *The Idea of Phenomenology*, translated by Lee Hardy, 1–13. Dordrecht: Kluwer Academic, 1999.

Heidegger, Martin. *The Basic Problems of Philosophy*. Translated by Albert Hofstadter. Revised edition. Bloomington and Indianapolis: Indiana University Press, 1982. First published in German in 1975.

———. *Being and Time*. Translated by John Macquarrie and Edward Robinson. Oxford: Blackwell, 1962.

———. *Contributions to Philosophy (From Enowning)*. Translated by Parvis Emad and Kenneth Maly. Bloomington and Indianapolis: Indiana University Press, 1999.

————. *On Time and Being*. Translated by Joan Stambaugh. New York: Harper and Row, 1972.

————. *Pathmarks*. Edited and translated by William McNeill. Cambridge: Cambridge University Press, 1998.

————. *Sein und Zeit*. Tübingen: Max Niemeyer Verlag, 2006. First published in 1926.

————. *Towards the Definition of Philosophy*. Translated by Ted Sadler. London and New Bruswick, NJ: Athlone, 2000.

————. *Wegmarken*. Frankfurt am Main: Vittorio Klostermann, 1976.

————. *Zur Bestimmung der Philosophie*. Frankfurt am Main: Vittorio Klostermann, 1987. Lectures given in 1919.

Henry, Michel. *C'est Moi la Vérité: Pour une Philosophie du Christianisme*. Paris: Éditions de Seuil, 1996.

————. *The Genealogy of Psychanalysis*. Translated by Douglas Brick. Stanford, CA: Stanford University Press, 1993.

————. *I am the Truth: Towards a Philosophy of Christianity*. Translated by Susan Emanuel. Stanford, CA: Stanford University Press, 2003.

————. *Incarnation: Une philosophie de la chair*. Paris: Éditions du Seuil, 2000.

————. *Incarnation: A philosophy of flesh*. Translated by Karl Hefty. Evanston, IL: Northwestern University Press, 2015.

Herbert, George. *The Poems of George* Herbert. Oxford: Oxford University Press, 1961.

Hill, Michael. *Social Security Policy in Britain*. London: Edward Elgar, 1990.

Hirsch, Donald. *Could a "Citizen's Income" work?* York: Joseph Rowntree Foundation, 2015. www.jrf.org.uk/publications/could-citizens-income-work.

Hooker, Morna D. *From Adam to Christ*. Cambridge: Cambridge University Press, 1990.

Huang, Di. "Normativity and Teleology in Husserl's Genetic Phenomenology." *Husserl Studies* 38 (2022) 17–35.

Husserl, Edmund. *Analyses Concerning Passive and Active Synthesis: Lectures on Transcendental Logic*. Translated by Anthony J. Steinbock. Dordrecht: Springer Science + Business Media, 2001.

————. *Cartesian Meditations: An Introduction to Phenomenology*. Dordrecht: Springer Netherlands, 1999. Originally published in 1950.

————. *The Idea of Phenomenology*. Translated by Lee Hardy. Dordrecht: Kluwer Academic, 1999.

————. *Ideas Pertaining to a Pure Phenomenology and to a Phenomenological Philosophy: First Book, General Introduction to Pure Phenomenology*. Translated by F. Kersten. The Hague: Martinus Nijhoff, 1983.

————. *Logical Investigations*, volume 1. Abingdon: Routledge, 2001: Translated by J.N. Findlay from Edmund Husserl, *Logische Untersuchungen*, Halle: M. Niemeyer, 1900/1901. References that give only the paragraph and page number refer to chapter 11 of the 'Prolegomena' to the *Logical Investigations*; for other chapters of the 'Prolegomena' the chapter number is given as well (for instance: 1, §6, 19); references to the 'Introduction' between the Prolegomena and the Investigations are given as 'I', followed by the paragraph and page numbers; and references to the first two Investigations are given as I1 or I2 respectively, followed by the paragraph and page numbers.

————. *Philosophy of Arithmetic: Psychological and Logical Investigations with Supplementary Texts from 1887–1901*. Translated by Dallas Willard. Dordrecht: Springer Netherlands, 2003.

Jackson, Andrew and Ben Dyson. *Modernising Money: Why the Monetary System is Broken and How it can be Fixed*. London: Positive Money, 2013.

Janicaud, Dominic. *Phenomenology and the Theological Turn*. New York: Fordham University Press, 2001.

Jeremias, Joachim. *The Parables of Jesus*. London: SCM, 1963.

Jordan, Bill, Simon James, Helen Kay and Marcus Redley. *Trapped in Poverty? Labour-market Decisions in Low-income Households*. London and New York: Routledge, 1992.

Journet, Charles. *The Meaning of Grace*. London: Geoffrey Chapman, 1960.

Kant, Immanuel. *Critique of Practical Reason*. Translated by T.K. Abbott. New York: Prometheus, 1996.

———. *Critique of Pure Reason*. Translated by Werner S. Pluhar. Indianapolis, IN: Hackett, 1996 [References are given as follows: page number in the first edition of the German text (A), published in 1781; page number in the second edition of the German text (B), published in 1787; page number in Pluhar's English translation]

———. *What is Enlightenment?* Translated by Mary C. Smith. Originally published in 1784. http://www.columbia.edu/acis/ets/CCREAD/etscc/kant.html.

Käufer, Stephan. "Logic." In *A Companion to Heidegger*, edited by Hubert L. Dreyfus and Mark Wrathall, 141–55. Malden, MA: Blackwell, 2005.

Kenny, Anthony. *Descartes: A Study of his Philosophy*. Bristol: Thoemmes, 1997.

Kidd, Chad. "The Skeptical Origins of Husserl's Transcendental Phenomenology." *Husserl Studies* 37 (2021) 169–91.

Kőműves, Zsófi, Chris Thoung and Jakub Zagdanski. *Macroeconomic Implications of a Basic Income*, Cambridge: Cambridge Econometrics, 2022. https://www.camecon.com/what/our-work/the-macroeconomics-of-basic-income/.

Kopytoff, Igor. "The Cultural Biography of Things: Commoditization as Process." In *The Social Life of Things: Commodities in Cultural Perspective*, edited by Arjun Appadurai, 64–91. Cambridge: Cambridge University Press, 1986.

Kotowicz, Zbigniew. *Gaston Bachelard: A Philosophy of the Surreal*. Edinburgh: Edinburgh University Press, 2016.

Kuhn, Thomas S. "A Function for Thought Experiments." In *Scientific Revolutions*, edited by Ian Hacking, 6–27. Oxford: Oxford University Press, 1981. First published in 1964.

———. *The Structure of Scientific Revolutions*. Chicago: Chicago University Press, 1962.

Küng, Hans. *Justification*. London: Burns and Oates, 1981.

Lafont, Cristina. "Hermeneutics." In *A Companion to Heidegger*, edited by Hubert L. Dreyfus and Mark Wrathall, 265–84. Malden, MA: Blackwell, 2005.

Larsen, Christian Albrekt. *The Institutional Logic of Welfare Attitudes: How Welfare Regimes Influence Public Support*. Aldershot: Ashgate, 2006.

Leask, Ian G. and Eoin G. Cassidy, eds. *Givenness and God: Questions of Jean-Luc Marion*. New York: Fordham University Press, 2005.

Lee, Seung Cheol. "The (Anti-)Social Gift? Mauss's Paradox and the Triad of the Gift." *European Journal of Social Theory* 23 (4) (2020) 631–48.

Levinas, Emmanuel. *Entre Nous: Essais sur le Penser-à-l'Autre*. Paris: Grasset, 1991.

———. *Entre Nous: Thinking of the Other*. Translated by Michael B. Smith and Barbara Harshav. New York: Columbia University Press, 1998.

———. *God, Death, and Time*. Stanford: Stanford University Press, 2002.

————. *Humanism of the Other*. Translated by Nidra Poller. Urbana, IL: University of Illinois Press, 2006.

————. "Is Ontology Fundamental?" Translated by Peter Atterton. *Philosophy Today*, 33 (2) (1989) 121–29. (Also in Emmanuel Levinas, *Basic Philosophical Writings*, edited by Adriaan T. Peperzak, 1–10, Bloomington: Indiana University Press, 1996 and 2008; and in Emmanuel Levinas, *Entre Nous: Thinking of the Other*, translated by Michael B. Smith and Barbara Harshav, 1–11. New York: Columbia University Press, 1998.

————. "L'Ontologie est-elle Fondamentale?" *Revue de Métaphysique et de Morale* 56 (1951) 88–98.

————. *The Levinas Reader*, edited by Sean Hand, Oxford: Blackwell, 1989.

————. *Le Temps et L'Autre*. Paris: Quadrige / Presses Universitaires de Paris, 1991.

————. *Time and the Other*. Translated by Richard A. Cohen. Pittsburgh: Duquesne University Press, 1987.

————. *Totalité et Infini: Essai sur l'extériorité*. La Haye: Martinus Nijhoff, 1961.

————. *Totality and Infinity: An Essay on Exteriority*. Translated by Alphonso Lingis. Dordrecht: Kluwer Academic, 1991.

Lucas, J. R. "Pelagius and St. Augustine." *Journal of Theological Studies* N.S. 22 (1) (1971) 73–85.

Luft, Sebastian. "From Being to Givenness and Back: Some Remarks on the Meaning of Transcendental Idealism in Kant and Husserl." *International Journal of Philosophical Studies* 15 (3) (2007) 367–94.

MacKinlay, Shane. *Interpreting Excess: Jean-Luc Marion, Saturated Phenomena, and Hermeneutics*. New York: Fordham University Press, 2010.

Mallard, Grégoire. *Gift Exchange: The Transnational History of a Political Idea*. Cambridge: Cambridge University Press, 2019.

Marion, Jean-Luc. *Au Lieu de Soi*. Paris: Presses Universitaires de France, 2008.

————. *À Vrai Dire: Une Conversation*. Paris: Les Éditions du Cerf, 2021.

————. *Being Given: Toward a Phenomenology of Givenness*. Translated by Jeffrey L. Kosky. Stanford: Stanford University Press, 2002.

————. *Believing in Order to See: On the Rationality of Revelation and the Irrationality of Some Believers*. Fordham University Press, 2017.

————. *Brève Apologie Pour un Moment Catholique*. Paris: Bernard Grasset, 2017.

————. *A Brief Apology for a Catholic Moment*. Translated by Stephen E. Lewis. Chicago: The University of Chicago Press, 2021.

————. *Cartesian Questions: Method and Metaphysics*. Translated by John Cottingham, Jeffrey L. Kosky and Stephen Voss. Chicago: University of Chicago Press, 1999.

————. *Certitudes Négatives*. Paris: Bernard Grasset, 2010.

————. *Courbet, ou, La Peinture à l'Oeil*. Paris: Flammarion, 2014.

————. *Cours sur la Volonté*. Edited with Christophe Perrin. Louvain-La-Neuve: UCL Presses Universitaires de Louvain, 2014.

————. *La Croisée du Visible*. Paris: Quadrige/Presses Universitaires de France, 2013. First published in 1991.

————. *The Crossing of the Visible*. Translated by James K.A. Smith. Stanford: Stanford University Press, 2004.

————. *Descartes*. Paris: Bayard, 2007.

————. *Descartes's Grey Ontology: Cartesian Science and Aristotelian Thought in the Regulae*. South Bend, IN: St. Augustine's, 2022.

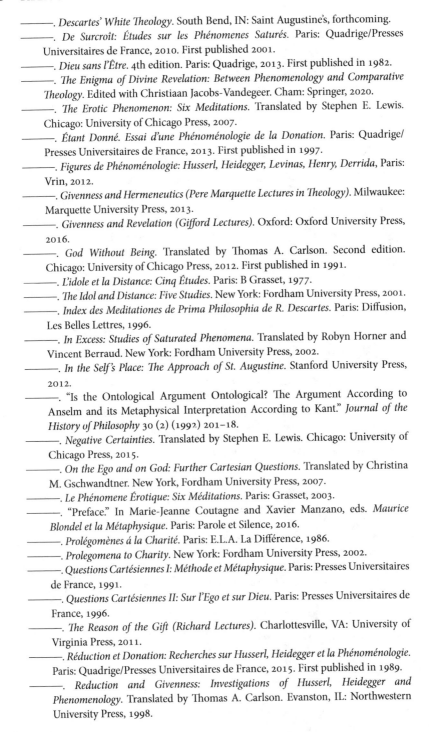

————. *Descartes' White Theology*. South Bend, IN: Saint Augustine's, forthcoming.

————. *De Surcroît: Études sur les Phénomenes Saturés*. Paris: Quadrige/Presses Universitaires de France, 2010. First published 2001.

————. *Dieu sans l'Être*. 4th edition. Paris: Quadrige, 2013. First published in 1982.

————. *The Enigma of Divine Revelation: Between Phenomenology and Comparative Theology*. Edited with Christiaan Jacobs-Vandegeer. Cham: Springer, 2020.

————. *The Erotic Phenomenon: Six Meditations*. Translated by Stephen E. Lewis. Chicago: University of Chicago Press, 2007.

————. *Étant Donné. Essai d'une Phénoménologie de la Donation*. Paris: Quadrige/ Presses Universitaires de France, 2013. First published in 1997.

————. *Figures de Phénoménologie: Husserl, Heidegger, Levinas, Henry, Derrida*, Paris: Vrin, 2012.

————. *Givenness and Hermeneutics (Pere Marquette Lectures in Theology)*. Milwaukee: Marquette University Press, 2013.

————. *Givenness and Revelation (Gifford Lectures)*. Oxford: Oxford University Press, 2016.

————. *God Without Being*. Translated by Thomas A. Carlson. Second edition. Chicago: University of Chicago Press, 2012. First published in 1991.

————. *L'idole et la Distance: Cinq Études*. Paris: B Grasset, 1977.

————. *The Idol and Distance: Five Studies*. New York: Fordham University Press, 2001.

————. *Index des Meditationes de Prima Philosophia de R. Descartes*. Paris: Diffusion, Les Belles Lettres, 1996.

————. *In Excess: Studies of Saturated Phenomena*. Translated by Robyn Horner and Vincent Berraud. New York: Fordham University Press, 2002.

————. *In the Self's Place: The Approach of St. Augustine*. Stanford University Press, 2012.

————. "Is the Ontological Argument Ontological? The Argument According to Anselm and its Metaphysical Interpretation According to Kant." *Journal of the History of Philosophy* 30 (2) (1992) 201–18.

————. *Negative Certainties*. Translated by Stephen E. Lewis. Chicago: University of Chicago Press, 2015.

————. *On the Ego and on God: Further Cartesian Questions*. Translated by Christina M. Gschwandtner. New York, Fordham University Press, 2007.

————. *Le Phénomene Érotique: Six Méditations*. Paris: Grasset, 2003.

————. "Preface." In Marie-Jeanne Coutagne and Xavier Manzano, eds. *Maurice Blondel et la Métaphysique*. Paris: Parole et Silence, 2016.

————. *Prolégomènes á la Charité*. Paris: E.L.A. La Différence, 1986.

————. *Prolegomena to Charity*. New York: Fordham University Press, 2002.

————. *Questions Cartésiennes I: Méthode et Métaphysique*. Paris: Presses Universitaires de France, 1991.

————. *Questions Cartésiennes II: Sur l'Ego et sur Dieu*. Paris: Presses Universitaires de France, 1996.

————. *The Reason of the Gift (Richard Lectures)*. Charlottesville, VA: University of Virginia Press, 2011.

————. *Réduction et Donation: Recherches sur Husserl, Heidegger et la Phénoménologie*. Paris: Quadrige/Presses Universitaires de France, 2015. First published in 1989.

————. *Reduction and Givenness: Investigations of Husserl, Heidegger and Phenomenology*. Translated by Thomas A. Carlson. Evanston, IL: Northwestern University Press, 1998.

————. *La Rigueur des Choses: Entretiens avec Dan Arbib*. Paris: Flammarion, 2012.

————. *Sur l'Ontologie Grise de Descartes: Science Cartésienne et Savoir Aristotélicien dans les Regulae*. Second edition. Paris: Lirairie philosophique J. Vrin, 1981.

————. *Sur la Pensée Passive de Descartes*. Paris: Presses Universitaires de France, 2013.

————. *Sur le Prisme Métaphysique de Descartes: Constitution et Limites de l'Onto-théologie dans la Pensée Cartésienne*. Paris: Presses Universitaires de France, 1986.

————. *Sur la Théologie Blanche de Descartes: Analogie, Création des Vérités éternelles et fondement,* Paris: Presses Universitaires de France, 1981

————. *Le Visible et le Révélé*. Paris: Les Éditions du Cerf, 2005.

————. *The Visible and the Revealed*. New York: Fordham University Press, 2008.

Matsaganis, Manos. "Benefits in Kind and in Cash." In *The Routledge Handbook of the Welfare State*, edited by Bent Greve, 84–93. London and New York: Routledge, 2013.

Matsaganis, Manos and Chrysa Leventi. "Pathways to a Universal Basic Pension in Greece." *Basic Income Studies* 6 (1) (2011) 1–20.

Mauss, Marcel. *Essai sur le Don*. Aigle: FV Éditions, 2021. First published 1923–24.

————. *The Gift: The form and reason for exchange in archaic societies*. Translated by W.D. Halls. London: Routledge, 1990.

McArthur, Daniel. "Why Bachelard is not a Scientific Realist." *The Philosophical Forum* 33 (2) (2002) 159–72.

Mellor, Mary. *Money: Myths, Truths and Alternatives*. Bristol: Policy Press, 2019.

Merleau-Ponty, Maurice. *Phenomenology of Perception*. London and New York: Routledge, 2012.

Moffatt, James. *Grace in the New Testament*. London: Hodder and Stoughton, 1931.

Moltmann, Jürgen. *The Church in the Power of the Spirit*. London: SCM, 1977.

Moran, Dermot. *Introduction to Phenomenology*. London and New York: Routledge, 2000.

Moreau, Joseph. "Remarques sur l'Ontologie Aristotélicienne." In *Études Aristotéliciennes: Métaphysique et Théologie*, edited by Pierre Aubenque et al., 229–63. Paris: Librairie Philosophique J. Vrin, 1985.

Murray, Charles. *Charles Murray and the Underclass: The Developing Debate*. London: Institute of Economic Affairs, 1996. (Contains 'The Emerging British Underclass', first published in 1989, and 'Underclass: The Crisis Deepens', first published in 1994).

————. *In Our Hands: A Plan to Replace the Welfare State*. Washington, DC: AEI, 2006.

————. *Losing Ground: American Social Policy, 1950–980*. New York: Basic, 1984.

O'Connor, Patrick. "Lecture 1—Husserl's Phenomenology." Unpublished lecture, no date.

Oman, John. *Grace and Personality*. Second edition, Cambridge: Cambridge University Press, 1919.

O'Neill, John. "What Gives (with Derrida)?" *European Journal of Social Theory* 2 (2) (1999) 131–45.

Owens, Joseph. "The Relation of God to World in the *Metaphysics*." In *Études sur la Métaphysique d'Aristote*, edited by Pierre Aubenque, 207–28. Paris: Libraire Philosophique J. Vrin, 1979.

Panoff, Michel. "Marcel Mauss's 'The Gift' Revisited." *Man* NS5 (1) (1970) 60–70.

Papanicolaon, Andrew and Peter Gunter, eds. *Bergson and Modern Thought*. London: Harwood Academic, 1987.

Patrick, Ruth. "Wither Social Citizenship? Lived Experiences of Citizenship In/ Exclusion for Recipients of Out-of-work Benefits." *Social Policy and Society* 16 (2) (2017) 293–304.

Peperzak, Adriaan. *To the Other: An Introduction to the Philosophy of Emmanuel Levinas*. West Lafayette, IN: Purdue University Press, 1993.

Percy, Andrew. "Universal Basic Services." In *The Palgrave International Handbook of Basic Income*, edited by Malcolm Torry, 219–22. Cham: Palgrave Macmillan, 2019.

Peterson, Christopher. *Monkey Trouble: The Scandal of Posthumanism*. New York: Fordham University Press, 2018.

Polt, Richard. "*Ereignis.*" In *A Companion to Heidegger*, edited by Hubert L. Dreyfus and Mark Wrathall, 375–91. Malden, MA: Blackwell, 2005.

Portes, Jonathan, Howard Reed and Andrew Percy. *Social Prosperity for the Future: A Proposal for Universal Basic Services*. London: Institute for Global Prosperity, University College London, 2017. https://www.ucl.ac.uk/bartlett/igp/sites/bartlett/ files/universal_basic_services_-_the_institute_for_global_prosperity_.pdf.

Prevot, Andrew. "The Gift of Prayer: Toward a Theological Reading of Jean-Luc Marion." *Horizons* 41 (2) (2014) 250–74.

Privitera, Walter. *Problems of Style: Michel Foucault's Epistemology*. New York: State University of New York Press, 1995.

Purcell, Michael. *Levinas and Theology*. Cambridge: Cambridge University Press, 2006.

Rahner, Karl. *Grace in Freedom*. London: Burns and Oates, 1969.

Ravaisson, Félix. *De L'Habitude*, Paris: Allia, 2007.

———. *Of Habit*. London: Continuum, 2008.

Raventós, Daniel and Julie Wark. *Against Charity*. Petrolia, CA: Counterpunch, 2018.

Rayment-Pickard, Hugh. *Impossible God: Derrida's Theology*. Aldershot: Ashgate, 2003.

Rees, B. R. *Pelagius: A Reluctant Heretic*. Woodbridge: Boydell, 1988.

Rider, Robert. "A Game-theoretic Interpretation of Marcel Mauss' The Gift." *Social Science Journal* 35 (2) (1998) 203–12.

Robinson, J.A.T. *The Body: A Study in Pauline Theology*. London: SCM, 1952.

Rosen, Matt. "The Givenness of Other People: On Singularity and Empathy in Husserl." *Human Studies* 44 (2021) 333–50.

Rotenstreich, Nathan. *Synthesis and Intentional Objectivity: On Kant and Husserl*. Dordrecht: Springer Science + Business Media, 1998.

Ruin, Hans. "Contributions to Philosophy." In *A Companion to Heidegger*, edited by Hubert L. Dreyfus and Mark Wrathall, 358–74. Malden, MA: Blackwell, 2005.

Sabourin, Eric. "Marcel Mauss: From the Gift to the Issue of Reciprocity." *Revista Brasileira de Ciências Sociais* 23 (66) (2008) 131–38.

Sahlins, Marshall. *Stone Age Economics*. Chicago: Aldine Atherton, 1972.

Sanders, E.P. *Jesus and Judaism*. London: SCM, 1985.

———. "Jesus and the Sinners." *Journal for the Study of the New Testament* 19 (1983) 5–36.

———. *Paul, the Law and the Jewish People*. Philadelphia: Fortress, 1983.

Schelling, Friedrich Wilhelm Joseph. *The Unconditional in Human Knowledge: Four early essays, 1794–1796*. Translated by Fritz Marti. Lewisburg: Bucknell University Press, 1980.

Schneider, Eric C., Arnav Shah, Michelle M. Doty, Roosa Tikkanen, Katharine Fields and Reginald D. Williams II. *Mirror, Mirror 2021: Reflecting Poorly: Health Care in the U.S. Compared to Other High-income Countries*. New York: The Commonwealth Fund, 2021. https://www.commonwealthfund.org/publications/ fund-reports/2021/aug/mirror-mirror-2021-reflecting-poorly.

Seneca. *How to Give: An Ancient Guide to Giving and Receiving.* Translated by James S. Rom. Princeton and Oxford: Princeton University Press, 2020.

Serres, Michel. *The Natural Contract.* Translated by Elizabeth MacArthur and William Paulson. Ann Arbor: University of Michigan Press, 1995.

Sheehan, Thomas. "Dasein." In *A Companion to Heidegger,* edited by Hubert L. Dreyfus and Mark Wrathall, 193–213. Malden, MA: Blackwell, 2005.

Siegel, James. "False Beggars: Marcel Mauss, 'The Gift,' and its Commentators." *Diacritics* 41 (2) (2013) 60–79.

Sigaud, Lygia. "The vicissitudes of The Gift." *Social Anthropology* 10 (3) (2002) 335–58.

Simons, Massimiliano. "The Many Encounters of Thomas Kuhn and French Epistemology." *Studies in History and Philosophy of Science* 61 (2017) 41–50.

Skemp, J. B. "The Activity of Immobility." In *Études sur la Métaphysique d'Aristote,* edited by Pierre Aubenque, 229–45. Paris: Librairie Philosophique J. Vrin, 1979.

Smolin, Lee. *Time Reborn: From the Crisis of Physics to the Future of the Universe.* London: Penguin, 2013.

Soffer, Gail. "Revisiting the Myth: Husserl and Sellars on the Given." *The Review of Metaphysics* 57 (2) (2003) 301–37.

Spence, Thomas. *The Meridian Sun of Liberty, or the Whole Rights of Man Displayed and Most Accurately Defined.* London: T. Spence, at no. 8 Little Turnstile, High Holborn, 1796.

———. *The Rights of Infants.* London: T. Spence, at no. 9 Oxford Street, lately removed from no. 8 Little Turnstile, 1797.

Spicker, Paul. *The Idea of Poverty.* Bristol: Policy, 2007.

Statham, Rachel, Henry Parkes and Casey Smith. *Universal Basic Services: Building Financial Security in Scotland.* Edinburgh: Institute for Public Policy Research Scotland, 2022. https://www.ippr.org/research/publications/universal-basic-services-scotland.

Stefano, Vincini. "The Epistemological Contribution of the Transcendental Reduction." *Husserl Studies* 37 (1) (2021) 39–66.

Steinbock, Anthony. "Personal Givenness and Cultural *A Prioris.*" In *Space, Time and Culture,* edited by David Carr and Cheung Chan-Fai, 159–76. Dordrecht: Springer Science + Business Media, 2004.

Svallfors, Stefan. "Welfare States and Welfare Attitudes." In *Contested Welfare States: Welfare Attitudes in Europe and Beyond,* edited by Stefan Svallfors, 1–24. Stanford, CA: Stanford University Press, 2012.

Thielicke, Helmut. *The Waiting Father.* Translated by J. Doberstein. San Francisco: Harper and Row, 1959.

Thomson, Iain. "Ontotheology? Understanding Heidegger's Destruction of Metaphysics." *International Journal of Philosophical Studies* 8 (3) (2010) 297–327. https://doi.org/10.1080/096725500750039291

Tiles, Mary. "Technology, Science, and Inexact Knowledge: Bachelard's Non-Cartesian Epistemology." In *Continental Philosophy of Science,* edited by Gary Gutting, 157–75. Malden, MA: Blackwell, 2005.

———. "What does Bachelard mean by *rationalisme appliqué? Radical Philosophy* 173 (2012) 24–26.

Titmuss, Richard. *Commitment to welfare.* London: George Allen and Unwin, 1968.

———. *The Gift Relationship: From Human Blood to Social Policy.* London: Allen and Unwin, 1970.

Tonkens, Evelien, et al. "Introduction: Welfare State Reform, Recognition, and Emotional Labour." *Social Policy and Society* 12 (3) (2013) 407–13.

Torrance, T.F. *The Doctrine of Grace in the Apostolic Fathers.* Edinburgh: Oliver and Boyd, 1948.

Torry, Malcolm. *101 Reasons for a Citizen's Income: Arguments for Giving Everyone Some Money.* Bristol: Policy, 2015.

———. "Action, Patterns and Religious Pluralism." *Theology* CVI (830) (2003) 107–18.

———. *Actological Readings in Continental Philosophy.* Eugene, OR: Resource, forthcoming.

———. *Actology: Action, Change and Diversity in the Western Philosophical Tradition.* Eugene, OR: Resource, 2020.

———. *Basic Income: A History.* Cheltenham: Edward Elgar, 2021.

———. *Basic Income—What, Why, and How?* Cham: Palgrave Macmillan, 2022.

———. "Do we Need Basic Income Experiments?" *Basic Income Studies* 16 (1) (2021) 39–54.

———. "An Essential Dimension of the Social Minimum." In *Specifying and Securing a Social Minimum in the Battle Against Poverty,* edited by Toomas Kotkas, Ingrid Leijten and Frans Pennings, 31–46. Oxford: Hart, 2019.

———. *The Feasibility of Citizen's Income.* New York: Palgrave Macmillan, 2016.

———. *A Modern Guide to Citizen's Basic Income: A Multidisciplinary Approach.* Cheltenham: Edward Elgar, 2020.

———. "Primary Care, the Basic Necessity: Part I: Explorations in Economics." In *Handbook of Primary Care Ethics,* edited by Andrew Papanikitas and John Spicer, pp. 369–76. Boca Raton, FL: Taylor and Francis, 2018.

———. "Primary Care, the Basic Necessity: Part II: Explorations in Ethics." In *Handbook of Primary Care Ethics,* edited by Andrew Papanikitas and John Spicer, pp. 377–84. Boca Raton, FL: Taylor and Francis, 2018.

———, ed. *The Palgrave International Handbook of Basic Income.* Cham: Palgrave Macmillan, 2019.

———. *Static Microsimulation Research on Citizen's Basic Income for the UK: A Personal Summary and Further Reflections.* EUROMOD Working Paper EM13/19. Colchester: Institute to Social and Economic Research, 2019. https://www.iser.essex.ac.uk/research/publications/working-papers/euromod/em13-19.pdf.

———. *Two Feasible Basic Income Schemes for the UK, and a Feasible Pilot Project for Scotland.* CeMPA Working Paper 7/22. Colchester: Centre for Microsimulation and Policy Analysis, University of Essex, 2022. https://www.microsimulation.ac.uk/publications/publication-547284/.

———. "Two Kinds of Ambiguity." *King's Theological Review* 3(1) (1980) 24–28.

———. *Why we Need a Citizen's Basic Income: The Desirability, Feasibility and Implementation of an Unconditional Income.* Bristol: Policy, 2018.

Tracy, David. "Foreword." In *God Without Being* by Jean-Luc Marion, translated by Thomas A. Carlson, second edition, xi–xvii. Chicago: University of Chicago Press, 2012. First published 1991.

Wagner, Richard E. *Fiscal Sociology and the Theory of Public Finance: An Exploratory Essay.* Cheltenham: Edward Elgar, 2007.

Walker, Carol. "For Universalism and Against the Means Test." In *Fighting poverty, inequality and injustice: A manifesto inspired by Peter Townsend,* edited by Alan Walker, Adrian Sinfield and Carol Walker, 133–52. Cambridge: Polity, 2011.

Walker, Robert, et al. "Poverty in Global Perspective: Is Shame a Common Denominator?" *Journal of Social Policy* 42 (2) (2013) 215–33.

Wallenfang, Donald. *Emmanuel: Levinas and Variations on God with Us*. Eugene, OR: Cascade, 2021.

Ward, Graham. "Introducing Jean-Luc Marion." *New Blackfriars* 76 (1995) 317–24.

Watson, Francis. *Paul, Judaism and the Gentiles*. Cambridge: Cambridge University Press, 1986.

Webb, David. *Heidegger, Ethics and the Practice of Ontology*. London and New York: Continuum, 2009.

Webb, Stephen. *The Gifting God: A Trinitarian Ethics of Excess*. New York: Oxford University Press, 1996.

Weeks, John F. *The Debt Delusion: Living Within our Means and Other Fallacies*. Cambridge: Polity, 2020.

Welfare Reform Team, Oxford City Council. *Evaluation of European Social Fund Pilot Project 2014–2015*. Oxford: Oxford City Council, 2016. www.oxford.gov. uk/downloads/file/2119/welfare_reform_european_social_fund_project_ evaluation_report.

White, Stuart. *The Civic Minimum: On the Rights and Obligations of Economic Citizenship*. Oxford: Oxford University Press, 2003.

———. "Reconsidering the Exploitation Objection to Basic Income." *Basic Income Studies* 1 (2) (2006) 1–24.

Widerquist, Karl and Grant S. McCall. *Prehistoric Myths in Modern Political Philosophy*. Edinburgh: Edinburgh University Press, 2017.

Wilk, Richard R. and Lisa Cliggett. *Economies and Cultures: Foundations of Economic Anthropology*. Second edition. New York and London: Routledge, 2018.

Williams, Heath. "Is Husserl Guilty of Sellars' Myth of the Sensory Given." *Synthèse* 199 (3–4) (2021) 6371–89.

Williams, N. P. *The Grace of God*. London: Longmans, Green, 1930.

Wollaston, Arthur. "Introduction." In René Descartes, *Discourse on Method and Other Writings*, 7–32. Harmondsworth: Penguin, 1960.

Wrathall, Mark A. "Unconcealment." In *A Companion to Heidegger*, edited by Hubert L. Dreyfus and Mark Wrathall, 337–57. Malden, MA: Blackwell, 2005.

Yarnold, Edward. *The Second Gift: A Study of Grace*. Slough: St. Paul Publications, 1974.

Zizioulas, John. *Being as Communion: Studies in Personhood and the Church*. London: Darton, Longman and Todd, 1985.

Index

213